ADVANCE PRAISE FOR

Methodology and Praxis: Thinking with Patti Lather

"Beyond offering an overarching explication of Patti Lather's work over the years, this volume puts her concepts and sharp theorizations to work in strategic fashion. In this sense, the volume's chapters are more engaged than descriptive, more challenging than representative. As a whole, *Methodology and Praxis* offers a wonderful and productive zigzag between the more macro orientation of concept creation and micro engagement with critical practices in material context."

Dr. Aaron M. Kuntz
Dean & Frost Professor of Education and Human Development
Florida International University

"How does one study the work of Dr. Patti Lather? With deep curiosity, a readiness to engage in debates about subjectivity, and an unflinching commitment to interrogating what knowledge means in a post-structural world. And of course, with love—for Patti as both a human being and a model of what it means to be a scholar.

I remember the first time I read *Getting Lost*—I didn't know a scholar could write so boldly about the unknown, about failure, and about the pursuit of knowledge grounded in a feminist commitment to radical (re)thinking. Patti's work gave language to what so many of us were feeling but hadn't yet learned how to articulate.

Thank you to the authors who have taken up the challenge of thinking with Patti Lather in *Methodology and Praxis: Thinking with Patti Lather*. This is not a book you read once and shelve. It's a book you keep close, return to often, and allow to stretch your thinking, unsettle your assumptions, and demand more of you each time."

Dr. Bettina L. Love,
acclaimed author of the New York Times bestseller
Punished for Dreaming

"By introducing feminist poststructuralism and posthumanism into the mainstream of educational research, Patti Lather's writings helped education scholars understand that research doesn't just produce knowledge, but also subjects, identity, aporia, and proliferating relational possibilities. Her impact on contemporary education scholarship would be difficult to overestimate. Her influence, however, extends well beyond the influence of her individual publications. She was also a remarkable advisor and mentor to many of the leading scholars of critical and postcritical qualitative methodology of the last 30 years. She inspired countless additional scholars in her many public addresses with her incisiveness and the easy pleasure she takes in discourse about theory. In all these ways Patti Lather helped build a worldwide multigenerational community that continues to support ambitious and imaginative thought about social inquiry. This book both celebrates and enacts these features of her legacy, by bringing together the voices of many who have been influenced by her and by inviting Dr. Lather to reflect on a remarkable career. It is essential reading for anyone interested in critical and postcritical research methods."

Jerry Rosiek
Professor of Education Studies
Affiliated Professor in the Department of Philosophy
Affiliated Professor in the Department of Indigenous, Race, and Ethnic Studies
College of Education, University of Oregon

Methodology and Praxis

Methodology and Praxis

Thinking with Patti Lather

Edited by Gabriel Huddleston
and Robert J. Helfenbein

(mep) Myers
Education
Press

GORHAM, MAINE

(mep) Myers Education Press

Copyright © 2025 | Myers Education Press, LLC

Published by Myers Education Press, LLC
P.O. Box 424 Gorham, ME 04038

Myers Education Press is an academic publisher specializing in books, e-books, and digital content in the field of education. All of our books are subjected to a rigorous peer review process and produced in compliance with the standards of the Council on Library and Information Resources.

Library of Congress Cataloging-in-Publication Data available from Library of Congress.

13-digit ISBN 978-1-9755-0644-5 (paperback)
13-digit ISBN 978-1-9755-0645-2 (library networkable e-edition)
13-digit ISBN 978-1-9755-0646-9 (consumer e-edition)

Printed in the United States of America.

All first editions printed on acid-free paper that meets the American National Standards Institute Z39-48 standard.

Books published by Myers Education Press may be purchased at special quantity discount rates for groups, workshops, training organizations, and classroom usage. Please call our customer service department at 1-800-232-0223 for details.

Cover design by Dutton and Sherman Design.
Cover art by Asilia Franklin-Phipps, 2024. www.asiliafranklin.com

Visit us on the web at www.myersedpress.com to browse our complete list of titles.

DEDICATION

For our families, whose unwavering love and support sustain us; our students, whose curiosity and engagement inspire us daily; and our colleagues, whose intellectual fellowship and camaraderie enrich our academic journey.

CONTENTS

ACKNOWLEDGMENTS

IN MANY WAYS, THIS entire book and the project of putting it together is an acknowledgment—an acknowledgment of what it is to learn, what it is to teach, what it is to study, what it is to do these things *not* alone but together. What we think will become clear when readers engage with these reflections and provocations is that a scholarly life is much more than a series of papers, presentations, or syllabi; it is a way of being in the world that is necessarily in relation (whether we admit that or not) and always impactful in ways beyond our intentions or even our most daring hopes. While we, the editors, need to acknowledge, recognize, and thank the numerous people that encouraged and made this work possible—key here would be Patti Lather herself, Chris Myers of Myers Education Press, and the inspiring students[1] of Gabe's Inquiry Seminar: *Research as Praxis—The Work of Dr. Patti Lather,* whose engagement with and enthusiasm for Patti's work sparked the initial idea for this book—it seems important to note that all the authors involved, in the varied ways in which they chose, acknowledge a wider work that traverses our lifetimes, our shifting subjectivities, and the spaces that enable our interactions. Our daring hope in offering this to the world is rooted in a joyously uncertain understanding that our effort of *thinking with Patti Lather* only continues, begins anew, and becomes something not yet.

Note

1. Elissa Bryant, Jonathan Crocker, Jayme Del Mario, Mang Kim, Ryan Peterson, Kelcia Righton, Rachel Solomon, and Nicole Weinberg.

A Glass of Wine with Patti

GABRIEL HUDDLESTON AND ROBERT J. HELFENBEIN

IT MAY BE A cliché to call this work a labor of love, but our editorial view is that this challenge will disappear once readers dive into the collection of scholars, reflections, and contributions both academic and personal. There can be no doubt that Patti Lather remains a prominent and prolific scholar whose work has been influential in shaping multiple fields, challenging conventional understandings of research and knowledge, and advocating for explicitly political interventions related to social justice and equity in education. We intentionally sought out a diverse group of scholars to contribute to the conversation on the impact that her work had on them developmentally but also in terms of how it pushes work forward now. What we received (and, we hope, what you will soon read) are extremely powerful delineations of an unparalleled scholarly career but also deeply personal notes on Dr. Lather as teacher, mentor, colleague, confidant, and friend. To value that approach, we too begin with more than one story on the life of a scholar.

Much like many of the authors collected here, we begin with a personal note. "A glass of wine with Patti. . . ." This phrase signifies our admiration, respect, and relationship with Dr. Patti Lather. It became a connection between us as Gabe embarked on his academic journey as a doctoral student, with Rob as his advisor and eventual dissertation chair. Rob introduced Gabe to Lather's scholarship in a qualitative inquiry class, but it was later that he introduced him to Patti personally. Gabe first met her at the *Journal of Curriculum Theorizing*'s annual conference, also famously known as "Bergamo." Given her renowned work, it's unsurprising she was there. Despite the conference's relatively small attendance (approximately 120 each year), it boasts an impressive list of academic scholars.

As one attendee put it, "Bergamo is your bookshelf come to life." With scholars including Watkins, Britzman, Ayers, Schubert, Love, Stovall, Berry, Miller, and Taliaferro Baszile attending (to name a few), meeting others at Beramo can be surreal. The presence of Patti Lather only intensifies this feeling. Introduced as Rob's student, Gabe cherished his moments with Dr. Lather (later Patti), particularly during Bergamo's social hours where they discussed high school football from a critical feminist perspective. As Gabe progressed through his Ph.D. coursework and dissertation, Dr. Lather became Patti to him, and Rob's student became Gabe to her. Soon, all three were finding space at the American Educational Research Association (AERA), exchanging ideas over food and wine.

This personal connection to Patti is significant to both of us, but it's further amplified by our intellectual engagement with her work. Gabe recalls writing a book review of *Troubling the Angels* (1997) and realizing his desire for "more Patti" was due to the intentional methodological choices she made to center the voices of the women in the book. Later, Gabe taught a graduate seminar—Research as Praxis: The Work of Patti Lather. Held in-person after the peak of the COVID-19 pandemic, the course was a haven from the ongoing global unrest. Patti and one of the authors in this book, Dr. Janet Miller, occasionally joined the class. The class was diverse, with master's and doctoral students from various programs. One of the students, Dr. Elissa Bryant, is a chapter author in this book. While all students engaged with Patti's work in unique ways, her work consistently sparked intense examination of research methods. As one student exclaimed, "I didn't know what a methodologist did before this class, and now I think I am one!"

At times, Patti's work challenged the notion of emancipatory research, while at other times, it empowered students to rethink research and methodological choices—refusing to accept traditional terminology such as validity and data on its face, but rather, attempting to reinscribe those terms with new sensibilities. Research methods transformed from being perceived as infallible truths to, borrowing a phrase from Stuart Hall (1996), "angels with which to be wrestled."

The journey with Patti didn't stop in the classroom, but extended beyond it. *A glass of wine with Patti* has become a euphemism to capture the complex tapestry of dialogue, challenging and enriching our understanding of research. Each conversation, literal or otherwise, with Patti was a new learning experience, one that held the potential to ignite a new idea or inspire a different perspective. The most distinct aspects of these dialogues were the depth and breadth of the topics covered. We discussed everything from research methodologies and contemporary academic trends to the intricate details of Patti's work and its impact. We dissected her concepts, grappled with her theories, and sought to understand her vision of research as a transformative force. No question was too small or too large to warrant our attention, and every discussion fueled our intellectual curiosity.

While the majority of this collection focuses on the extensive work on critiques of method and implications of philosophical developments on methodology, we also want to point to Patti Lather's impact and influence on/in cultural studies. As both of us engage in cultural studies work, it seems important to note that *Getting Smart* (1991) and *Troubling the Angels* (1997) both became widely popular in cultural studies coursework and noted by cultural studies scholars. Her title, at one point at least, at The Ohio State University was Professor of Cultural Studies and Education. It could be argued that taking on these questions of method and what could be called "the science wars" were natural cultural studies projects—taking on the conflation of education policy, the marketization of education, and computational logics. A rather recent special issue project put forth "a cultural studies of numeracy" (Lather, 2016) and pointed to new avenues for the (post)critical. Again, as evident in this collection, a marker of this distinguished career was its continual movement: from Deleuze and Derrida to Butler and Barad. Patti always seemed to be ahead of the curve, anticipating the next theoretical "turn." The project was always to put theory to work, to see how it might help us, our participants, and our communities. These are lessons we learned from Patti. They represent a commitment that animates our work now and moving forward.

The chapters in this collection, when taken as a whole, chart a similar path wherein reflections on Patti's contributions open up into considerations for future research in education and beyond. Some chapters are written from the vantage points of Patti's contemporaries—detailing personal relationships intertwined with complex investigations into theory, research, and praxis. Others put Patti's ideas "to work" in research, demonstrating how this approach yields no easy answers, but rather, more questions. These questions, when asked, reveal their necessity for meaningful research.

Janet Miller's chapter offers a deeply personal and scholarly reflection on her relationship with Patti. It highlights the pivotal role of this relationship in their academic beginnings and the broader field of curriculum studies. Miller's narrative vividly illustrates how immersing oneself in critical theory, particularly feminist theory, can profoundly impact a scholar both personally and professionally. The collaborative work between **Chris Smithies** and Patti on their groundbreaking publication, *Troubling the Angels*, is explored in Smithies' chapter. This reflection delves into how their meaningful research partnership not only transformed them personally but also revolutionized approaches to sensitive topics and marginalized communities in research.

Examining Lather's contributions to feminist theory and pedagogy, **Susan Adams** highlights how her work has bridged the gap between feminist thought and educational practice. Adams demonstrates how Lather's insights have encouraged more inclusive and empowering teaching methods. **Lisa Mazzei** delves into Lather's engagement with post-humanist theories and new materialisms. Her chapter examines how Lather's later work expanded our understanding of agency, subjectivity, and the role of the non-human in education research.

The critique of scientism in education research forms the core of **Harry Torrance**'s contribution. Torrance analyzes how Lather's work challenged positivist paradigms and advocated for more diverse and critical approaches to educational inquiry. In **Sam Rocha**'s chapter, readers are offered a deeply personal and reflective account of the author's relationship with his mentor. Rocha explores various dimensions of erudition as exemplified by Lather, from her pedagogical approaches to her scholarly work, providing insights into the complexities of academic mentorship and intellectual growth.

A collaborative reflection on the evolution of post-qualitative research is provided by **Elizabeth de Freitas**, **Kate O'Brien**, and **Nathalie Sinclair**. Their chapter engages with Lather's work to explore the complex relationship between qualitative and quantitative research methods. The authors delve into Lather's concept of the "incalculable" and her critique of traditional research paradigms, offering fresh perspectives on how we might reimagine the qual/quant entanglement in social inquiry.

Investigating Lather's contributions to post-qualitative research, **Maggie MacLure**'s chapter highlights how Lather's work bridged critical theory, cultural studies, and education research. MacLure explores how this integration offers new ways to understand the cultural dimensions of education practices and policies. **Elissa Bryant** explores the embodied practice of

Jiu-Jitsu as a form of anti-violent discourse and a means of grappling with
the complexities of anti-racist work. Drawing on the work of Lather and
Karen Barad, Bryant offers a "matterphorical" approach to understanding
Jiu-Jitsu as an embodied praxis for engaging with the (im)possibilities of enacting anti-racist, anti/de-colonial work as a white settler-scholar.

Sarah Sterner focuses on Lather's influence on poststructuralist thinking
in education. Her chapter explores how Lather's engagement with poststructuralist theories reshaped our understanding of knowledge production and
the researcher's role in qualitative inquiry. The profound impact of Lather's
work on education research methodologies is the subject of **Deborah Britzman**'s chapter. In it, she explores how Lather's innovative approaches challenged traditional notions of validity and data collection, pushing researchers to reconsider their methodological choices and embrace more nuanced,
reflexive practices.

Collectively, these chapters provide a rich and nuanced exploration of
Patti Lather's far-reaching impact on education research, feminist theory,
poststructuralism, and cultural studies. They illuminate the expansive scope
and profound depth of her influence—from her bold challenges to established methodological norms to her transformative reshaping of our understanding of knowledge production in education. Our engagement with
Patti, both personal and scholarly, continues to shape the academic paths
we tread. She has become a beacon of inspiration, guiding us through the
labyrinth of academia with her wisdom and insights. Her influence is not
just confined to our academic pursuits but permeates our approach to life,
teaching us to question, to probe, to never stop learning, but also to care
deeply about the people we encounter along the way.

As we continue our journey, we carry Patti's lessons with us, ones that
remind us to remain open to new ideas, to embrace change, and to always
strive for intellectual growth and development. The memories of our times
with Patti, the glasses of wine, the laughter, the debates, and the quiet moments of reflection, are all etched into our minds. They serve as reminders
of our shared journey, a journey that has been as enlightening as it has been
rewarding. And as we move forward, we look to Patti's work, her words,
and our shared experiences with her as a source of inspiration and guidance.

References

Hall, S. (1996). Cultural studies and its theoretical legacies. In D. Morley & K.H. Chen (Eds.), *Stuart Hall: Critical dialogues in cultural studies*, 262–275. Routledge.

Lather, P. (1991). *Getting smart: Feminist research and pedagogy with/in the postmodern.* Routledge.

Lather, P. (2016). Post-face: Cultural studies of numeracy. *Cultural Studies ↔ Critical Methodologies, 16*(5), 502–505. https://doi.org/10.1177/1532708616655771

Lather, P., & Smithies, C. (1997). *Troubling the angels: Women living with HIV/AIDS.* Westview/HarperCollins.

CHAPTER ONE

Entanglings: Feminisms, Qualitative Research, Curriculum, and Generosities of Friendship

JANET L. MILLER

Prelude(s)

I arrive at the entryway of a small conference room, peek in.

Glancing up from the head table, she invites: "Up here, have a seat."

I settle into a creaky wooden chair, quickly search the room. She responds: "They all creak."

Half-giggling, I open my notebook. She shuffles a plethora of pages in what I assume is a final ordering of all that she wants to say in this session.

The wall clock clicks time into place.

She nods: "I'll start."

I smile: "Great."

I'm her only audience member.

I listen intently throughout the session's hour to intricate textual webbings that spin together women studies' perspectives; critical theories; chunks of qualitative research à la Egon Guba; and touches of curriculum thought. All this signaled by her paper's title, the one that has drawn me into this room: "Do Good Girls Make Good Teachers? Gender and the Shaping of Public School Teaching."

I lean forward in my wooden chair, shiver slightly—must be the early autumn air.

******

I'm here conjuring rememberings filtered through 45 subsequent years of conversing, teaching, researching, writing, and conferencing. In particular, I'm retroactively interpreting that slight shiver, that barely discernible movement and moment that accompanied my listening to an academic paper that abounded with theories and data analyses, all of which pondered her main question: "Do Good Girls Make Good Teachers?"

Filled with 1979 versions of feminisms and U.S. women's studies viewpoints, in particular, the paper also grappled with critical theories as interpreted then in the U.S. by mostly white male curriculum theorists. All swirled together with her varied critiques of quantitative educational research as I then understood it: that is, a mostly immalleable research domain of fixities, hierarchies, and supposedly absolute, non-contradictory, objective stances and answers. A world that, for me, suddenly became unsettled by not-quite-yet-fully-formed articulations of a declared feminist wishing to especially call both patriarchy and quantitative research to account.

In those fragmentary moments, I sensed shimmers of thinking differently—a thinking that I did not fully grasp but knew that I did not want to ignore.

All this offered to me in that meager conference room by then-first-year doctoral student, Patti Lather.

Histories: Bergamo, Feminisms, Curriculum

Patti's and my first encounter transpired in Autumn 1979, at a conference center known as Airlie House located in Virginia, just outside Washington, D.C. This was the site where William Pinar, as founder and editor, and I, as managing editor of a new journal called *JCT: Journal of Curriculum Theorizing*, hosted the second official *JCT*-sponsored curriculum theorizing conference. Already established as an annual event, the Airlie conference was part of a burgeoning movement identified as the U.S. reconceptualization of curriculum studies.

In fact, the reconceptualization's traceable beginnings were marked by a number of curriculum theorizing conferences held even prior to Bill

Pinar's organizing, in 1973 at the University of Rochester, NY, a conference entitled Heightened Consciousness, Cultural Revolution and Curriculum Theory (Pinar, 1974). That conference functioned, in great part, as a formal pronouncement of the growing vitality of the U.S. curriculum field's re-conceptualization, wherein no conception of curriculum could ignore the lived—the existential, political, racialized, gendered—experience of those who taught and studied it. The resultant *JCT*'s journal-supported gatherings over the ensuing 45-plus years have come to be known colloquially as The Bergamo Conferences (See Kridel, 1996; Miller, 1978, 1999, 2000; Pinar, 1975, 2004).

These were the parameters of the academic world into which I entered in the mid-1970s, having taught English from 1966 through 1973 in class-rooms filled with high school juniors and seniors. During the latter part of those classroom teaching years, I earned my M.A. in English and education from the University of Rochester, with Bill Pinar serving as my advisor. In 1977, I was awarded my Ph.D. from The Ohio State University (OSU).

As part of my doctoral studies double major, I studied early on with sev-eral faculty in humanities education-English, but my primary interest was in working with Donald Bateman, who was quite well-known in English education circles for his research on transformational grammar.

But it was not this topic that solidified my interest in working with Don. Rather, it was Don, as full professor, who was impressively re-imagining his own career interests, especially in areas that fostered what we now might call *social justice-oriented scholarship*. In spring semester of the second year of my studies, Don, taken with Paulo Freire's (1970) *Pedagogy of the Op-pressed*, invited me to co-teach that book for a quite large Master's seminar group.[1]

I also had the privilege of studying with curriculum theorist Paul Klohr, whose main intellectual interests during my years at OSU focused on varia-tions of existentialism and phenomenology. These were the theoretical lens-es that Paul advocated as particularly appropriate for reconceptual curricu-lum theorizing, especially that which employed autobiography as a primary mode of inquiry.

Among his many supportive acts for his doctoral students, Paul provid-ed constantly updated reading lists and bibliographies beyond those he re-quired for our doctoral courses and seminars. Given that overload of intel-lectual wealth, students often sought individual meetings with Paul during his office hours. Paul met with all in his Ramseyer Hall office, often gazing out his office's windows as means to muse a bit before answering a student's question—and I must admit that many times, that student was me.[2]

By the time I heard Patti deliver her paper at that 1979 Airlie conference, I was an assistant professor immersed in my teaching, researching, writing, and advising obligations. Simultaneously, I was committed to the ever-increasing work involved as managing editor of *JCT* as well as co-organizer of the annual *JCT*-sponsored curriculum theory conferences.

Having completed my dissertation research focused on existential phenomenological philosopher of education, Maxine Greene, and her influences on the U.S. curriculum reconceptualization, I remained moved as well by Greene's unwavering declaration that she indeed was a feminist. Greene (1978) framed her feminist analyses as predicaments of women, especially as she wrote about the histories of women in U.S. education. In those histories, she examined countless examples of the subordination of women teachers by the almost exclusively white men in administrative positions, who dictated moral and pedagogical imperatives that women teachers were expected to enact. Maxine Greene thus constantly urged women—and indeed challenged all educators—to work toward taking action to repair as well as to create positive change:

> There must be critique. There must be ongoing demystification, as there must be an enlarging conversation among those who have had the courage to identify themselves as subordinate, as oppressed. [Further,] connection[s] between the kind of subordination imposed on women and the kind of subordination imposed on schoolchildren must be exposed. (Greene, 1978, pp. 240–41)

Studying Maxine's action-oriented feminist perspectives did challenge me to respond, even as small as my acts might be in working against subjugation of any and all deemed *other*. I thus worked to approach Greene's provocations—as well as Lather's—as vital aspects of my teaching, researching, writing, and *JCT*-managing editor commitments. I vowed, at the very least, to attend to *difference* as both concept and embodiment.

But it was listening to Patti at that Airlie House curriculum theorizing conference, and subsequently conversing with her first at Airlie and then at early Bergamo conferences, that further and primarily propelled my continuing studies of feminisms, especially as these both proliferated and diverged. But influenced too by slogans of *solidarity, sisterhood,* and *community* especially prominent in the U.S. women's movement during the 1960s and '70s, I wanted to examine aspects of feminisms that could illuminate efforts as well as questionings that might address one of my then-main academic preoccupations: that is, possibilities and impossibilities of working toward teacher- and qualitative research-oriented national and international curriculum communities.[3]

Simultaneously, I continued to study the work of curriculum feminists who were theorizing primarily from psychoanalytic, phenomenological, or critical theory perspectives. Indeed, throughout the 1970s, 1980s, and into the 1990s, curriculum feminists researched, for brief example: how gendered meanings and their associated and often inequitable practices were constructed, reproduced, researched, and represented in education contexts; and how pervasive impacts of *patriarchy* affected dominant constructions of *good* teaching and curriculum that ironically too often resulted in maintaining the *feminization* of teaching.

Tiny Interlude

I'm hoping—both here and throughout this writing—that these brief yet situated entwinings provide "good enough brief versions of particular histories" for considering the kinds of questions that Patti Lather has urged us all to ask about feminisms, post qualitative research, and curriculum as a broad field of study.

Assembling: Conferences, Classrooms, Suitcases

In no way am I assuming that I am able to narrate with authority any definitive "beginnings" of the reconceptualization, or of varying feminist perspectives and theories—or of Patti's or my early academic work, or of our first encounter. The subject's lack of transparency to itself, and the ways that one is always already given over to others and to the norms that structure one's recognition—these conditions indeed shatter any possibilities of my offering temporally fixed and fully articulated narrations of what can only be considered as partial, fragmented, elusive memories arising from a non-unitary self. Clearly, according to Judith Butler (2005), narratives of such can only be, simultaneously, the precondition for a subject who both names and can only provide retroactive orderings of its own still-illusive subjectivity.

However, even before I read and continue to read Judith Butler, Patti was pushing me to consider the risks of qualitative research that claims *narrative* as a mode of inquiry, as a way of knowing, and as representational writing. Patti reminded me that in such work, too often a qualitative researcher/narrator is positioned, or is simply assumed to be a fully conscious *self* who can speak with certainty about *what happened* as well as about the *meanings* and *implications* for *others* of such. Patti instead pushed all qualitative researchers to deeply consider the incalculable, the messy, and the responsibilities of not knowing in all our work.

Recalling that shiver, then, I slowly moved to interrogate my uses of an always conscious "I" who supposedly functioned as "fully aware" in my own early autobiographical work in curriculum studies. But I also had to address centuries of autobiography as a mode of literary and personal inquiry that supported that genre as one already functioning as a major U.S. curriculum discourse within the reconceptualist movement (Pinar et al., 1995).

But as I continued to examine implications of an autobiographical self that remains at least partially opaque to itself, I also attempted to attend to Butler's caution: that is, the self's opaqueness still does not license the self to flagrantly do what it wants or to ignore its relations to others.

Patti has never ignored such.

Rather, throughout her career, in the very sharing of her thinking, Patti has performed her work as one form of an accounting of a self that is not in her total possession. She indeed has offered her scholarship as means of acknowledging that version of her "self" in her relationship to others as well as to the fields of inquiry that comprise and compel her scholarship.

All of these emphases have affected her work with generations of eager doctoral students who have lined up to take Patti's introductory and advanced qualitative research classes that she offered as part of her professorial teaching load at The Ohio State University. And having also attended many academic conferences with Patti over the years, I can verify that, following the concluding remarks of all session presenters, numerous attendees would rush the presenters' table to grab one of Patti's printed-out versions of her presentation. She also willingly constructed a sign-up sheet for those who failed to secure a copy.

In fact, early on in our careers, we had to print out copies of our AERA papers to bring to our program sessions. Thus, many of us would load our stapled paper copies into various-sized suitcases, which we then would lug to all our sessions, not to mention to restaurants and cafes before or in-between sessions.

Perhaps the most vivid of our suitcase adventures occurred when Patti and I searched for a quick breakfast in New Orleans before our early morning session. We sat in Café du Monde, enjoying morning clouds scuttling by as well as our chicory coffee and beignets. Then: glancing at my watch, I sound the alarm: "We're almost late, grab the check."

By that time, we were sharing our table with our session's other presenters. My major lingering images of this professional almost-disaster include us dragging our suitcases over cobbled streets, then cradling them in our arms for a bit, then pulling again (no roller suitcases back then), and finally straggling into our conference presentation room. We were five—or maybe it was more like eight minutes late in starting the session. And for sure, we all needed a few deep breaths.

Meanwhile, one of us had lost her suitcase key; the rest of us flung open our suitcase lids and started to pile our papers onto the presentation table, all the while requesting that everyone wait until the end of the session before attempting to grab one or more papers. I'm not sure whose paper pile diminished first.

I *do* know for sure, however, that Patti has received, over the decades of her career, gobs of professorial emails containing conference-centered inquiries and requests—or just plainly interested questions about her scholarship. I take all this as further evidence of Patti's vast influences on both enlarging and complicating the fields of qualitative research, of feminisms, and of curriculum studies.

Positing my slight shiver on that now long-ago late autumn afternoon, as vaguely sensed then, I mean to signal a sort of recognizing as well as an unhinging provoked by Patti and her work. Whatever that shiver entailed . . . that initial encounter with Patti and her thinking, and the generosities she enacted right there, turned me toward decades of totally new glimpses that I could carry away in directions and modes of inquiry *that I myself could both imagine and enact.* This was and is her gift.

Patti's Wildly Prolific Academic Journeys

So, what should be evident by now is that I can't tell this "Patti and Janet first-meeting-and-beyond tale" straight, so to speak. That opening Airlie vignette, for example, is simply one swirling re-membering, a gathering of selves that can never fully recover nor articulate the absolute conditions of our emergences. Throughout this writing, then, I can only gesture toward some always-further entanglings, rather than attempting to delineate "the way it was or is now."

A few of these tangles did involve coincidentally coinciding life-contexts that affected Patti's and my initial conversations following her Airlie House presentation. But in supposedly just reciting these as "facts," I am quite aware that the embodied intensities and entanglements of that early shiver—correlated since then over long distances of time and space—flow through my diffractive rememberings and recitations, including these:

Patti grew up in rural South Dakota and completed her M.A. in American studies at Purdue University in 1972. Although a school administrator, in evaluating her substitute teaching, had declared her a threat to all school children in America, Patti, subsequently and successfully, did teach high school English, history, and American studies in a small town in Indiana. This was during a time in which teachers' creations of their own course syllabi were expected. Patti thus incorporated, for example, all manner of women's literature as well as history into a two-hour time block in the high school schedule entitled American Studies, among other curricular innovations.

Patti's doctoral studies at Indiana University, under the guidance of curriculum scholar Norman Overly, were officially within the field of curriculum and instruction. But Patti's intellectual interests were lodged more firmly in the scholarly arenas of her two chosen minors: one in women's studies, and the other in inquiry methodology, which enabled her to study with the renowned qualitative researcher and theorist, Egon Guba. Patti's Ph.D. was awarded from Indiana University in 1983; her dissertation was entitled *Feminism, Teacher Education and Curricular Change: Women's Studies as Counter-Hegemonic Work* (which indeed contained elements of that Airlie House paper, "Do Good Girls Make Good Teachers?"). Obviously, even in the late 1970s and into the early 1980s, Patti was exploring "the promise of thinking and doing otherwise" (Lather, 2017, p.168).

Patti's major mentor, Norman Overly, had been a doctoral student of Paul Klohr's at The Ohio State University. Productive discontinuities continued to abound in 1988, when Patti, then a professor at Mankato State University in Minnesota, accepted a professorial position at OSU within the Department of Curriculum and Instruction.

And Her Institutional Constraints

During those OSU decades, Patti attained the rank of full professor with tenure. She also joined academic colleagues in either resisting or composing (depending on the then-vacillating political environments) departmental reconfigurations, all of which involved pronounced programmatic struggles among various faculty members. These resulted in the dropping of the curriculum & instruction label in favor of "Social Foundations," (much to Patti's chagrin, given that she had proposed the title, "Cultural Studies of Education"). Eventually, the department settled on "Educational Policy and Leadership." Within these time- and power-intensive reorganizational efforts, Patti also maintained her professorial status and teaching commitments as part of the Graduate Faculty of Women's Studies and of Comparative Studies Departments (Lather, 2006).

Empower-Abilities

Early in her academic career, Patti argued for, as well as critiqued, a *democratized process of inquiry* that supposedly is characterized by negotiation and reciprocity. She worked her initial conceptualizations of qualitative research as those that could pay close attention both to research and to teaching in order to produce what Patti then termed *emancipatory knowledge*. Such knowledge, she postulated, not only could empower the researcher/teacher, the student, and educational studies writ large, but also could and should empower *"the researched."* All this theorizing was further developed in her significant *Harvard Educational Review* article, "Research as Praxis" (Lather, 1986), where she argued for as well as theorized qualitative research designs that could demonstrate a *democratized process of inquiry* characterized by negotiation and reciprocity.

In that very same year, five classroom teachers who had successfully completed their doctoral studies asked me if we six could continue our meetings and discussions of various current scholarship perspectives. I was happy to agree—and immediately mimeographed copies of "Research as Praxis" for all.[4]

These teachers were especially interested in anything that could further illuminate their understandings of the empowering possibilities of being and becoming emancipatory teacher researchers, especially because four of the five were choosing to return to their elementary, middle, or high school classrooms, even as they returned with their doctoral degrees. The fifth member of our informal group study did intend to pursue an academic position, but still wished to be part of our group discussions.

Many of our gatherings featured all five, worrying that if our group disbanded and they returned to their various schools or moved into a new academic position, they would lose all capacity to teach and research in emancipatory ways. But the entire group also had not been shy about sharing their fears that they never could fully enact those ways. They especially couldn't quite imagine how they could work toward emancipatory pedagogy and curriculum, given the returns of neo-liberally imposed constraints on their time within their schooling contexts, including their students' needs, their administrators' expectations, and the intense daily work of teaching.

Patti, in fact, worked diligently to refuse the recharged positivism of a neoliberalism that threatened to squelch my fellow researchers. Patti especially has fought against assimilation, as well as the reduction of the qualitative to an instrumentalism fashioned to meet the demands of an audit culture. Even more, she has insisted on the importance of both epistemological and ontological wrestlings in qualitative research methodologies; she has called out the unthought in how research-based knowledge is conceptualized and produced; and she has pushed us all to move into the messy doings of science, a science of indeterminacy that embraces the unpredictable as well as the potentialities of always becoming.

Further, Patti has contested normalized borders, and she has challenged current educational practices that force understanding too quickly, asking of herself and all her readers involved in qualitative research to trace our complicities in hopes of moving toward some place that might be called "feminist efforts toward a double science" (Lather, 2017, p. 50)—both science and not science. Such imaginaries, she argued, contribute to proliferations of eccentric kinds of science that can address questions of practice in relation to postfoundational theories

As prelude, Patti had been wrestling openly with her desire to employ critical thought into varying forms of emancipatory action. Her first book, *Getting Smart* (1991), continued that line of thinking in that Patti worked toward a praxis-oriented approach to inquiry, even as she also understood that emancipatory aspirations were not innocent of issues of power and control. And in the following decades, Patti was daring us all to engage in qualitative research that would have us embrace "getting lost" (Lather, 2007)—we then must confront unanswerable questions and the necessary experiences of the unknown and of the responsibilities of not knowing. Notably, Patti had argued early on that "not knowing" opens us to possibilities of doing differently in order to engage in committed, self-reflexive, and critical work that situates inquiry as it is lived.

Another Scene, Perhaps a Situated Inquiry As It Was Lived

In one summer in the early 1990s, Elizabeth Ellsworth, our friend Mimi Orner, and I were bemoaning the mandated conference formats, posturings, and equilibrium-seeking research condensations that AERA, as a prime example, seemed mostly to produce. We three were longing for some places/spaces in which to deeply explore our varied work in totally emergent and yet sustained ways. We thus concocted an invitation to some fellow feminists to travel to our farmhouse outside Madison, WI for a weekend in August. And we included, as an enticement, a non-structured suggestion that each of us would get two exquisite hours of the others' undivided attention devoted to our individual work during our non-retreat weekend.

Liz and I picked vegetables from the garden, huddled over the wall phone discussing menus with Mimi, ordered soft drinks and wine, and scrubbed the farmhouse—all in service of the August arrival of five other feminist researchers who worked in differing disciplinary as well as institutional settings.

When it was her turn, Patti decided that she would stage her two hours of exquisite attention time—what she later named her *Naked Methodology* (Lather, 1998) as a situated practice—in the old farmhouse's second-floor, skylight-illuminated, small bathtub jacuzzi. The rest of us sat around the tub, which was elevated a bit on a wooden platform onto which Liz and I, several years before, had painstakingly cut and then cemented each turquoise tile.

As she soaked in the tub, we each, in turn, addressed bare Patti with questions about her "angels" research in collaboration with Chris Smithies and women with HIV/AIDS (Lather & Smithies, 1997). As the late afternoon sun slanted through the skylights above, Patti made it quite clear to us that her nudity did not imply full transparency of the researcher, or of her audience members, or of her eventual readers. Instead, her nakedness was a mask that she invited us to interrogate as an aspect of indeterminacy, as a way to become accountable to complexity, accountable to thinking the limits.

That Wisconsin farmhouse *Naked Methodology* encounter indeed was about bodies literally affecting one another and generating intensities: interfacing, not as objects meeting but as multiplicities emerging from interactions; clothed interrogators all huddling around the tub and with Patti naked in the tub—human bodies, discursive bodies, bodies of thought.

But unlike the self-contained Cartesian body, whose interiority supposedly holds all thoughts, sensations, and feelings, all those bodies could not be easily disentangled from the other "bodies" they affected and by which they were affected. Indeed, we were bodies in stasis and in motion, contingent fields that moved with continual changes of place among constituent particles and forces. Simultaneously, we were mired, not necessarily bounded, not precisely separate. Indeed, what Patti eventually named as her *Naked Methodology* (Lather, 1998) was productive, I believe, of what Kathleen Stewart (2003) describes as transpersonal connections of some kind that have unpredictable and even unimaginable impacts.

Patti indeed has engaged all these issues and more with a critical eye, always wary of how power operates in the production of any one supposed truth. Her scholarship, by extension, has enabled generations of education researchers to imagine, propose, and work to enact paradigm proliferations that challenge any one version of dominant authority.

Among The Generosities . . .

No matter what I have variously and incompletely attempted to highlight as primary in Patti's scholarship, that initial shiver in 1979 in the Airlie House conference room still hovers throughout my multiple returnings to Patti's work—as well as to her arresting titles and concepts that still draw us in: Research as praxis and research as praxis 2.0, fertile obsession, voluptuous validity—and what I continue to interpret as an ache of angel wings . . .

Our subsequent years of talking, of participating together on conference panels, of reading one another's academic writing, of supporting each other's professional and personal efforts—all have affected my academic work, including my teaching, advising of doctoral students, and participating in national and international curriculum studies' organizational as well as theorizing efforts.

As one who has drawn upon Patti Lather's scholarship in numerous ways, I also have witnessed, across decades, Patti's generosity as she readily has attended to colleagues' and students' questions, dilemmas, conundrums, and worries about the unknowable in the conceptualizing and doing of qualitative and post-qualitative versions of education research.

These generosities also have reinforced, I believe, her researching of a plethora of questions regarding what it means to do research in the human sciences. For example, she has examined conceptions and possibilities of social justice within and after identity politics. She also has intensively and multiply questioned the nature of validity in research; of conceptions of self, self-reflexivity, and gender; of voice, experience, and representation; and, in recent iterations, what Patti has called Qualitative Research 2.0—what comes next (Lather, 2013).

Patti's initial academic work thus gestured toward what was to eventually become an overarching preoccupation—that is, to explore the practices of the social sciences within the contexts of post-foundational theories (Lather, 2002).

In particular, she more recently has utilized insights from feminist science studies, a field that critiques the hegemony of science as a deeply gendered knowledge-making system wherein science itself is a contested site. Her employments of feminist theories and research in relation to that contested site within education research thus enabled her to pose possibilities in which a different science might take form. Patti has theorized that "different science" as that which complicates any linearity as well as untroubled claims to objectivity and truth. This, then, is a science of an indeterminacy that not only is less imperialistic, but also is one that grows out of practical engagement with a world that recognizes a different ontology of knowing. This is a science that is more cognizant of contingencies, instabilities, histories, and relationalities (Lather, 2016).

Further and simultaneously, it is Patti who has consistently reminded us, in these still-current moments of government intrusion:

- That "this IS your father's paradigm;" (Lather, 2004);

- That we, more than ever, need to lean toward and into the side of the messy and staying lost;

- And that we also need to engage with/in a relational ontology, with a thinking through the body in the ruins of empire.

Indeed, Patti, in an immanence of doing, continues to invent proliferating possibilities for enacting a daily and future life of difference as yet another way to imagine enacting post-qualitative research.

So, I quickly have noted various aspects of my own academic work in relation to returning again and again to Patti's scholarship. But I've been unable to do so without also interrogating my assumptions and biases toward influences of our 45 or so years of edifying engagements, for these too still reflect effects of that first shiver I felt in 1979.

My now-multiple shivers in fact are ongoing, infused as they are with all kinds of feminisms and curriculum studies; with the post, post-posts-double-posts and their attached conversations and debates in relation to (post) qualitative research; with the busyness, challenges, losses, and enjoyments of daily life—and with a friendship that sustains.

Notes

1. I'm grateful still for what I learned from Don Bateman in that seminar and beyond—not just about Freire's dialogical encounter and *conscientization*, but also about how to re-think and re-imagine beyond what I too quickly took as the confines of academe.

2. I am thankful for Paul's gift of angel wing begonias (mine bloom still), dug from his garden when I moved, as one of his new doctoral students, into my Alhambra Court apartment on North High Street, a few blocks north of the OSU campus. As he did for all his students, Paul carved out numerous office hour appointments with me, sipping tea as he elucidated differences among the phenomenological tenets of Hegel, Husserl, and Heidegger, for example. Paul's multiple influences on generations of curriculum doctoral students remain incalculable.

3. These included my work for the annual Bergamo conferences as well as for *JCT* (1978–1998). Also included are my elected offices in the American Educational Research Association (AERA): chair of the SIG "Critical Issues in Curriculum," (1988–1990); Division B's (Curriculum Studies) secretary (1990–92); and AERA's vice president for Division B (1997–2000). I also brought these emphases as well as questionings of *community* in relation to my work as inaugural president (2004–2007) of the American Association for the Advancement of Curriculum Studies (AAACS), an affiliate of the International Association for the Advancement of Curriculum Studies (IAACS). In addition, I engaged in six years of collaboratings with five other teacher-researchers who, as classroom teachers, wished to study possibilities of becoming—or not—"empowered and empowering" educators (Miller, 1990).

4. In agreeing to meet with those five, I had no idea that we would continue our every three-to-four week meetings for six years. In retrospect, this group remains paramount in my understandings of what perhaps may be possible—albeit in fits and starts and disagreements and power relation struggles as well as in-depth sharings of fears, frustrations and joys—when a

group willingly agrees to collaborate. (This agreeing was not mandated in any way, as too often happens in schools when teachers are tapped by an administrator to "collaborate with others to develop curriculum," for example.)

I did have to deal with my own worries about imposition, in particular, as group members (all my recently graduated or almost graduated doctoral students) often expected that I would remain *the leader*, something I truly did not wish to be. But indeed, I too easily often fell back into that very role. All this was ripe for the six of us to discuss Patti's "Research as Praxis" (Lather, 1986) article many times: to note our ebbs and flows, our stubborn insistences about certain issues and not others, our often-floating definitions of *teacher-researchers*, and our just as stubborn insistences that we, as diverse and opinionated as we were/are, indeed were always-becoming collaborating/collaborators.

References

Butler, J. (2005). *Giving an account of oneself.* Fordham University Press.

Freire, P. (1973). *Pedagogy of the oppressed.* (M. B. Ramos, Trans.). The Seabury Press.

Greene, M. (1978). *Landscapes of learning.* Teachers College Press.

Kridel, C. (1996). Hermeneutic portraits: Section editor's notes. *JCT: Journal of Curriculum Theorizing, 12*(4), 41.

Lather, P. (1983). *Feminisms, teacher education and curricular change: Women's Studies as counter-hegemonic work* [Doctoral dissertation, Indiana University].

Lather, P. (1986). Research as praxis. *Harvard Educational Review, 56*(3), 257–277.

Lather, P. (1991). *Getting smart: Feminist research and pedagogy with/in the postmodern.* Routledge.

Lather, P. (1998). Naked methodology. In V. Olesen & A. Clark (Eds.). *Revisioning women: Feminist cultural and technoscience perspectives* (pp. 136–154). Routledge.

Lather, P. (2002). Postbook: Working the ruins of feminist ethnography. *Signs: A Journal of Women in Culture and Society, 27*(1), 199–227.

Lather, P. (2004). This IS your father's paradigm: Government intrusion and the case of qualitative research in education. *Qualitative Inquiry, 10* (1), 15–34.

Lather, P. (2006). The foundations/cultural studies nexus: An emerging movement in the curriculum studies field. *JCT: Journal of Curriculum Theorizing,* (Summer), 25–40.

Lather, P. (2007). *Getting lost: Feminist efforts toward a double(d) science.* State University of New York Press.

Lather, P. (2013). Methodology-21: What do we do in the afterward? *International Journal of Qualitative Studies in Education, 26*(6), 634–645.

Lather, P. (2016). Top ten+ list: (Re)thinking ontology in (post) qualitative research. *Cultural Studies/Critical Methodologies, 16*(2), 125–131.

Lather, P. (2017). *(Post)critical methodologies: The science possible after the critiques.* Routledge.

Lather, P., & Smithies, C. (1997). *Troubling the angels: Women living with HIV/AIDS.* Westview Press.

Miller, J. L. (1978). Curriculum theory: A recent history. *JCT: Journal of Curriculum Theorizing, 1*(1), 28–43.

Miller, J. L. (1990). *Creating spaces and finding voices: Teachers collaborating for empowerment.* State University of New York Press.

Miller, J. L. (1999). Curriculum reconceptualized: A personal and partial history. In W. F. Pinar (Ed.), *Contemporary curriculum discourses: Twenty years of JCT* (pp. 498–508). Peter Lang.

Miller, J. L. (2000). What's left in the field: A curriculum memoir. *Journal of Curriculum Studies, 32*(2), 253–266.

Pinar, W. F. (Ed.). (1974). *Heightened consciousness, cultural revolution and curriculum theory: The proceedings of the Rochester conference.* McCutchan.

Pinar, W. F. (Ed.). (1975). *Curriculum theorizing: The reconceptualists.* McCutchan.

Pinar, W. F. (2004). *What is curriculum theory?* Lawrence Erlbaum.

Pinar, W. F., Reynolds, W. M., Slattery, P., & Taubman, P. M. (1995). *Understanding curriculum: An introduction to the study of historical and contemporary curriculum discourses.* Peter Lang.

Stewart, K. (2003). The perfectly ordinary life. *Scholar and feminist on line, 2.1*(Summer).

CHAPTER TWO

A Grace Note to *Troubling the Angels*

CHRIS SMITHIES

"Hey Chris, Everything is Data" (Lather, personal communication, 1992).

THESE WORDS BEGAN MY collegial relationship and eventual deep and abiding friendship with Patti Lather. I am Patti's co-author of *Troubling the Angels* (Lather & Smithies, 1997). Patti commented recently that she "worked more intimately with me than any other human being on the planet"(Lather, personal communication, March 7, 2024). We had the opportunity to share a fully collaborative research partnership that was a change, an opening, and a catalyst for both of us. Patti was an academic, a faculty member at The Ohio State University, and I was a psychologist, steeped in application and community. We became co-researchers, co-authors, and friends, and made it all work. We hope that *Troubling the Angels* has served as a model and an inspiration for similar collaborations between scholars and practitioners.

Launched in 1992, our relationship was never entirely ours alone. It was always infused with the stories, struggles, and victories of women living with HIV/AIDS, a then-deadly disease. We worked and learned in the shadow of a worldwide deadly siege that impacted millions of people. More recently, we endured the COVID-19 pandemic, so it has taken effort to remember the battles won and lost to HIV/AIDS.

In 1988, I was working as a staff psychologist at the University of Cincinnati. I organized a support group for women living with HIV/AIDS, the first such group in Ohio. I knew little about HIV/AIDS and remember a stranger bolting when she heard me ask for a book on the topic at a local bookstore. That was a lightweight introduction to the stigma and fear that was associated with the virus.

We met weekly on Wednesday evenings and named ourselves Womancare. The group grew quickly from two members to ten or more and initially included a former nun, a graduate student, a business executive, an older grandmother, and several mothers. Their backgrounds were diverse by race, income, spirituality, and age. Several lived in suburbs, others lived in the poorest area of the city. However, the commonality of their positive HIV/AIDS statuses made for quick and deep bonding. There was intimate sharing, and there were tears, hugs, and a lot of joking and laughter. For some members, Womancare was the most support they had received in any form for years. That group became an oasis of safety and community. We made hospital visits, organized retreats, spoke to groups, traveled to view the AIDS quilt in Washington, D.C., attended funerals, and celebrated a lot of birthdays.

In the safety and warmth of the support group, members found their voices, some expressing themselves genuinely for the first time in their lives. By 1990, they determined that they had a lot to offer to the outside world regarding their experiences living with HIV/AIDS. They wanted to share their knowledge, personal growth, and deep insights. A book, they decided, was the best way to amplify their newly found voices. That community of women was on a mission to help others, to reach out, to leave a legacy. They assumed I could author the book with them, that I would know how to make it happen. I had no idea how to make it happen. I knew I could not approach this task alone.

Enter Patti Lather

Patti, a deep thinker and typically a lone ethnographer, was looking for a project when a mutual colleague introduced us in 1991. Patti and I met and chatted, not knowing we were launching a collaboration, and soon, a friendship that would last our lifetimes. It was clear immediately that we shared feminist values and vision, but I was protective of the support group members who were now clamoring for a book. While I knew Patti was a qualitative researcher and a feminist, could she understand and respect the privilege of being let into the women's intimate circle? Could she handle tears, hugs, the touchy-feely stuff?

Patti's Immersion Experience

I invited Patti to join support group members from several Ohio cities for a weekend retreat. I organized the retreat and have still marveled that we gathered at a convent in Indiana. Fortuitously, Patti's car broke down, so she had to ride with me from Columbus. This was a lot of time together, but we talked the entire trip. I expected to be intimidated by Patti, but found her to be warm, funny, interested in my work, and very smart.

Patti struggled with the intensity of the retreat, the openly loving connections shared by women who were living day-to-day in isolation, fear, and often, shame. She realized that the participants assumed that she was HIV+. When and how to make this distinction? It happened spontaneously in the smoker's alley, relieving her of undercover status.

Privately, Patti shared that she was uncomfortable at the retreat and briefly escaped to the adjacent cemetery, a final resting ground for the Catholic sisters, for time to process it all. I was not surprised and valued her honesty. She endured her discomfort with curiosity and a touch of spirituality. During the closing session, the attendees gathered in a huge and sustained group hug. Patti, touched by this image of strong and connected women, saw angels. The image remained with her and became integral to her effort to understand survivorship.

By the end of Patti's immersion experience, I knew she was all-in, that I could trust her to honor these women in all respects. I was excited about our pending partnership. Our charge was simple: to get their stories out.

Patti had no reservations regarding collaboration. Reassured by our easy bonding, she decided early on that I would be easy to work with and that was "terribly important"(Lather, personal communication, March 7, 2024). Typically, Patti worked alone, but adapted well to having a co-researcher, experiencing relief that she did not have to do all the work herself, learning to let it flow. Becoming involved in the world of HIV/AIDS was an unexpected pivot in her life. Little did she know she would be holding hands, singing songs, witnessing tears, and eating cake while doing research. Or that she would find herself "twitching" for days after we visited a dying mom in her home (Lather & Smithies, 1997, p. 154).

Though Patti referred to herself as "somewhat a hired hand," this was not the case (Lather, personal communication, March 7, 2024). Our respective skill sets were quite different and equally necessary for this research. Patti was rooted in the academy and had experience with publishing, grant writing, networking, and especially, ethnographic field methods. As a clinical psychologist, I was established and trusted in the HIV/AIDS community and provided unique access to enthusiastic study participants. We shared identities as feminists, and our work and lives reflected those deeply held political and social values. Feminism meant giving voice to an underrepresented group, refusing to objectify, to categorize, or to hold up for expert scrutiny. Rather, we believed that we were privileged to be witnesses, "giving testimony to what is happening to these women" (Lather & Smithies, 1997, p. 127). Qualitative methodologies rooted in feminism combined with a devastating but unique crisis of opportunity allowed and required us to empower participants to speak their truth, to document their experiences, and to collaborate with them. Our intent was never to persuade or push any woman toward feminist identification. However, during the support group process in general, and the research process in particular, members expressed feelings of empowerment, pride, and sisterhood. Patti and I may have been feminist role models, but in truth, we were privileged, HIV-negative women graced with access and opportunity during a tragedy. These women let us in while facing almost inevitable death sentences. Patti and I spoke often of our responsibility to listen, organize, write, and publish, knowing that our participants were, as Linda B. emphasized, "on deadline, you know." She also reminded us that "Statistics are human beings with the tears wiped off" (Lather & Smithies, 1997, p. xxvi).

Naked Methodology

How could we do this work? Figuring this out was at the heart of our collaboration. And there was no better place to do this than in the hot tub on my back porch, a sign of the times in the 1990s. We would unwind from our otherwise busy lives and have both deep and pragmatic conversations about purpose and methodologies. Initially, we planned to conduct individual interviews with members of HIV/AIDS support groups in Cincinnati, Columbus, Dayton, and Cleveland. In preparation, we met with members of Womancare, the Cincinnati support group, to elicit their ideas for a protocol of questions for the individual interviews. The conversation that evening was notably enthusiastic and dynamic, with the women themselves expanding the discussion in unexpected and interesting directions. This exciting evening, combined with our commitment to participant inclusion at all stages of the study, significantly changed the trajectory of our research.

I suggested to Patti that we switch the interview methodology from individual interviews to group interviews. Patti agreed and suddenly we had a new design for our study. We knew this would mean more complicated analyses, organization, and presentation. But as anticipated, group interviews significantly enriched the interview experiences for the participants and for the co-researchers and brought energy and sisterhood into the data. We conducted group interviews throughout 1992 and 1993, traveling to Cincinnati, Columbus, Dayton, and Cleveland. Participants signed consent forms and agreed that discussions could be recorded. Patti and I sometimes prompted dialogue, but much of the data flowed from conversations among the group members.

Data analysis required hours of organizing narratives around emergent themes that included life after diagnosis, relationships, making meaning of living/dying with HIV/AIDS, and support groups. Independently, Patti collected AIDS-related educational information and resources. She discovered culturally and politically relevant poetry and art. Ever the scholar, she found "cooling comfort to escape from the intensity of fieldwork to library stacks" where she pursued angelology, Rilke, Benjamin, and more. Her essays were deep and dense and difficult for me to understand. But I found provocative gems and insights and mostly understood the intent of her scholarship. Patti wrote that the work of *Angels* was to "make the text say more and other about something as absurd and complicated, as untimely as dying in the prime of life of a disease of global proportions" (Lather & Smithies, 1997, p. 235). Her essays eventually became the angel intertext chapters, lending intellectual integrity and academic reach to *Troubling the Angels*.

Format for The Book

How could we present such a mix of data, analyses, education, reflections, art, and angel essays? Patti was the mastermind of design and created the innovative multi-layered format for the book. Narratives by the women had to be highlighted and were centralized along the upper halves of pages. Our analyses and commentary appeared in smaller font at the bottom of the pages. Interspersed were factoid boxes, which included information on HIV/AIDS, as well as poetry, contributed mostly by the participants, and art. The angel intertext chapters were separate, bridges to deeper reflection and understanding.

We were authoring this book for a very wide audience, and the multi-layered format allowed us to accomplish this goal of wide reader accessibility and relevance. Patti's format prioritized participants' stories for readers who were HIV+ as well as their loved ones and caregivers. Commentary by the co-researchers included our process, reflections, and reactions to all that we heard and learned. We discussed the qualitative research design and ethnographic study methods, with the intention to be instructive to future researchers. For the student, the survivor, the professional, *Troubling the Angels* provided HIV/AIDS education, context, and inspiration. And Patti's angel intertexts provided a deep dive into the existential and philosophical realms.

With the passage of time, many participants became ill, and some succumbed to AIDS. The survivors became impatient waiting for the book. We wanted to share the progress we had made and keep participants engaged with the research process. To accomplish this, Patti published a desktop draft of the book, titled *Troubling Angels*. Participants in the Cincinnati support group, who first envisioned this entire project, were the first to receive copies. Across all the support groups, members were ecstatic to hold that book in their hands and to see their own words in print. They had compliments, comments, and criticisms, and we sought this feedback.

To collect this new data, we conducted member checks in a group interview format. We listened to and recorded their positive as well as critical feedback. Those meetings further extended our commitment to include participants as collaborators rather than subjects. We relied on this added layer of accountability to further guide our work, especially regarding the angel intertexts and the title of the book.

Clipping Wings and Troubling Title

"Clipping the angels' wings" was Patti's expression for how we addressed my discomfort with the length and depth of the angel intertext chapters. I was concerned that the angels would de-centralize women who were struggling in earthly lives to manage doctor appointments, medical tests and hospitalizations, relationships, children, financial strain, grief, and fear. I was both right and wrong, as we learned from the member checks. Some participants felt confused or distracted by the angel intertexts; some ignored them. Other women found them beautiful, spiritual, and comforting. Patti listened to all the feedback and decided to "clip" some wings while also standing by her "stubborn attachment to the necessary angels." This process of feedback, collaboration, and compromise involving co-researchers and participants epitomized and defined feminist mission and methodologies.

Troubling Angels or Troubling THE Angels?

At the conclusion of that first retreat, there was that magnificent moment, a sustained group hug in a candlelit room. Patti saw angels and as she learned more, she came to view the women as *troubling angels*, burdened with the mission to wake us up, to worry us, to trouble us to be better selves/researchers/friends/family. She proposed the book title *Troubling Angels*, evoking her inclination to be a troublemaker, to stir the pot, to push and protest. During the member check, one woman stated, "Troubling has a negative connotation and could be softened" (Lather & Smithies, 1997). I was worried by the implication that women living with HIV/AIDS were trouble, a result of trouble, or ongoing trouble. As a trouble mender, my mission was always toward connection, empowerment, support, and understanding. Patti and I worked to understand the perspective of the other but neither of us was relenting on the title. We could not think of another title but after a long walk and much thought, I suggested *Troubling THE Angels*. Patti's first comment was "Hmm . . ." and that was encouraging. Soon Patti said the "the" would do "just fine." We were mutually satisfied with the compromise that managed to reflect different perspectives that were always vital to the entire research endeavor.

Publication: *Troubling the Angels*, Westview Press, 1997

Data collection took a long time, and data analysis was slowed in 1995 by my three-month stay in Paraguay, required to adopt my daughter. That was also the year of the introduction of Highly Active Antiretroviral Therapy (HAART) that dramatically reduced AIDS mortality and HIV transmission. By 1997 and the publication of *Troubling the Angels*, AIDS in the United States had shifted from a crisis of suffering and death to virus management and restored health. This was a stunning, rapturous miracle, and it significantly changed the relevance and meaning of five years of research and collaboration. *Troubling the Angels* became a historical documentation of women affected by HIV/AIDS during the worst part of the AIDS crisis. It was a collection of memoirs by the deceased and a retrospective journal of suffering, fortitude, and sisterhood for the survivors.

"It's Been a Helluva Trip" (Sidle, personal communication, April 7, 2024)

Preparing to write this chapter required rereading *Troubling the Angels* and remembering not just the work of our collaboration but also the work of caring for and loving the women in the support groups. I experienced a renewed sense of grief and loss as I recalled the individual women who died, thinking about all they suffered, all they have missed, and all those who have missed them. *Troubling the Angels* was hardly a bestseller or a commonplace read, but Patti and I have taken comfort knowing that their voices have been out there in some small way, and that we facilitated that opportunity.

I shared my sadness with Patti. She reminded me that "everything is data," including my grief, which became a case of writer's block. It was both difficult and gratifying to look back. Only Patti traveled on this journey with me. It was never just research collaboration but included dealing with a lot of hard stuff. There was no investigator distancing or safe objectivity. We were not HIV+ but we were in the trenches, together. What had started in 1992 as a promise to share the voices and experiences of diverse women coping with a devastating disease had continued to be a catalyst for our own reflection and friendship.

Simultaneous with writing this reflection, I received an email from a woman who was an early member of the Cincinnati support group and a participant in the research. This synchronicity was perfect and relieved my sadness. I submitted prompts to Linda, and she responded with insights, vivid memories, and wit. This extension of member participation pleased me. Linda, known in the book as Linda B, now Linda Sidle, was infected at age 39 by her since-deceased husband. Now in her seventies, Linda shared that she was still working, living in her hometown, and had taken back her family name (and gave permission for her full name to be used here). In 2013, on World AIDS Day, she came out at work as HIV+, to "hugs, tears, and acceptance" from her co-workers. She has been a steadfast AIDS activist, at one time traveling to Congress to ask for funding and meeting the mother of Ryan White. She traveled to Florida to speak to a class that read *Troubling the Angels*. She worked for the IRS for ten years and used an inheritance to buy a tobacco farm. She remarried, and fifteen years later, "I tossed him into the front yard (literally)" (Sidle, personal communication, April 7, 2024).

Linda recalled that first retreat that tested Patti: "I remember so well the retreat we had in Indiana at the Catholic sisters' [home] where the showers were cold. . . . But all of us were together . . . a rare gift in those days. We struggled to have a support group. It was magical." She goes on to add:

> Do you two ladies realize you are forever on the frontier of this disease just by writing a book, bringing all these women together from the four corners of the state of Ohio: Ponder that for a while. And look at us now, wearing Depends and orthopedic shoes. I still have both knees though. (Sidle, personal communication, April 7, 2024)

Very few researchers have had the heartwarming opportunity to receive such validation from a research participant. It has touched Patti and me deeply. This is the grace note to our research, our collaboration, and our friendship.

Future Possibilities

Troubling the Angels was a unique collaboration between an academic and a community-based practitioner. Why did it work? Patti and I were mutually rooted in feminism, so we shared a value system. This was fundamental to every decision, every method, and every aspect of our process. Beyond that, our training and skill sets were quite different but complementary for this research. I provided mission and access, and Patti provided methods and professional connections. I envisioned a reach to caregivers, family members, helping professionals, and support for HIV+ women, especially those enduring HIV/AIDS in isolation. Patti envisioned a book that would speak to the women themselves and to an intellectual community of researchers and educators.

We succeeded in bridging what has been a wide divide between the ivory tower and communities. Comments came in from a wide and diverse audience. Patti would periodically shoot me an email with a thoughtful reaction, a rave review, appreciation, or a request to present our work at a conference.

Most important to our work were the women, our participants, who expressed ownership of the process and the book. They were open, thoughtful, articulate, and connected to one another. Some described the inclusive process as therapeutic. Some, expecting abbreviated lives, found that the book gave meaning to their experiences. Many participants loved the book, others liked parts of it, and many chose to give the book to friends and family.

One participant gave the book to her doctor, who mostly treated gay men, and told him he had to read it. And to Patti's surprise and pleasure she said, "This was the first thing I wrote that my mother engaged with"(Lather, personal communication, March 7, 2024).

Research does not usually conclude with a happy, much less joyous, ending. With highly effective medication, soon widely available in the United States, HIV became undetectable for most HIV+ people. It is ironic that what we studied, in part, was now a managed factor in the lives of survivors. While HIV medications required diligence and usually came with side effects, women went on to lead healthy lives, to pursue education, careers, marriages, and parenthood. We have wondered what has been the impact of this survival, 30 years after facing a death sentence? Linda addressed this:

> We all get a cross. It's a cross we bear but a cross we share with all those who see us carry this cross. Our respective crosses are not only our lessons but the lessons for others. I find myself asking God how He could see His way to let me remain after losing so many friends. . . . Later this month I will get my first HIV shot. Cabenuva. Once a month. No more daily pills. Ladies, it's been a helluva trip." (Sidle, personal communication, April 7, 2024)

Patti and I hold hope that our successful collaboration will inspire other academics and community practitioners to find one another and form partnerships. We discovered that methodology that promotes inclusion, transparency, and trust revealed "data" that would not have surfaced with traditional methodology.

Troubling the Angels would never have been researched and published without Patti Lather, my collaborator and dear friend. Together, and with the support group women, we chronicled the tragic and the beautiful. We could not be more grateful that the sea change in survival transformed our collaboration from a documentation of living and dying with HIV/AIDS to one of miraculous recoveries, unexpected futures, and enduring sisterhood[1].

Afternote

In loving memory of Charlene, Diane, Jane, Kathleen, Lori, Louisa and her young daughter, and Nancy.

Note

1. Special thanks to Patti Lather, Louise Douce, Peg Mosher, and Sandy Shullman, for their encouragement and insights when I had writer's block. And to Ruth Fassinger for extensive and invigorating review of a first draft.

Reference

Lather, P., & Smithies, C. (1997). *Troubling the angels: Women living with HIV/AIDS.* Westview.

Note

CHAPTER THREE

Troubling the Researcher and Researching My Praxis

Susan R. Adams

Introduction

IN 2009, WHILE ENROLLED in a language education doctoral program, I was simultaneously directing a university-based federal grant in which I taught graduate courses for practicing middle and high school educators. The goal of the grant and of the courses was to improve instructional conditions for English language learners. My early assumption was that I would design a dissertation study that would demonstrate some sort of learning outcome or perspective shift that resulted from the graduate courses I was teaching. This sentiment was shared by both my chair and the professor teaching my research class. My assignment was to write a paper in which I began framing this prospective research study from an epistemological and methodological perspective based on what we had been reading. Nevertheless, I sensed something was amiss. I really struggled with how to write this paper.

With the imminent paper deadline looming and a cursor blinking at me on an empty page, I squandered a great deal of time clicking through hyperlinks, scouring reference lists, randomly skimming articles, and following my curiosity wherever it drew me. Nothing seemed to be exactly what I was looking for, but the search was far more pleasant than staring at the blank page in a panic. After a few hours of task avoidance, I tumbled into Patti Lather's 1986 classic, "Research as Praxis." I had been actively avoiding reading this article precisely because several classmates and a mentor or two had urged me to read it, and if I am honest, I did not enjoy being told how much I would love Lather's work. I did not know anything about Lather; I just did not like being told what to read. But on this late Saturday night, with a ticking deadline clock looming large in my imagination, I took a deep breath and clicked the link.

As I read "Research as Praxi" (Lather, 1986), I felt like I was falling fast down a rabbit hole not unlike Alice's. I had no idea where this hole was taking me, but the light from the surface was barely visible and I knew, *absolutely knew*, that I was in trouble. Deep trouble. This article was not on the reading list in my major, which was literacy, culture, and language in education. I did have the fleeting thought that none of the philosophy we were reading felt like a good fit for the study I was imagining and remembered the shocked look on my chair's face when I once asked her innocently if we all had to situate our research project in those theorists.

Here is but a small sampling of the words which rocked me to the core:

> An emancipatory social research calls for empowering approaches to research whereby both researcher and researched become, in the words of feminist singer-poet Chris Williamson, "the changer and the changed." For researchers with emancipatory aspirations, doing empirical research offers a powerful opportunity for praxis to the extent that the research process enables people to change by encouraging self-reflection and a deeper understanding of their particular situations. (Lather, 1986, p. 263)

My heart pounded as I realized that this study might require more from me than just a lot of reading, writing, and hard work. It might demand something more from me than academic excellence.

> I argue that we must go beyond the concern for more and better data to a concern for research as praxis. What I suggest is that we consciously use our research to help participants understand and change their situations. (Lather, 1986, p. 263)

Oh, now you have my attention, Patti Lather. As I thought about the challenges facing K–12 teachers, I shared your desire to create time and space in which teachers could think deeply and work together to make changes that matter to them and to their students.

> If it is to spur toward action, theory must be grounded in the self-under-
> standings of the dispossessed even as it seeks to enable them to reevaluate
> themselves and their situations. This is the central paradox of critical the-
> ory and provides its greatest challenge. The potential for creating recipro-
> cal, dialogic research designs is rooted in the intersection between people's
> self-understandings and the researcher's efforts to provide a change-en-
> hancing context . . . whereby the people for whom the theory is supposed
> to be emancipatory can participate in its construction and validation.
> (Lather, 1986, p. 269)

Yes, this is what I was seeking: research and learning that is co-con-
structed and cooperatively analyzed by the teachers, my research participants. Every teacher I know has been on the receiving end of professional
development designed to fix them and even to *teacher-proof* instruction. I
believe that teachers are capable of doing this demanding work given the
right conditions.

> Catalytic validity represents the degree to which the research process reori-
> ents, focuses, and energizes participants toward knowing reality in order to
> transform it, a process Freire (1973) terms conscientization. . . . The argu-
> ment for catalytic validity is premised not only within a recognition of the
> reality-altering impact of the research process, but also in the desire to con-
> sciously channel this impact so that respondents gain self-understanding
> and, ultimately, self-determination through research participation. (Lather,
> 1986, p. 272)

Teachers as self-determining agents building classrooms in which learners experience the same kind of respect and autonomy? Yes, please!

As I read, my heart rate skyrocketed and, in my mind, exploded a new
consciousness of the implications of my positionality, of my own hidden
needs and fears, and of my potentially abusive application of research study
participants' words and stories. I had been preparing to do research *to* and
on my participants, but what I realized now is that I was ethically obligated
to do research *with* and *for* my participants.

I felt lost. I felt found. I felt scared, challenged, inspired, and elated.
Lather's words articulated who I aspired to be as a researcher. However,
this new clarity was far afield of the paradigms and philosophies we were
reading in my language education classes. I could see how the language edu-

cation and Lather's ethic should be connected, but this was unlike anything else I was reading in my coursework. And this felt like a problem.

Breathless and shaky, I emailed my professor late on that Saturday night (with the paper due in 24 hours) and hoped to catch her attention with the subject line, "HELP! Talk me off the ledge!". In the body of the email, I explained my situation and, wonder of all wonders, my professor replied while I was still sitting at my desk. She extended my deadline by four days and was receptive to Patti Lather's influence because she had studied at The Ohio State University and knew of Patti's reputation as a scholar. With her blessing, I did the best I could in four days to get my head around the basic ideas and implications of "Research as Praxis." In preparation for writing this chapter, I re-read that paper and while I did not set the academic world on fire with my brilliance, it is still quite clear that I was making a firm declaration of my intentions for my dissertation to be rooted in the methodological commitments I discerned in Lather's work. Already I was taking deliberate steps off the prescribed path of language education and into a field of study I did not even have a name for.

The Backstory

While I am intrigued by philosophy, and indeed have earned a Ph.D., I am not a true philosopher by any stretch of the imagination. This is not me being modest. My background is teacher education, more specifically in language education and secondary teaching. Most of my studies have focused on improving instruction for students in foreign language and English as a Second Language (ESL) classrooms. Even in my language education graduate courses, the focus was on utilizing discourse analysis (Gee, 2014), the New London Group's creation of multiliteracies (1996), or on current applications of Vygotsky's (1978) Zone of Proximal Development (ZPD) with very little interrogation of underlying philosophy. It was a revelation to actually *read* Vygotsky directly instead of simply reading someone else's interpretation of the ZPD. Our readings were grounded in the social construction of meaning, but even that grounding did little to excavate the underlying philosophies.

My professional work took an unexpected turn in the early 2000s when I shifted away from Spanish teaching into an ESL high school classroom while the district in which I taught was swept up in the chase for one of the earliest Bill and Melinda Gates Small Schools grants. I was selected to serve as a team and building representative as we prepared our portfolios for the grant application. As a result, I was invited into spaces that were completely new to me at the district level. We were provided with some puzzling professional development opportunities, most of which were of little use to me as the primary portfolio writer for my team. But a major component of our experiences included a five-day workshop as an introduction to what was cryptically called Critical Friends Groups, also known as CFGs and now referred to in my work as Intentional Learning Communities (ILCs).

I have written elsewhere (Adams & Peterson-Veatch, 2012; Adams & Breidenstein, 2024) about the life-changing excitement of the learning I experienced, but for the sake of this chapter, the connection between "Research as Praxis" and ILCs is that much of the focus of the workshop was unlearning, excavating assumptions, noticing biases, and questioning traditional ways of engaging with students and colleagues. The ILC work asked me to pay attention to the impact of my underlying beliefs on students, particularly on students of color. I was challenged to question the efficacy and outcomes of exerting my teacherly authority and power over students. We were asked to de-privatize our teaching practices with our colleagues and to trust one another with our vulnerabilities. These questions were quite shocking to a good midwestern, first-generation college, pink-collared, high school teacher who suddenly realized her complicity with the deep inequities of public K–12 education. As I learned about ILCs and then read "Research as Praxis" (Lather, 1986), I was struck deeply by how close I had come to obediently going through the motions of designing a study that would do nothing more than advance my own professional goals.

This ILC experience changed the way I organized my classroom learning community. I began showing my puzzled ESL students my agendas and asking for feedback. I attempted to co-negotiate classroom norms which were completely culturally inaccessible to my students hailing from five continents. Perhaps most importantly, my new unlearning and re-learning caused me to notice my own biases and prejudices during hallway interactions with students who were not in my classes. I tried new ways of talking to kids who were wandering the halls, changing my stance from hallway monitor to hallway facilitator. I asked "Honey, what is going on? How can I help?" with a friendly tone instead of barking "Where are you supposed to be?" and got astonishing results. Often the students would tell me exactly what was going on and why they were not in class. This usually led to thoughtful conversations that culminated with me walking them to their classrooms and joyfully announcing to their irritated teacher, "Look! I found Josh and he now has a pencil AND a textbook!" Sometimes the truth was that the teacher was secretly hoping Josh would not show up for class, but what I discovered is that Josh now saw me as an adult who cared about his well-being and whom he could seek out for help in other situations. In the cafeteria, instead of demanding that students take their trays back and dump their trash, I began circulating with a trash can, offering to take the trash for them like a waitress in a restaurant. Some students were happy to hand me their trash; others were horrified and insisted they would make sure their whole table got cleared. Either way, the results pleased the cafeteria workers and completely changed the tone of our lunch period.

Small, but persistent steps such as these were slowly changing the culture of our small school team of students and teachers. We used the ILC principles to develop our meeting agendas and ILC protocols to do data analysis from an equity lens to evaluate our students' learning. This was no easy feat at a school infamous for its multigenerational dropout rates and abysmal standardized testing scores—a school that was once listed in a national newspaper as one of the "Top 24 Failing High Schools." We were not yet moving the needle, but some of us were changing the school by changing ourselves first.

In the years following this five-day training, I had zealously jumped at every opportunity to get involved with the organization which housed the work and with the facilitators I deeply admired. I pursued pathways to be certified as a national facilitator—a recognition which had just been bestowed upon me a few months before I stumbled onto "Research as Praxis. (Lather, 1986).

Reading Lather took me down, down, down several layers into the deep underlying beliefs I hold as a teacher and as someone trying to position herself as an emerging researcher. And because I encountered Lather's work with very little preparation, I read everything I could and held on for dear life. I had to Google names of philosophers she referenced and referred to like old friends. I had to read, reread, and stop regularly to ask myself, "What is Patti talking about here? And what does it mean for my research?"

This unexpected detour into philosophy woke up some anger in me. Why didn't I know this? How was I supposed to catch up and get my head around such complex ideas at the end of my doctoral coursework? But as Patti herself says in several places in her Patti-way, once you know, you do not get to *not* know the truths she is revealing in the questions she is asking. I had to accept that there was no going back and that I had just chosen a much harder path for myself than I originally imagined. For me, this was a moment of getting clear about what research integrity means from the very beginning of conceptualizing a study in which humans are the focus.

Now What? Implications in My Research Methodology

So, I read. I read everything I could get my hands on (Lather, 1986; Lather, 1991; Lather, 2001; Lather, 2007; Lather, 2012; Lather & Smithies, 1997). I slugged my way through complex texts, googling references that were unknown to me in a frantic attempt to fully grasp what Lather meant. To keep her unique speech patterns in my head, I listened to YouTube recordings until I could "hear" Patti in my mind as I read again. *Engaging Science Policy* (Lather, 2012) was so challenging I shut my office door and read the entire book aloud to myself very slowly, stopping regularly to ask myself what in the world Patti was talking about. I am not sure I could pass an Accelerated Reader™ quiz on the book, but I got through it.

I stalked Patti Lather at conferences. I took notes when she gave keynotes. I listened to old Internet recordings of lectures. And I got to meet her several times in person, most notably at the *JCT* Bergamo conferences where she was a beloved fixture, and where several times she gave riveting and hilarious keynote addresses. More than once I cautiously approached Patti to tell her that she was getting me into a lot of trouble. Quite predictably, she roared with laughter and assured me she expected nothing less.

While "Research as Praxis" woke me up, what perhaps influenced me even more was the stance taken by Lather and co-researcher, Chris Smithies, in *Troubling the Angels* (1997). While Lather is rarely explicit about research methods in other publications, I was riveted by the level of detail articulated by Lather and Smithies as their study of women with HIV/AIDS unfolds more like a novel and less like a dry, predictable recounting of a clear research series of steps. And most notably for me, the participants spoke into the project from the beginning and demanded that Lather and Smithies produce a book they might actually *want* to read, or what they described as a "K-Mart book" (Lather & Smithies, 1997) that a normal person could pick up and read rather than a highbrow academic publication that would feel inaccessible and irrelevant and in which the participants might not even recognize themselves.

This research approach, sometimes described by Lather as emancipatory participative research, illuminated for me a possibility of doing research *with* a group of teachers rather than doing research *to* a group of teachers. This idea of co-constructing a research study made complete sense to me from an ILC perspective as well. The underlying principles of ILCs are grounded in a deep respect for the educator participants' capacities to craft their own agendas, determine what they want to study, identify their own goals, and actively determine the direction of their own groups. ILCs created spaces in which teachers could decide for themselves what was of most importance, what the data means, and how to make instructional design changes in response to their findings rather than simply allowing an authority figure (a principal, a district leader, or worse, an external researcher) to explain the problem and mandate a response. I felt the two pieces click into place in my mind like puzzle pieces and knew my study could not take advantage of my power as a researcher at the expense of teacher participants. I could not fall into the temptation Lather describes, citing Visweswaran, as "the university rescue mission in search of the voiceless" (Visweswaran, 1994, p. 69, cited in Lather, 2001, p. 202).

I was designing an ethnographic study focused on understanding the meaning of race-based teacher professional development. I was mindful of my awkward positionality as a participant in the professional development experience, as a member of our group, as a convener of our group, and as a researcher attempting to represent what the participants wanted to say about their individual and collective experiences during and in the years following the professional development experience. Lather and Smithies'(1997) commitments to getting out of the way of the women in *Troubling the Angels* provided some guidance, but a major difference between us is that I was not simply a researcher asking to tell the story; I was also a participant, a fellow teacher, and the person who facilitated our group meetings. It was not going to be enough to do some basic member checking.

Doubled Epistemology: Turning the Lens on Myself

Lather (1986) insists that "the goal of emancipatory research is to encourage *self-reflection and deeper understanding* on the part of the persons being researched at least as much as it is to generate . . . knowledge" (p. 266, emphasis added). I was intrigued by the question of what I might learn about myself in the process of writing a dissertation, and it seemed simple enough in those early days to agree that after I completed my analysis of the data, I would examine myself with the same lens and write about what I discovered.

I was intrigued by Lather's (2001) challenge to commit to a doubled epistemology "where the text becomes a site of the failures of representation, and textual experiments are not so much about solving the crisis of representation as about troubling the very claims to represent" (p. 201). I believed I was prepared to "Problematize the researcher as 'the one who knows,'" (Lather, 2001, p. 202, citing Judith Butler, 1993), but Lather (2001) also describes ethnography (my selected methodology) as "Placed outside of mastery and victory narratives [in which] ethnography becomes a kind of self-wounding laboratory for discovering the rules by which truth is produced" (p. 202).

The anticipation of that textual failure trembled within me as I grasped the impossibility of the task before me, yet I had to say *something* in order to complete my dissertation. And I was determined to tell a faithful story of our shared and individual experiences and of our becoming a people, an *ethnos*, which is what gradually drew me away from phenomenology and into ethnography.

And while I innocently believed that I understood what I was taking on in the early days of designing the study and writing my methodology chapter (2013), the truth is I had no idea what darkness would be waiting for me later as I wrote what I believed to be the final chapter. In the early days, I was focused on being "accountable to complexity" (Lather, 2009, p. 202-3) and naively overlooked the conclusion of the sentence which warns that, "thinking the limit becomes the task, and much opens up in terms of ways to proceed for those who know both too much and too little" (Lather, 2001, p. 203). I was struck by the poetry and brilliance of the language but neither heard nor heeded the clear caution about the ugly truth about research and researchers embedded in those pretty words.

And this "discovering the rules by which truth is produced" (Lather, 2001, p. 202) is what led me into a dark turn as I neared the finish line. I began to understand the fragility of the entire research enterprise. My study participants actively joined me in conducting more than ten hours of interview text analysis, even to the point of co-creating categories. I created multiple versions of graphics attempting to show the complicated relationships between themes before they agreed that I finally got it right. But they entrusted the ultimate task of narrative writing to me. And while I felt that I did indeed have a firm grasp on the study group's conclusions, now I could see from the inside that at the end of it all, someone must take a stand and say what it all means. And this is where I began to melt down, but also to begin to wonder about the credibility of anything labeled "research." *Who gets to decide what anything means? What are we doing in the name of research? What exactly are we accomplishing?*

Suddenly, I also understood the strange game I was playing with my dissertation committee as I sought their approval and validation of my research results. The reality of myself as a researcher who "know[s] both too much and too little" (Lather, 2001, p. 203), but who must convince the committee that I had indeed met the dissertation challenge and that I indeed did know *something,* exploded into my consciousness. As I did the self-imposed self-reflection I had promised to do, I employed the metaphor of dance that my study group had played with during their analysis. To my horror when I turned that lens on myself, I saw myself dancing a humiliating burlesque on an imaginary conference table while my committee members evaluated my form, my body, my costume selection, and my desirability. I now understood that my job in the final defense was to dance with confidence, to get naked *enough*, without getting *too naked*, and to pretend that this performance was not at all weird or awkward. Once you see this image in yourself and your willingness in your mind, you cannot unsee it.

Turning the dance metaphor lens upon myself was completely predictable when I returned again to Lather's insistence that the researcher cannot remain detached from the work of the study and its members. If I asked the study group to be vulnerable, I was obligated *a priori* by virtue of the methodological commitments I made to be vulnerable in exactly the same ways. If they were dancing, I must dance, too. If they were seeing things from new vantage points, I was understanding my own experiences from new perspectives, too. That was a very dark night of the soul for me. I was finally seeing the Ph.D. process clearly for the first time, and I was disgusted with the entire enterprise and with myself for desiring the approval of the people working in the system. I pounded out a scathing diatribe in which I raged about the game I had been playing with the academy and with my committee and left the chapter draft in a shared folder for nearly 24 hours, risking the possibility that my director might actually read it and see my pain and know the truth about me. But the next day I awoke with the sobering realization that each of the committee members was as entangled in my mess and my desire as I was. If I failed, the responsibility of the failure would have been as much theirs as my own. As I watched the committee members navigate their own relationships, I had a new sympathy for each of them as people who had once desired this same recognition and approval.

So, we went through the ritual of the command burlesque performance of the dissertation defense with each of us playing our expected part. And they roughed me up as expected, and I was successful, just as we all expected I would be. The completion of the Ph.D. was a happy milestone of accomplishment for a humble first-generation college girl like me. But something in me was permanently shifted away from the prior innocence with new insights into the messiness of research and of the teaching systems we participate in and the reciprocal benefits that bind and implicate all of us working in these systems as professors, scholars, and generators of "knowledge." As a member of the academy, I participate actively in my own versions of seeking validity and affirmation through writing proposals; publishing books, chapters, and articles; and presenting my work at conferences. I need the evidence of my contributions to advance myself in the academy, and the organizations need my travel dollars. I need other scholars to validate the quality and quantity of my contributions, and those scholars need to be seen as people trusted to make those judgments. There is a hidden version of a "pay to play" system in place that is easier to live with when we pretend there is no conflict of interest on anyone's part. But once you see the truths of the transactional nature of this academic system, you cannot unsee it. Or, as I have personally heard Patti Lather say in a multitude of ways and in multiples places, once you know, you do not get to not know.

Conclusion: Returning to the Present

More than ten years after my dissertation was completed, and as I quite literally await the imminent and expected good news of my promotion to full professor, I continue to notice the messiness of this enterprise of higher education and of my complicity in it. I am both grateful and guilty. I do my best to practice transparency in my teaching, scholarship, and service even as I simultaneously understand that I will rarely be rewarded for it and sometimes will pay a steep price. But as Patti Lather (1991) says, "there is no 'correct line' knowable through struggle. The struggle reconstitutes itself, and any useful theories of social change must deal with this fluidity" (p. 164). The institution of higher education is far more powerful, resistant, and long-lived than I am. It is bound to persist in resetting itself, but so will I also persist in calling it to be what it says it is, at least for as long as I am able.

I am currently serving as a director of Diversity, Equity, and Inclusion (DEI) for the College of Education at Butler University. This role might seem strange for a white woman to take on, but as a friend of mine likes to say, "Who am I to *not* do this work?". And as I am fond of saying in front of my university's president, I just want our university to be what it says it is. So, in this DEI role, I have remained true to all that I learned during my dissertation study about co-creating spaces in which learners can do what they believe needs to be done. I have refrained from settling for DEI programming and events and have chosen instead to build and sustain Intentional Learning Communities in which my colleagues create spaces of vulnerable reflection and choose which aspects of their teaching need application of our learning. I have selected and convened a small group of colleagues who serve as facilitators and as DEI Fellows. We spent our first year building our own learning community by discovering together how to create conditions and relationships in which real change can be cultivated and sustained.

This sort of learning is messy and imperfect, to be sure. There is no roadmap; we are making our road by walking it. There is no preset curriculum; we are guided instead by the power of our own questions. It is very difficult to "prove" that we have done anything. But after three years, this idea and these practices continue to evolve and grow as we figure it out together. The fact that we are still together, still working and learning, and still committed to making our teacher education classrooms spaces of equitable and accessible learning is its own kind of evidence.

Patti Lather's influence took root in a fertile place in my soul that was ripe for just such an encounter at that moment of my personal, academic, and professional life. Her ethics, honesty, brilliance, humor, and ferocity continue to inspire me to be better, to do better, and to make the institution and the world better. I sometimes feel her hand on my shoulder and hear her laughter of delight when situations are complicated by the intersections of power, responsibility, relationships, and ethics. That is the moment in which I take a deep breath and remind myself that we humans can figure out almost anything when we choose to tackle it together with respect, with truthfulness, with collegiality, and with joy. For the inspiration and challenge she has exploded into my life, I extend my deep respect and profound gratitude.

References

Adams, S. (2013). *The meaning of race-based professional development: A critical feminist ethnography*. (Publication No. 1324465698) [Doctoral dissertation, Indiana University]. ProQuest Dissertations Publishing.

Adams, S. R., & Breidenstein, A. (Eds.). (2024). *Exploring meaningful and sustainable intentional learning communities for P–20 educators*. IGI Global.

Adams, S. R., & Peterson-Veatch, R. (2012). "Critical friendship" and sustainable change: Creating liminal spaces to experience discomfort together. In J. Faulkner (Ed.), *Disrupting pedagogies and teaching the knowledge society: Countering conservative norms with creative approaches* (pp. 32–45). IGI Global.

Butler, Judith. 1993. *Bodies That Matter: On the Discursive Limits of "Sex."* Routledge.

Gee, J. (2014). *An introduction to discourse analysis: Theory and method*. Routledge.

Lather, P. (1986). Research as praxis. *Harvard Educational Review, 56*(3), 257–277.

Lather, P. (1991). *Getting smart: Feminist research and pedagogy with/in the postmodern*. Routledge.

Lather, P. (2000). Drawing the line at angels: Working the ruins of feminist ethnography. In E. St. Pierre (Ed.), *Working the ruins: Feminist poststructural theory and methods in education* (pp. 284–311). Routledge.

Lather, P. (2001). Postbook: Working the ruins of feminist ethnography. *Signs, 27*(1), 199–227.

Lather, P. (2007). *Getting lost: Feminist efforts toward a double(d) science*. State University of New York Press.

Lather, P. (2009). Getting lost: Feminist efforts toward a double(d) science. *Frontiers: A Journal of Women Studies, 30*(1), 222–230. https://www.jstor.org/stable/40388724

Lather, P. (2012). *Engaging science policy: From the side of the messy*. Peter Lang.

Lather, P., & Smithies, C. (1997). *Troubling the angels: Women living with HIV/AIDS*. Westview/HarperCollins.

The New London Group. (1996). A pedagogy of multiliteracies: Designing social futures. *Harvard Educational Review, 66*(1), 60–92.

Visweswaran, K. (1994). *Fictions of feminist ethnography*. University of Minnesota.

Vygotsky, L. L. (1978). *Mind in Society: The development of higher psychological processes*. Harvard University Press.

CHAPTER FOUR

Getting Lost: Or How I Ended up Waiting for Deleuze in a Welsh Pub

LISA A. MAZZEI

> Getting Lost *abstracts a philosophy of inquiry from an archive of work in order to move toward a fruitful sense of dislocation in our knowledge projects.*
>
> (Lather, 2007, p. 1)

I SHOULD HAVE SEEN it coming, but of course, that is the beauty of not knowing. An unexpected encounter with "a fruitful sense of dislocation" began in my early graduate student days. I landed in my Ph.D. program a few short years after Patti Lather started teaching qualitative methodology at The Ohio State University. The first course that sent me reeling seemed rather innocuous in its naming, Introduction to Qualitative Research in Education, but it was anything but. Part methodology, part philosophy—disorienting, intoxicating, and exhilarating.

In my reading and writing of this chapter, I have returned to publications that I have not visited in years, but that remain fresh in their urging of a "less comfortable social science," (Lather, 2017, p. 33), a "science that is about-to-be" (Lather, 2017, p. 12), and a movement of "research in many different and, indeed, contradictory directions in the hope that more interesting and useful ways of knowing will emerge" (Lather, 2017, p. 26). It is this admonition to seek dislocation, to attune to the not yet, and to think with philosophical concepts that has been, and continues to be, a dominant force in my own work.

Paradigms All the Way Down

The introductory course mentioned above was framed as an introduction to paradigms, theories, and exemplars: in other words, not a study of mere method or technique, but the philosophical underpinnings of epistemological claims and how these guide approaches to inquiry. Assignments, while grounded in the context of research practice, were always to be positioned in terms of the methodological implications and learnings. As students, we were constantly asked to consider how an author was situating themselves theoretically and how this was enacted in the work. While *method* was always an underlying consideration, it was not method from a merely utilitarian approach. It was more an examination of what becomes askable and knowable given the knowledge claims made possible within a particular paradigm.

Those many innovative thinkers who have gone on to contribute much to challenging received knowledge and practices were taught this from the start. We were taught to think methodologically and to carefully consider the limit of our preconceived notions of knowledge, research, and method. We were thrust into a "philosophy of inquiry" that urged movement "toward a fruitful sense of dislocation in our knowledge projects" (Lather, 2007, p. 1). We were taught to always be thinking with, and about, the ontological and epistemological assumptions that were informing the work. During my time at Ohio State, the constellation of burgeoning scholars that have gone on to make substantive interventions into qualitative methodology was tremendous.[1]

Patti was in the midst of her work with Chris Smithies on their book, *Troubling the Angels* (Lather & Smithies, 1997) during this time, and as students, we were treated to glimpses of her thinking and writing as she brought pieces of her work and thought into class and seminar discussions. It was a vibrant scholarly community with Professor Lather as a hub of connections and ideas. She created the possibility of this assemblage that produced more interesting and useful ways of knowing.

This immersion in philosophical texts and methodological considerations planted the early seeds for what I developed in my collaborative work with Alecia Jackson that we named *thinking with theory* (Jackson & Mazzei, 2012, 2023). In other words, we think performative accounts and philosophical concepts together in a *plugging in* process methodology. As we wrote in the second edition of the book:

> Plugging in is a production of the new: the assemblage in formation. This is a dramatic, profound shift from social science knowledge with its hierarchical, empirical demands for recognizable representation to an ontology in which experimentation is privileged. *Thinking with theory* then, emerges as assemblage, *attaching itself to philosophy* [emphasis added] rather than the dogmatic image of thought in conventional qualitative research. (Jackson & Mazzei, 2023, p. 2)

We further explain that these philosophical concepts, which provoked thought, were not just those that we happened upon in the writing of the book. Instead, they were "philosophical concepts that we had studied and thought with for years" (Jackson & Mazzei, 2023) beginning with our doctoral studies. This began with my studies with Patti, and Alecia, as a doctoral student advised by Elizabeth St. Pierre.

Deconstructing Voice (or Theorizing Silence)

In 1993, validity underwent a poststructural reckoning in the article, "Fertile Obsession: Validity after Poststructuralism" (Lather, 1993). Writing in the introduction, Patti described the article as working "at the edges of what is currently available, in moving toward a science with more to answer to in terms of the complexities of language and the world" (Lather, 1993, p. 673). This obsession with validity, while not new in her work, was now to be rethought "in light of antifoundational discourse theory" (Lather, 1993, p. 674). In other words, she was subjecting the received notion of validity, conditioned by the legacy of postpositivism, to a poststructuralist reading in order to rupture it as a regime of truth (Foucault, 1982).[2] These are my words, not hers, but this is *deconstruction in a nutshell* as described by Spivak (1976):

> To locate the promising marginal text, to disclose the undecidable moment, to pry it loose with the positive lever of the signifier; to reverse the resident hierarchy, only to displace it; to dismantle in order to reconstitute what is always already inscribed. Deconstruction in a nutshell. (p. lxxvii)

Patti (1993) continued in her description of her *fertile obsession*:

> Rather than jettisoning "validity" as the term of choice, I retain the term
> in order to both circulate and break with the signs that code it. What I
> mean by the term, then, is all of the baggage that it carries plus, in a dou-
> bled-movement, what it means to rupture validity as a regime of truth, to
> displace its historical inscription. (p. 674)

Deconstruction in a nutshell, perhaps?

Inspired by this doubled-movement, this dismantling and examination of what was always already coded in my received knowledge of data and analysis, I encountered my own "stuck place" that provoked a more interesting and fruitful line of inquiry. This line of inquiry began with my dissertation in which I considered, with a group of white teachers, how one's racial identity as a white person impacted curricular decisions and work as teachers. What is not so surprising now, but was in the mid-1990s, is that the white teachers, including myself, had given little consideration of themselves as having a racial identity. Having mostly lived in a world of white privilege, they/we were produced as unable to express themselves/ourselves as *Other*. What presented itself in the conversations was an articulation of racial identity and whiteness in the form of silence, both literal and metaphorical. What was I to do with reams of "data" that failed to name, according to this regime of truth, what it was, and how this racial identity was functioning? How could I account for "voice" in the form of silence? How might I work at the edge of what was currently available?

Because of the philosophical orientations of my methodology classes and an immersion in philosophical texts, especially for me the writings of Derrida, I began to consider the absent presence, and so began my lengthy obsession with and theorization of silence as presence and voice as present in both the spoken and unarticulated. Although I had been schooled to work against the desire to find truths in the words spoken by the teachers with whom I worked, I was still operating within a regime of truth that gave preference to things seen and heard as intelligible, and thus, knowable. What was necessary in order to find a more fertile way of knowing was to move toward this fruitful sense of dislocation.

A dislocation that prompted a need to invent methodological strategies and rationales that would work the *against* with more vigor than the *within*.

This was a decades-long "creation of a way of thinking" (Colebrook, 2002, p. 20), in a historical displacement of research, data, and voice.[3]

Waiting for Deleuze

Because Patti has her pulse on everything, it seems, she knew scholars at Manchester Metropolitan University[4] in the UK and things that were happening there before I did. I had applied for a research fellowship and was on my way to Manchester, having never even visited England, much less Manchester, along with three cats, my husband, our books, and kitchen accoutrements—all the essentials. I had not been in England very long when I received an email from Patti. Short and to-the-point as she often is, the message read: "I think you should attend this and tell me about it." The "this" was the first ever Deleuze Camp to be held at Cardiff University in July 2007, taught by Ian Buchanan, Claire Colebrook, Paul Patton, Greg Lambert, and Dan Smith. Why not, I thought? Elizabeth St. Pierre had long been thinking with Deleuze in ways that I found very provocative, and I had never quite gotten myself to do any focused study of his solo work or his collaborative writing with Guattari, so off I went—and was I in for a surprise! On the Saturday before the camp started, as the rain pelted down only as it can on the west coast of Wales, I found myself in a Welsh Pub—the best place to be on a rainy Saturday afternoon with a nice pint and a bag of crisps. I was surrounded by people speaking Welsh (with the exception of my husband, Phillip) as we watched Rugby on the tele (something else that I knew nothing about), and I found this a fitting metaphor for thinking about what *Getting Lost* (Lather, 2007) has meant to me both personally and intellectually.

My colleagues at MMU teased me about going to Deleuze *boot camp* as they fondly dubbed it.[5] In preparation for boot camp, I spent three months with a stack of books marked with pages to read in advance. The itinerary I received for the week consisted of lectures M–F from 10–12; 1–3; and 4–6, with a one-hour break for lunch at noon and, yes, tea from 3–4. Among the 40 attendees, there were two others from education, with the rest primarily being philosophy students from Europe. There were a few, and I mean very few, women, and the rest were what I call *philosophy boys*. You know the type: young, smart, cocksure, and quoting from memory passages from *Milles Plateau*.[6] At first, I had no idea what *Milles Plateau* was—it wasn't on the reading list! But I soon figured that out, keeping my ignorance to myself. I called Phillip, my wonderful partner in this journey, during the lunch break on the first day and told him that I was taking the first train back to Manchester because I didn't understand anything that was being said and didn't see any hope on the horizon of that changing. Fortunately for me, he talked me off the ledge and into staying for the remainder of the camp. I spent the rest of the week trying to keep up, furiously taking notes that I still refer to, and noting all the texts that I wanted to go back to and re-read now that I had some concepts and notes to help me navigate the terrain. Who knows what kind of unintelligible response I gave to Ian Buchanan when he asked me about my research and what desiring machines the teachers in my study were plugging into.[7] It must not have been too bad since he still speaks to me but, boy oh boy, was I pushing into unknown territory!

Like my first encounters digging deep into philosophical texts as part of my doctoral education (recalling the glorious term guided by Patti Lather and Mary Leach in which a handful of us read nothing but Gayatri Spivak's (1976) translator's preface to Derrida's *Of Grammatology*), I knew that in reading and thinking with these texts by Deleuze and Guattari, something was happening that I needed to pay attention to. Just like being a new doctoral student in Introduction to Qualitative Research where I first encountered continental philosophy, what it was I was not able to name, but there were intensities and affects that could not be ignored.

For the next year, I did nothing but read Deleuze, and didn't utter any ideas in public until the following September when I was invited to present on a panel at the British Education Research Association conference to talk about how I was using Deleuze in my work—so I did as you advised, Bettie, and Laurel.[8] I used writing to help me figure out what I was thinking, and how I was *thinking with* Deleuze—a phrase that has "stuck" in terms of my current work with Alecia Jackson as we describe what we do in our encounters with performative accounts and philosophical texts as a *plugging in* and *thinking with*.

When Alecia and I were conceptualizing the first edition of *Thinking with Theory*, one of our aims was to counter simplistic and mechanistic approaches to analysis that did little to "critique the complexities of social life . . . [that] preclude dense and multi-layered treatment of" social phenomena (Jackson & Mazzei, 2012, p. vii). Further, we wished to create a text that we could use in our own teaching. A text that would attend to the methodological, epistemological, and ontological implications of doing philosophically-informed inquiry; an approach which mirrored some of the teaching and learning that I first encountered as a doctoral student in the qualitative methodology courses that I took with Patti as the instructor.

While we accomplished what we set out to achieve in the book, it is also that which has guided the curriculum and teaching of qualitative methodology courses that has stayed with me in my own mentoring of doctoral students. In the methodology sequence that I developed with Jerry Rosiek, my colleague at the University of Oregon, the courses are organized around philosophical traditions (e.g., interpretivist; critical; poststructural; posthumanist). In each course, the emphasis is not on methods or approaches, but rather the way in which language, experience, the subject, agency, and representation are enacted differently according to the paradigmatic assumptions.

Patti was doing this all along—teaching us to think with philosophical texts. Alecia and I named it and described what it looked like as we did it, but the early seeds were planted in that first methodology class with Patti. Alecia and I did what I had learned from my adventures with Patti and then with Deleuze and Guattari. We asked, not what does it mean but, how does it work and what does it produce? Whether mapping on a Deleuzian plane or considering "a shift from what we can know about an object (method and epistemology) to what a particular object does when we enact inquiry" (Jackson & Mazzei, 2017, p. 726), I am doing what I learned long ago, beginning with my qualitative methodology courses under Patti's tutelage. I am using philosophical concepts as a way to ask previously unthought questions, not about meaning, but about what is happening in a postfoundational approach that "stays open to makings and reconfigurations" (Jackson & Mazzei, 2024, p. 2).

Getting Lost, Again

In the acknowledgements for my first book, I thanked Patti Lather for prompting me to "get lost" and sending me on my way. I hope she knows how indebted I am to her, and perhaps she understands how many of her practices have stuck with me in my reading, writing, teaching, researching, and mentoring of my own doctoral students. I am grateful to have this opportunity to continue on this journey of getting lost that began for me in earnest in 1993 and that I hope will continue with many of you for years to come.

In the spirit of getting lost, and in an everlasting state of discomfort, I end this chapter with a Top Ten List. This is a nod to a paper first presented at the International Congress of Qualitative Inquiry, subsequently published in *Cultural Studies ↔ Critical Methodologies* (Lather, 2016), and appearing at the end of the selected works text that I have previously mentioned (Lather, 2017).

Top Ten Things I Learned from Patti Lather

1. In order to work the against, you need to know what you are refuting.

2. All knowledge is contingent.

3. Never settle—always complicate that which is mistaken for an easy sense.

4. Find your feminist colleagues.

5. Read philosophy, and then read some more.

6. Never take the familiar path.

7. Interdisciplinarity is the key to innovative methodological thinking.

8. The privilege of getting to do this work cannot be overstated.

9. The joy and challenge of working with students fosters thought and newness.

10. Attune to the "not yet" in a post, post, post world.

Notes

1. Preceding me by a couple of years was Jim Scheurich. Overlapping with me was Wanda Pillow, Bettie St. Pierre, Kate McCoy, and Cynthia Tyson, to name a few. And brilliant feminist faculty, also thinking at the limit, that I was privileged to encounter: Mary Leach, Cynthia Dillard, Gia Hinkle, Laurel Richardson, Suzanne Damarin, and Marge Cambre.

2. What Foucault (1982) refers to in this article as *régime du savoir*.

3. See for example, Mazzei 2004; 2007; 2013; 2016.

4. Not once, but twice in my scholarly development I found myself in the center of a hub of intellectual connectives and thinking at the limit. The intellectual assemblage that was the Education and Social Research Institute at Manchester Metropolitan University in the mid-2000s was extraordinary. I could write another paper on the way in which ideas sparked and thought took flight.

5. The *boot camp* to which I refer was the first Deleuze Camp, organized by Ian Buchanan, held at Cardiff University in 2007. I am indebted to Harry Torrance, then director of the Education and Social Research Institute (ESRI), who approved funding for my attendance at this event. Also to Maggie MacLure for her extended mentoring and others in the "Becoming a Problem" research group; Rachel Holmes, Christina MacRae, and Liz Jones who along with Maggie read the Deleuze Cinema books with me over the course of the next year. Both Harry Torrance and Maggie MacLure are contributors to this volume and have been/continue to be important to my scholarly development.

6. I refer here to the untranslated title of Deleuze & Guattari's (1987) *A Thousand Plateaus: Capitalism and Schizophrenia.*

7. Ian Buchanan is an Australian scholar who founded the Deleuze Camp, Deleuze Conference, and *Deleuze Studies* journal.

8. See Richardson & St. Pierre, 2008, where they discuss writing as inquiry.

References

Colebrook, C. (2002). *Gilles Deleuze*. Routledge.

Deleuze, G., & Guattari, F. (1987). *A thousand plateaus: Capitalism and Schizophrenia*. University of Minnesota Press.

Foucault, M. (1982). The subject and power. *Critical Inquiry, 8*(4), 777–795.

Jackson, A.Y., & Mazzei, L.A. (2012). *Thinking with theory in qualitative research: Viewing data across multiple perspectives*. Routledge.

Jackson A. Y., & Mazzei, L. A. (2017). Thinking with Theory: A New Analytic for Qualitative Inquiry. In Denzin, N. & Lincoln, Y. (Eds.), *The Sage Handbook of Qualitative Research* (5th edition). Sage Publications.

Jackson, A.Y., & Mazzei, L.A. (2023). *Thinking with theory in qualitative research 2nd ed.* Routledge.

Jackson, A.Y., & Mazzei, L.A. (2024). Postfoundational inquiry after method: Reorientations, enactments, and opening. In L. Mazzei & A. Jackson (Eds.), *Postfoundational approaches to qualitative inquiry*, 1–22.

Lather, P. (1993). Fertile obsession: Validity after poststructuralism. *The Sociological Quarterly, 34*(4), 673–693.

Lather, P. (2007). *Getting lost: Feminist efforts toward a double(d) science*. SUNY Press.

Lather, P. (2016). Top ten+ list: (Re)thinking ontology in (post)qualitative research. *Cultural Studies ↔ Critical Methodologies, 16*(2), 125–131.

Lather, P. (2017). *(Post)critical methodologies: The science possible after the critiques*. Routledge.

Lather, P. & Smithies, C. (1997). *Troubling the Angels: Women Living With HIV/AIDS*. Westview/HarperCollins. A CHOICE Outstanding Academic Book of the Year, 1998.

Mazzei, L.A. (2004). Silent listenings: Deconstructive practices in discourse-based research, *Educational Researcher, 33*(2), 26–34.

Mazzei, L.A. (2007). *Inhabited silence in qualitative research: Putting poststructural theory to work*. Peter Lang.

Mazzei, L.A. (2011). Desiring silence: Gender, race, and pedagogy in education. *British Educational Research Journal, 37*(4), 657–669.

Mazzei, L.A. (2013). A voice without organs: Interviewing practices in posthumanist research. *International Journal of Qualitative Studies in Education, 23*(6), 732–740.

Mazzei, L.A., & Jackson, A.Y. (Eds.). (2024). *Postfoundational approaches to qualitative inquiry.* Routledge.

Richardson, L., & St. Pierre, E.A. (2008). Writing: A method of inquiry. In N. Denzin & Y. Lincoln (Eds.), *The SAGE handbook of qualitative research* (4th ed.), 473–499.

Spivak, G. (1976). Translator's Preface. In J. Derrida, *Of grammatology* (pp. ix–lxxxvii) (G. Spivak, Trans.). Johns Hopkins University Press. (Original work published 1967).

CHAPTER FIVE

Can the Center Hold? Patti Lather, Praxis, and Policy

HARRY TORRANCE

Introduction

PATTI LATHER IS PROBABLY best known as a social theorist and methodologist, particularly for bringing feminist, post-structuralist, and more recently, post-humanist and new materialist perspectives to bear on approaches to qualitative research and claims to knowledge (Lather, 1991; 2007). However, she has also consistently engaged in discussions about how research participants can be involved in research procedures and how the research process can generate critical knowledge for social action, rather than expert knowledge to drive professional practice (Lather, 1986; Lather & Smithies, 1997). Latterly, she has developed this enduring interest to challenge government assumptions about definitions of science, research, and the role of experimental design in producing evidence about 'what works' in social research, particularly educational research (Lather, 2004a; 2010). This chapter reviews and explores this engagement with debates about science, politics and policy, and reflects on the problems and possibilities of working across theoretical, methodological, and disciplinary boundaries. The chapter works with Lather's (2004a) call for critical researchers to take a "policy turn . . . with a focus on program evaluation as a particularly cogent site where a policy relevant counterscience might be

worked out" (p. 22); and the chapter will move in and out of my own encounters with Patti and her work, to identify and explore the breadth of her
intellectual ambition in engaging with this task.

Early Encounters

I first came across Patti's work when reading her 1986 *Harvard Education Review* paper, "Research as Praxis." It both did, and did not, connect
with my own interests in what was then known as Democratic Evaluation
(MacDonald 1974/2010) and Illuminative Evaluation (Parlett & Hamilton,
1972), both, now, long since lost in the mists of time. These overtly political
and qualitative approaches to evaluation emerged from increasing disappointment with the use of experimental techniques in educational evaluation in the 1960s. Field experiments had been undertaken in the 1960s and
1970s to evaluate new approaches to curriculum, teaching, and learning,
deriving from the objectives movement in curriculum design (Campbell &
Stanley, 1963; Tyler, 1949).

However, these had led to considerable disillusionment with experimental methods as the confounding problems of diverse implementation and
interaction effects produced evaluations which showed no significant difference between control and experimental groups (more of which later). In addition to trying to produce more illuminative and useful approaches to evaluation, Democratic Evaluation also raised questions of power and validity
—who is in a position to evaluate, and who is evaluated? Who claims to
know, how do they know, and on what grounds are their inquiries claimed
to be legitimate? These questions were addressed by qualitative fieldwork
procedures involving respondent validation of primary data and negotiation
of draft reports. MacDonald's (1974/2010) original articulation of democratic evaluation argued that it should be:

> An information service to the whole community about the characteristics
> of an educational program . . . the democratic evaluator recognises value
> pluralism and seeks to represent a range of interests . . . techniques of data
> gathering and presentation must be accessible to non-specialist audiences .
> . . The criterion of success is the range of audiences served. (pp. 249–250)

Of course times change and this formulation of evaluation presupposes that data can be gathered and diverse interests represented in a fairly straightforward, realist fashion, when in fact this is precisely one of the key issues at stake. The overlap with Lather's interest in participatory and emancipatory research is clear however, as outlined in the introduction to her *Harvard Educational Review* paper:

> The primary objective of this essay is to help researchers involve the researched in a democratized process of inquiry characterized by negotiation, reciprocity, empowerment—research as praxis. (Lather, 1986, p. 257)

I was particularly interested in Lather's (1986) concern to "discuss the implications of searching for an emancipatory approach to the human sciences" (p. 257); and taken with her question, "What is the relationship between data and theory in emancipatory research?" (p. 262). Here the issues of validity and whose understandings and interpretations have most warrant are of central concern. She further argued: "Dialectical practices require an interactive approach to research that invites reciprocal reflexivity and critique, both of which guard against the central dangers to praxis-oriented empirical work: imposition and reification on the part of the researcher" (Lather, 1986, p. 265).

Simply talking to people, interviewing research participants for example, wasn't/isn't enough: "A strictly interpretive, phenomenological paradigm is inadequate insofar as it is based on an assumption of fully rational action . . . false consciousness and ideological mystification may be present" (Lather, 1986, p. 269).

These are matters that remain of concern, though the issues are perhaps approached and understood differently than they once were (again, more of this, to follow). The 1986 paper, interestingly, and reflecting the Marxist and Gramscian implications of the idea of 'praxis,' drew on "feminist research, neo-Marxist critical ethnography and Freirean 'empowering' or participatory research" (p. 258), and framed the problem of validity in terms of taking "into account the deep structures . . . that shape human experience and perceptions, without committing the sin of theoretical imposition" (p. 262). Few, now, would talk in terms of *false consciousness* or *deep structures*, an indication once again that understandings can and do change, but the key issues persist of who knows, how do they know, and on what legitimate basis do they speak. The substance of my work in educational evaluation, however, was a long way from the feminist social critique which was the focus of Lather's paper and, as such, I didn't engage as much with the paper as perhaps I might. My doctoral research (with MacDonald) was in the field of student assessment and program evaluation. It was located in the qualitative case study tradition represented in the U.K. by the likes of Stenhouse (1978), Walker (1974), and Simons (1980, 1987), and in the USA by Stake (1978), House (1980), and Guba and Lincoln (1981). I was interested in how teachers and students understood the process of assessment and what was its impact on the curriculum, teaching, and learning. I particularly wanted to explore how teachers and students interpreted these processes, and how they might be developed collaboratively to underpin, rather than undermine, learning—a qualitative approach to the study of assessment, rather than a quantitative approach, which of course has dominated the field since its inception with mental testing in the 1920s and 1930s (Torrance, 1981).

Lather's 1986 paper spoke to my theoretical, methodological, and indeed political interests in terms of participatory approaches to research and who has the right to know and speak on matters of public policy, but of course did not directly address my substantive concerns and as such, perhaps, was noted as *interesting* but not directly *relevant*—background reading rather than something to engage with directly. As it happens, similar observations might be made of Lather's paper itself. She cites Kushner and Norris (1981) who come out of the same democratic evaluation tradition as myself (we were doctoral students together), along with Carr and Kemmis (1986), Guba and Lincoln (1981), and others, as reporting ways of involving research participants in research projects. However, their contributions are noted as interesting examples with little further comment, rather than multiple tributaries which might feed into a more shared and collaborative endeavor. Such are the difficulties of talking across disciplinary boundaries. Also, at that point in time, in 1986, we were safe in our newly constructed paradigms which were addressing the previous failures of positivism. We could read, think, research, and write, safe in the assumption that understanding in the social sciences was progressing just fine. We didn't need any new friends. . . . How wrong we were.

More Recent Engagements

Subsequently, the scholarly, philosophical ground from which Lather constructed her 1986 paper has been shaken to its core, indeed directly attacked, by government intrusion into what counts as *science* and *research*. Lather (1986) takes as given the post-positivist moment in which it was written, and looks to move beyond justificatory debate to ways in which validity and engagement with research participants can be conceived and enacted differently—what might working with participants as collaborators rather than subjects look like? Lather (1986) begins her paper with a quote from Mary Hesse: "The attempt to produce value-neutral social science is increasingly being abandoned as at best unrealizable, and at worst self-deceptive, and is being replaced by social sciences based on explicit ideologies" (p. 247).

Lather (1986) goes on to note that "postpositivism argues that the present orthodoxy in the human sciences is obsolete and that new visions for generating social knowledge are required" (p. 260). Thus: "A central task . . . becomes . . . the search for workable ways of establishing the trustworthiness of data in a new paradigm inquiry" (pp. 259–260). Hmm . . . if only . . . how little did we know . . . twenty years later we were fighting the *science wars* anew. As Patti herself put it, it was "déjà vu all over again" (Lather, 2010, p. 3).

Qualitative inquiry, and qualitative approaches to social research more generally, have now been under severe pressure from the *what works* science-based research and policy movement for 20 years and more. Experimental research, specifically Randomized Control Trials (RCTs), are routinely claimed to be the *gold standard* of scientific method (Torgerson & Torgerson, 2008), producing the "most rigorous evidence" (Slavin, 2002, p. 15) and identifying "what works best" (Goldacre, 2013, p. 4) for educational and social research. Qualitative research has once again been positioned as, at best, an adjunct to experimental research, as a *pre-scientific* stage of exploratory investigation and/or additional evidence gathering conducted before or alongside an experimental design in order to help interpret the experimental results (Cook & Payne, 2002; Shavelson et al., 2003). At worst, qualitative research is dismissed as of little value and not worth pursuing or funding (NCLB, 2002; WWC, 2020). The impact of such criticisms has perhaps been most acute in educational research, and in the United States, where "scientific" research has been extensively defined in US legislation, including insistence on "measurements or observational methods that provide reliable and valid data across evaluators and observers . . . evaluated using experimental or quasi experimental designs . . . with a preference for random assignment experiments. . . ." (NCLB, 2002). However, similar arguments have been made in the U.K. and elsewhere (Frederiksen & Beck 2010; Goldacre, 2013; Yates, 2004). Many responses and rejoinders have been published, both in what we might call a *first wave* of debate in the early 2000s and more recently as the arguments have been revisited and restated with renewed vigor in the U.S.A. and U.K. (Haynes et al., 2012; WWC, 2020; WWN, 2018). Torrance (2018, 2024) reviews the debate and the issues at stake at more length (see also Thomas 2016).

To many of us, renewed arguments that only RCTs could produce valid and reliable knowledge in the human sciences—*scientific* knowledge of *what works* in social and education policy—seemed woefully ignorant of not only the previous 20–30 years of detailed discussion in qualitative research, but of the previous hundred years in the development of social science. Certainly, as noted earlier, educational processes and outcomes in particular seem highly resistant to experimental evaluation designs, partly, at least, because they are the product of so many complex interacting variables. Interestingly, Campbell and Stanley's (1963) classic text *Experimental and Quasi-Experimental Designs for Research* notes regular periods of RCT advocacy and RCT disillusionment in education research, going back to McCall's *How to Experiment in Education*, published in 1923.

Willfully ignorant or not, the attack on qualitative approaches to research was sustained and, in the U.S.A., ensconced in legislation. Patti Lather became a key leader of the resistance, not just by publishing rejoinders and rehearsing old philosophical arguments, important as these were to the development of the debate, but by understanding the necessity to engage and the need to work across theoretical and disciplinary boundaries to oppose what could have been an existential threat to qualitative research. Lather understood the significance of the threat and the need to confront it, but also the opportunity it presented to work across boundaries with "program evaluators and policy analysts in order that these areas can become useful in fuzzying the lines between . . . empirical research, politics, and the philosophical renewal of public deliberation" (Lather, 2004b, p. 767). This is the essence and the ambition of Lather's contribution, not just to confront but also to engage, with policy concerns and with researchers in other fields similarly seeking to address complexity rather than reduce and control it: "to meet the obduracy of the problems and obstacles as the very way toward producing different knowledge and producing knowledge differently" (Lather, 2004a, p. 28). As she herself emphasizes: "I am not against scientific study of education. My issue is how the narrowly defined sense of science-based evidence . . . works to discipline educational research" (Lather, 2004b, p. 760). Furthermore "the degree to which the kinds of problems teachers face are open to solution by research is precisely the question" (Lather, 2004b, p. 763).

Lather's (2004a) first response did not simply try to repeat old philosophical arguments, though she did note her surprise at the turn of events: "I was . . . naive . . . that I would think the past 30 years of the social critique of science might actually shape contemporary thought about policy driven research" (p. 17).

Rather she sought to interrogate "the federal effort to legislate scientific method . . . as a backlash against the proliferation of research approaches of the past 20 years" (Lather, 2004a, p. 16). Reading it through the lens of Foucault, feminism, and postcolonialism, the paper tried to understand why diversity of research approaches was seen as so threatening by government. The paper made clear that, in Lather's view at least, this was not a debate about research quality and utility, but rather about the government urge to control: to control knowledge, policy, and populations. The subject of the government attack was not research quality but research diversity in terms of thought and action. Her argument was that the field was facing a "racialized masculinist backlash against the proliferation of research approaches" (Lather, 2004a, p. 15). The clue was in her title: "This IS Your Father's Paradigm."

My own view is rather more prosaic, though it certainly also regards the issues at stake as about control rather than quality—in whose interests was the attack launched? Part of the backdrop to the continuing debate is the uncertain status and legitimacy of both science *and* government at the present time. The role, purpose, and utility of science and scientific research is less agreed upon and less secure than it once was and, with respect to this, education research and social research can be seen to be located in a wider debate about scientific research and the role of science in society. Equally, government itself is under financial and ideological pressure 'to deliver' and to be seen to deliver, especially with regard to the provision of public services. Are public services still needed in their current form? If so, could they be better and more efficiently provided by other mechanisms and stakeholders? What reasons are there for state intervention in the lives of ordinary citizens? In this respect, government demands for 'evidence' is as much a demand for material to justify its own existence as it is a demand for the evaluation of particular policy alternatives. What is at stake is the legitimacy of policy intervention *per se*, and the continuation of a center-periphery view of policy making and policy implementation. In turn, it is almost as if researchers are now regarded by the state as directly employed technicians in the nationalized industry of knowledge production.

Of course, some in the research community do not seem uncomfortable with this position; indeed, many seem to see an opportunity to advance their particular vision of social science. And it is here that Lather's deployment of Foucault and ideas of governmentality identifies an important transactional apparatus between the state and the research community. Lather (2004a) notes the growth of the "grant economy" and observes that: "It appears that science, money, and politics have combined with prepositioned capability and sweetheart contracts . . . to court the increased federal role in the adoption of experimental methods . . . [in a] 'Faustian bargain' of the federal and corporate embrace" (Lather, 2004a, p. 22).

Clearly some researchers, in tandem with government itself, see an opportunity to reclaim and rehabilitate the role of *disinterested expert* in the context of 'evaluating' professional practice, albeit that their 'disinterest' is in fact very well-funded, so not disinterested at all.

Meeting and Working with Patti

I first met Patti in 2004 when she visited the Education and Social Research Institute (ESRI) at Manchester Metropolitan University, U.K. to speak at a seminar organized by Maggie MacLure. It marked the beginning of a long and continuing professional and personal friendship. At the time I was the director of ESRI and also co-editing, with colleagues, the *British Educational Research Journal* (*BERJ*). Patti accepted an invitation to join the newly created international editorial board of the journal and submitted a paper for publication (Lather, 2004b). As editors we thought it was timely and important to add international scholars to the Board, recognizing that similar research issues and policy initiatives were appearing in many different countries around the world, particularly in the U.K. and U.S.A. Patti and I met again at the inaugural meeting of the International Congress of Qualitative Inquiry (ICQI) in May 2005. Norman Denzin and colleagues had organized ICQI in recognition of the growing threat to qualitative research.

ICQI was organized as a direct response to the challenge, as the introduction to the edited book of the first congress makes clear:

> Around the globe, governments are attempting to regulate scientific inquiry by defining what is good science. Conservative regimes are enforcing evidence, or scientifically based biomedical models of research (SBR). These regulatory activities raise fundamental philosophical, epistemological, political and pedagogical issues for scholarship and freedom of speech in the academy. These threats constitute the conservative challenge to qualitative inquiry, the topic of this volume. (Denzin & Giardina, 2006, pp. ix–x)

Patti and I spoke in the same session at ICQI 2005 on threats to qualitative research and its relationship to policy ("Monsters of Evidence: Qualitative Research and the Globalization of Audit Culture") and subsequently in similar sessions at successive meetings of ICQI and the American Educational Research Association (AERA). Patti has also visited us at ESRI in Manchester to speak at our Summer Institute in Qualitative Research.

Such personal connections are not insignificant. Unlike twenty years previously, in 2004–2005 I found her perspective both interesting *and* relevant, and profoundly important with respect to building an international coalition and series of conversations about the nature of knowledge and its relationship to policy and practice. Patti's (2004b) *BERJ* paper reiterated her call to reach across disciplinary boundaries and argued for "a strategic infusion of those oriented towards critical theory and its concerns with the workings of power/knowledge into the ranks of program evaluation and policy analysis" (p. 767).

Extended conversations across successive conferences expand the nature of intellectual and political inquiry and 'seal the deal' with regard to reaching across disciplinary boundaries. Interestingly, Patti's *BERJ* paper specifically linked the new evidence movement to the "political technology" (Lather, 2004b, p. 762) of testing and accountability in education more generally. We have had many subsequent conversations about the emerging possibilities for what she calls "smart assessment," specifically, assessment procedures which might finally move away from the modernist obsession with measurement and classification towards processes and practices that might seek to identify and develop understanding, and the collaborative endeavour of learning. My (once again) rather more prosaic response is generally to agree with the aspiration (indeed I have written about it elsewhere, see Torrance 2017) but to note that in current political circumstances, probably the best we can hope for is slightly "less stupid" assessment than students endure at the present time (both quotes are from personal correspondence cited in Lather, 2016).

Control or Collaboration in Understanding and Pursuing Social Change?

Patti consolidated her thoughts on the government attack on qualitative research in her 2010 book *Engaging Science Policy: From the Side of the Messy*. Here, once again, we see not just a critical reaction to the evidence movement, but a more ambitious response to seize the opportunity to think differently about the relationship of research to policy: "My focus is on how qualitative research for policy might contribute to a social science of engagement, a social science that "matters" in struggles for a "deeper" democratic social order" (Lather, 2010, p. 2).

Drawing on her work in post-structuralism and new materialism, the book is a powerful call to engage with practice and the material in pursuit of what she terms "more complicated questions of what it actually means to use research" (Lather, 2010, p. 8). Her aim is to try "to be accountable to complexity while refusing to give up on praxis . . . where embracing not knowing is a condition of a less dangerous doing" (Lather, 2010, p. 15). The book rejects narrow definitions of science and the governmental rage for certainty, while acknowledging that social science research in general, and educational research in particular, should aspire to be more useful by exploring and building what a different sort of participative, democratic social order might look like. Such utility must include doubt and a commitment to continuous investigation, not proof. Knowing and not knowing should *both* contribute to what counts as an informed debate, as we acknowledge that our task is not to extinguish complexity and diversity but to learn to live with it, such that "constitutive unknowingness becomes a resource" (Lather, 2010, p. 9).

Thus, Lather's more expansive and enduring intellectual project goes beyond simply challenging the resurgence of a natural science model of social science research. Rather, she seeks to investigate the ways in which governmentality operates in the research-policy nexus and the ways in which research is disciplined when it threatens to produce profane and difficult knowledge from the margins, for the margins, rather than the center. The book restates the case, in new times, for research as a never-completed praxis, developing what she terms a different form of *scientificity*, that is, different ground on which science can be built. She rejects *scientism* but seeks a new *scientificity*, a new way in which research can confront and include uncertainty as part of its core legitimating practices: "My interest is in a scientificity that is about imperfect information where incompleteness and indeterminacy are assets . . . a scientificity of engagement grounded in a permanent facing of the undecidable" (Lather, 2010, p. 17). In turn she seeks to understand "how policy can produce possibilities for thought and action by embracing complexity and messiness" (Lather, 2010, p. 77).

The key insight here, and one that resonates completely with my original interests in democratic evaluation and policy analysis, is that dynamism and flux must be seen as inevitable components of social activity and policy, the constantly changing context in which policy and new social initiatives are understood and enacted, rather than considered as problems to be pinned down and eradicated with proven solutions about *what works*. One of the core problems with the *what works* movement is the assumption that research must precede the improvement of policy and practice. The *what works* movement seems to believe that the social world is essentially static, that it can be treated as somehow *standing still*, waiting for a solution to a problem to be found and implemented. The assumption seems to be that a particular issue can be identified as a topic of policy concern and solutions pursued in a relatively straightforward manner, while the circumstances of the identified issue remain static and constant. The linear model which it invokes, of problem identification, intervention, evaluation, and application/dissemination, takes too long and, ironically, not only does not work but, it might be argued, cannot work in a vibrant social world.

Indeed, we might go further and suggest that this is not only a problem for the *what works* movement; it might be argued that this is a core supposition and hence a core problem of most social research, including qualitative research. Social research looks backwards to investigate and evaluate what *has happened*, rather than looking forward to explore what *might happen*—as if social research, in and of itself, will lead to change. Large tracts of social research, including qualitative research, still operate with a linear and chronological set of assumptions with respect to the relationship between research, policy, and practice. The one (research) is assumed logically and necessarily to precede the other (changed policy and improved practice). The assumption is thus: identify problem, investigate problem, propose solutions, evaluate solutions (including, often, with qualitative and mixed methods research designs as well as RCTs), disseminate solutions, solve problem. The sequence of linked activity involves and assumes a seamlessly connected chain of problem-research-data-analysis-policy-solution. Except circumstances change, and the problems persist and re-emerge in new contexts and conditions. Lather alerts us to the fact that this linear model need not necessarily endure and indeed should not endure. We need a more iterative and dynamic model of the relationships among research, policy, and practice:

> To "take the side of the messy" is to counter faith in a naive and transparent social world, to work with empirical material in a way that pays attention simultaneously to language, bodies and material conditions, to present a mix of interpretations versus seeking consensus, both finding patterns and opening up closures. (Lather, 2010, p. 10)

The focus then, should be:

> on how qualitative work with a critical edge might improve the quality of practice . . . the task is to rethink the relation between empirical work and philosophy in a way that posits an engagement with not knowing as an ethical and political move. (Lather, 2010, pp. 10, 14)

Thus an epistemological imperative to value indeterminacy combines with a political imperative to value engagement, deliberation, and constant re-evaluation of current practice. The point is not to *solve* problems with *proof* but constantly to identify and reflect on social issues with the people concerned. What is at stake here is not only a different model of knowing and producing knowledge, but a different model of democratic engagement and producing policy. The currently deployed logic of using research to inform or even drive policy depends on assumptions of centralized decision-making. It assumes a classic, top-down, center-periphery model of social and economic development—research informs policy which determines practice. This model begs very severe questions about the democratic legitimacy of research and policy driving practice in this way, along with the many confounding problems and unintended consequences of practice being constantly conceived in this way and buffeted by such a model.

Interestingly enough, in light of my previous observations about *democratic evaluation*, Lather (2010) frames the issue in terms of "Democratic versus managerial accountability" (p. 48), and reviews various attempts to realize such activity in action. What is needed, she argues, is to build:

> deliberative practices into the midst of the messiness, contingency and ambiguity of our world. . . . [We need] a form of applied social science that can cope with the multiplicity of the social world. . . . The struggle is for an applied social science that can engage strategically with the limits and possibilities of the uses of research for policy toward improvement of practice. (Lather, 2010, pp. 48, 53)

As noted previously, key features of the practice of democratic evaluation were the use of qualitative fieldwork procedures involving respondent validation of primary data and negotiation of draft reports—direct engagement and deliberation with research participants about the nature of the problem and possible ways of approaching a different way of doing things. Of course, to reiterate, times change, and any parallels with "the side of the messy" are far from exact. Crucial however is the recognition that evaluation (and research) is an inherently political activity, and there is a distinct resonance with Lather's (2010) search for "a social science that integrates context dependency with practical deliberation . . . a social science that can contribute to society's practical rationality in clarifying where we are and where we want to be" (p.61).

The issue at stake is whether research and evaluation seek to act on behalf of government to try to solve people's problems for them or engage with people directly to explore and identify different ways to address social and economic issues: "to foster understanding, reflection and action instead of a narrow translation of research into practice" (Lather 2010, p. 62). Lather (2010) ends her book with a call to be open "to a politics of becoming" (p. 76) and "to show how subjects are materialized via iterative and intra-active agencies of time, place and individuals as co-constitutive of each other" (p. 85).

She cites examples of *democratic accountability* and *critical program evaluation* in action, and of course has tried to put such ideas into action in her own work including *Troubling the Angels* (Lather & Smithies,

1997). However, in many ways, citing examples is perhaps not the point. Of course, it is always helpful to have exemplars of what other ways of doing research might look like, and, as Patti herself insists "accessing the complexity and messiness of practice-in-context is the strength of qualitative research" (Lather, 2010, p. 10). But taking her injunction to view "time, place and individuals as co-constitutive of each other" (Lather, 2010, p. 85), the broader lesson is surely that it is the process, the struggle, which is as important as the specifics of each example. The point is always to keep possibilities open to the new, *praxis*, rather than *progress per se*. As Lather (2010) herself concludes: "What I am urging is that a diversity of approaches be instituted, each a factor in a complex web that builds capacities for micro-possibilities, instead of this big bang scaling up stuff" (p. 92).

Many of the theoretical and methodological matters that were thought to have been settled by the post-positivism of Lather's early career (1986) were not settled, are not settled, and indeed have been addressed without settlement by previous generations of researchers (Cowles, 2020; Jewett, 2020). The lesson of the reinvigorated *Science Wars* of recent years, and their reach into educational research, would seem to be that such matters can never be settled in absolute terms: They will and must be revisited and struggled over by successive generations of scholars. Out of that struggle, new knowledge will be generated, and new settlements and accommodations will be made. What is so significant about Patti Lather's effort to develop a much more situated, dynamic, and relational understanding of knowing and how it links to doing is that it provides a hugely valuable resource to help us think through these struggles, and how to realize the production and utilization of social scientific knowledge in action.

References

Campbell, D., & Stanley, J. (1963). *Experimental and quasi-experimental design for research*. Cengage Learning.

Carr, W., & Kemmis, S. (1986). *Becoming critical: Education, knowledge and action research*. Routledge.

Cook, T., & Payne, M. (2002). Objecting to the objections to using random assignment in educational research. In F. Mosteller & R. Boruch (Eds.), *Evidence matters: Randomized trials in education research* (pp. 150–178). Brookings Institution Press.

Cowles, H. (2020). *The scientific method*. Harvard University Press

Denzin, N. K., & Giardina, M. D. (Eds.). (2006). *Qualitative inquiry and the conservative challenge*. Left Coast Press.

Frederiksen, L., & Beck, S. (2010). Caught in the crossfire: Educational research in context. *International Journal of Research and Method in Education, 33*(2), 135–149.

Goldacre, B. (2013). *Building evidence into education*. London, Department for Education. https://www.gov.uk/government/news/building-evidence-into-education

Guba, E., & Lincoln, Y. (1981). *Effective evaluation*. Jossey-Bass.

Haynes, L., Service, O., Goldacre, B., & Torgerson, D. (2012). *Test, learn, adapt: Developing public policy with randomised controlled trials*. Cabinet Office Behavioural Insights Team, London. https://www.gov.uk/government/publications/test-learn-adapt-developing-public-policy-with-randomised-controlled-trials

Hesse, M. (1980). *Revolution and reconstruction in the philosophy of science*. Indiana University Press.

House, E. (1980). *Evaluating with validity*. Sage.

Jewett, A. (2020). *Science under fire*. Harvard University Press.

Kushner, S., & Norris, N. (1981). Interpretation, negotiation and validity in naturalistic Research. *Interchange, 11*(4), 26–36.

Lather, P. (1986). Research as praxis. *Harvard Educational Review 56*(3), 257–277.

Lather, P. (1991). *Getting smart: Feminist research and pedagogy with/in the post-Modern*. Routledge.

Lather, P. (2004a). This IS your father's paradigm. *Qualitative Inquiry, 10*(1), 15–34.

Lather, P. (2004b). Scientific research in education: a critical perspective. *British Educational Research Journal, 30*(6), 759–772.

Lather, P. (2007). *Getting lost: Feminist efforts towards a double(d) science*. State University of New York Press.

Lather, P. (2010). *Engaging science policy: From the side of the messy*. Peter Lang.

Lather, P. (2016). Post-face: Cultural studies of numeracy. *Cultural Studies ↔ Critical Methodologies 16*(5), 502–505.

Lather, P., & Smithies, C. (1997). *Troubling the angels: Women living with HIV/AIDS*. Westview Press.

MacDonald, B. (1974/2010). Evaluation and the control of education. In B. MacDonald & R. Walker (Eds.). (1974). *Innovation, Evaluation, Research and the Problem of Control*, pp. 9–22. SAFARI Interim Papers, Centre for Applied Research in Education, University of East Anglia, UK 1974; reprinted in H. Torrance (Ed.). (2010), *Qualitative research methods in education: Volume I: Theoretical origins of qualitative research methods in education*. Sage.

McCall, W. (1923). *How to experiment in education*. MacMillan.

No Child Left Behind (NCLB). (2002). *No child left behind act*. 115 STAT. 1965. http://www2.ed.gov/policy/elsec/leg/esea02/107-110.pdf

Parlett, M., & Hamilton, D. (1972). Evaluation as illumination: A new approach to the study of innovatory programmes, Occasional Paper No. 9. Centre for Research in the Educational Sciences, University of Edinburgh; reprinted in H. Torrance (Ed.). (2010), *Qualitative research methods in education: Volume I: Theoretical origins of qualitative research methods in education*. Sage.

Shavelson, R., Phillips, D., Towne, L., & Feuer, M. (2003). On the science of education design studies. *Educational Researcher, 32*(1), 25–28.

Simons, H. (Ed.). (1980). *Towards a science of the singular.* CARE Occasional Publications No. 10. Centre for Applied Research in Education, University of East Anglia.

Simons, H. (1987). *Getting to know schools in a democracy: The politics and process of evaluation.* Routledge

Slavin, R. (2002). Evidence-based education policies: Transforming educational practice and research. *Educational Researcher, 31*(7), 15–21.

Stake, R. (1978). The case study method in social inquiry. *Educational Researcher, 7*(2), 5–8.

Stenhouse, L. (1978). The study of samples and the study of cases. *British Educational Research Journal 6*(1), 1–6.

Thomas, G. (2016). After the gold rush: Questioning the 'gold standard' and reappraising the status of experiment and randomized controlled trials in education. *Harvard Educational Review 86*(3), 390–411.

Torgerson, C. J., & Torgerson, D. J. (2008). *Designing randomized controlled trials in health, education and the social sciences.* Palgrave Macmillan.

Torrance, H. (1981). The origin and development of mental testing in England and the United States. *British Journal of Sociology of Education 2*(1), 45–59.

Torrance, H. (2017). Blaming the victim: Assessment, examinations, and the responsibilisation of students and teachers in neo-liberal governance. *Discourse: Studies in the Cultural Politics of Education 38*(1), 83–96.

Torrance, H. (2018). Evidence, criteria, policy and politics: The debate about quality and utility in educational and social research. In N. Denzin & Y. Lincoln (Eds.), *The SAGE handbook of qualitative research* (5th ed.). Sage.

Torrance, H. (2024). Science, evidence and the development of policy and practice: Can qualitative research make a different contribution? In N. Denzin & Y. Lincoln (Eds.), *The SAGE handbook of qualitative research* (6th ed.). Sage.

Tyler, R. (1949). *Basic principles of curriculum and instruction.* University of Chicago Press.

Walker, R. (1974) *Classroom research: A view from SAFARI.* In SAFARI. Innovation Evaluation Research and the Problem of Control, ed. B. MacDonald and R. Walker, University of East Anglia, Norwich.

What Works Clearinghouse (WWC). (2020). *What Works Clearinghouse Standards Handbook, Version 4.1.* U.S. Department of Education, Institute of Education Sciences. https://ies.ed.gov/ncee/wwc/Docs/referenceresources/WWC-Standards-Handbook-v4-1-508.pdf

What Works Network (WWN). (2018). *The What Works Network Five Years On Cabinet Office.* https://assets.publishing.service.gov.uk/government/uploads/system/uploads/attachment_data/file/677478/6.4154_What_works_report_Final.pdf

Yates, L. (2004). *What is quality in educational research?* Open University Press.

CHAPTER SIX

The Uses of Erudition: Refections on Patti Lather

SAMUEL D. ROCHA

"*Theory is too often used to protect us from the awesome complexity of the world.*"

Patti Lather, *Getting Smart* (1991)

Introductory Context

I WANT TO TRY to reflect on the impact of Patti Lather's life and work upon my own. I use the word *try* in relation to the literary form of the essay. An essay is an attempt, a try, a rehearsal of sorts. I refer to the *life and work* of Lather and myself in relation to the literary forms of philosophical, intellectual, and spiritual biography, sometimes regarded as confessional literature, but also aware of the epistemic and psychological limits of self-disclosure, literary or otherwise. These limitations include the unreliability of personal memory and the looming potential for self-deception and other kinds of falsehood. These literary forms, with all their noted limitations, extend to any form of self-disclosure bracketed by a concern for types of academic formation, intellectual labor, and their various becomings. I have selected and will use *erudition* as the generative theme for these reflections.

For thematic context, I was a doctoral student at The Ohio State University from 2007 to 2010. Early in my program of study, I wandered down the hallway of Ramseyer Hall and found Lather's office. My memory does not recall whether this wandering was happenstance or suggested by Bill

Taylor, who had encouraged me to meet her. I also have a foggy recollection of one of her articles in *Educational Theory* posted to her closed door. Because *Educational Theory* was among the few journals I recognized as belonging to the field I was trying to enter, I saw her authorship there as another sign: I needed to familiarize myself with her and her work. I searched her name on the Internet and read several of the articles posted to her website. Soon thereafter, we met in her office. I recall seeing a large construction sign with a Derridean pun and piles of Xeroxed readings and writings stacked on the floor around her. She was loud and in a hurry, and she invited me to stop in again, which I did.

Lather's seminar on Michel Foucault was limited to 15 students and popular among students in her program and several other departments, especially geography and comparative studies. I was lucky to get a seat in that class and was introduced to Foucault there. I was also introduced to publishing and published my first two book reviews as a result. A panel of student work from that course was featured at the first Bergamo conference I attended. I do not recall when I asked her to serve on my committee, but I recall her noting that it would be an exception to her usual advisory conventions, but agreeing to do it nonetheless. I would later audit her course in feminist methodologies at her suggestion. At my first philosophy of education conference in 2009, the Kneller Lecture by Lorraine Code made more direct references to Lather than to any other name, which left me with another strong impression that Lather was very much within the fold of philosophy of education, however idiosyncratic that may have been within the politics of the disciplines. I never parted from that impression.

My impression of Lather as a philosopher is unremarkable within my own story, but I can see how it may seem odd to many who see Lather as a methodologist within qualitative research. I do not mean to quarrel with her reputation within the social sciences. Perhaps the title of *theorist* would serve as an intermediary position, but the issue, for me, is not of classification or nomenclature. The primary issue that Lather the philosopher introduces functions as our first entry into the theme of erudition, revealing a sense of erudition that resists parochial or provincial limitations upon the range of one's work and its impact.

I ended my program somewhat prematurely because one of my sources of funding ran out, and I recall her allowing for it with serious reservations about the quality of my graduate education received at Ohio State. For years thereafter, she would ask me whether I regretted going there. I did not understand that question until we had margaritas on her patio during my sabbatical year, which coincided with the COVID-19 pandemic, nearly ten years after I had left Ohio State. She asked the question—"Do you regret going to Ohio State?"—she had been repeating for a decade, and I finally confessed that I had never understood what she meant. She went on to explain her dismay at seeing my transcript and realizing that much of my program of study lacked a certain type of erudition I will discuss here and in the section to follow. That clarification made sense to me and also clarified that we are different philosophers, reliant on different approaches, while also, I would say, fairly focused on similar questions concerning the subject.

Our personal relationship has always been rooted in her deep understanding and acceptance. She recognized and named not only my religious identity but also my ethnic and class identity and more. I do not want to intrude any further, but I suspect her reasons for these recognitions emerged from certain biographical overlaps and sympathies. When I struggled to find my way into an idea, she would encourage me to work through what I already knew and had read, but she has always been frank about wondering whether my readings are sufficiently broad, especially within the social sciences and, above all, regarding qualitative theory and methodology. My arguments for a *pre-qualitative* approach to research through the humanities have been met with, and benefited from, strong scrutiny and critical argumentation from her.

It is from this partial context that these themes emerge. Some of them can be found within the literature, including a chapter I wrote and her critical response to it in *Philosophy and History of Education: Diverse Perspectives on Their Value and Relationship* (Errante et al., 2017). I initially considered writing this chapter as a response to that interaction. Although I chose a more anecdotal and thematic route instead, it may benefit the reader to become familiar with that exchange in addition to the contextual clues I have offered here in brief. To summarize, I argue that what has been called *post-qualitative* research in the social sciences is better understood as pre-qualitative scholarship in the humanities. Lather responded with a critique foregrounded by her concerns about the limits of my own erudition, especially, and admittedly, within the domain of qualitative research and the social sciences. In many respects, my studies with Lather, much like my sense of her as a philosopher, were idiosyncratic. My defense—

or, perhaps, my lament—of the humanities within education research, against the hegemony of the social sciences, including qualitative and even post-qualitative research, seemed, and perhaps still seems, a problem born of a lack of study and erudition.

My primary motivation to write this chapter is not theoretical nor an attempt to deconstruct or reinterpret Lather's work or impact within the various fields and disciplines where her work is studied. It is certainly not an apologia nor a response to the issues raised above. Of course, I realize that theorizing through thinking and interpretation through the use of language are inevitable, and I accept my proportional responsibility for them in their generic and unavoidable senses. However, in my heart of hearts, what I seek to do here is to reflect upon the life and work of Lather, my teacher and mentor and friend. I do not seek to memorialize nor, God forbid, eulogize her. This requires a lighter, more impressionistic touch, which is among the lessons I have tried to learn from Lather—a lesson I have struggled with and will continue to work on, even as I write this chapter.

Varieties of Erudition

There are a variety of senses of erudition that could be explored here, beginning with the basic and plain fact that Lather is a bookish person, a reading person, an educated person in the literary sense—an academic and intellectual. That sense of erudition may be more of a disposition or character study. As real as it is, it lacks sufficient concreteness to justify a study, but does set the stage for the uses of erudition to come.

The first use of erudition I will try to describe in Lather is pedagogical and curricular. I recall her textual approach to teaching Foucault. We began by reading the English translation of *The Order of Things* in full, making annotations in the text and margins. After a series of shorter articles and surveys of the secondary literature, we returned to *The Order of Things*, re-reading it with a writing instrument of a different color in hand, noting the difference between our first annotations and marginalia. This simple method taught me that erudition was not only a matter of breadth but also depth of analysis and understanding and, perhaps above all, tracking change and difference over time.

This pedagogical sense of erudition became more curricular in its dimensions when I slowly made better sense of some of her questions about my own course of study at Ohio State. Lather has a deeply American sense of doctoral education, steeped in a regime of intellectual coursework that qualifies the student in the content to follow for their comprehensive examination, dissertation, and future teaching. She would often encourage me to take courses in qualitative methodology, for example, not for the sake of my work in philosophy of education, but, instead, for the sake of my future ability to teach courses in methodology with some credibility.

Her approach to collegiate and graduate instruction is one that values and requires humanistic erudition. As we have seen, this approach contrasted with my more British course of study at Ohio State, bringing in transfer credits and doing a variety of directed readings. This British collegiate style is also more like the present Canadian graduate curriculum I work in today. I have learned to appreciate Lather's sense of humanistic erudition as a serious and effective guardrail against anti-intellectualism. In fact, as I reflect on this sense of humanistic erudition, I feel more and more aware of my own orientation towards folk and romantic anti-intellectualism. Her position on this has always been clear: there is no use nor place for anti-intellectualism in this work.

This is not to say there is nothing folksy about Lather. Far from it. Her prose has an ease to it and flows with expressions such as "just fine" and "like a duck to water." But she has also defended the rhetoric of erudition in dense theoretical writing against anti-intellectual, bad faith accusations that insist upon a particular form of "clarity." My point here is not to cast a portrait of an elitist sense of humanistic erudition, but, instead, and as we will see, a kind of faithful erudition that is also, in many respects, informal.

In her work as a scholar, the role of erudition selects primary and secondary texts which allow the scholar to make use of the expertise of another interpreter or translator. I recall her referral of my questions concerning Freud and psychoanalysis to the expertise of Deborah Britzman. This was not a casual referral. It was a specific reference to Britzman's treatment of the work of William James, my primary interest at that time. She had Britzman's Freudian work at hand and on offer to create a more constructive link between my interests, while making it very clear that the Freudian schema was not her own territory as a scholar. This introduces a third more scholastic sense of erudition which, again, has often produced tensions in my rather Protestant reliance on primary and direct textual interpretation— or unadorned ordinary-language argumentation. Her scholastic erudition is more Catholic in this respect than my own and carries a selective yet generous respect for the authority of a community of scholars, tracking the ongoing movement within the history of ideas.

Lather's scholarly approach to erudition has two inner movements that I, again, first observed in her teaching. She was never shy about making it clear when she regarded a particular text as canonical. I recall her occasionally making statements such as this one: "No one should be conferred a doctoral degree at this university if they have not read *The Structure of Scientific Revolutions.*"

I recall that one day, in my own class on political philosophy, I used Lather's rhetorical formula and asserted "No one can be considered an educated person if they have not read Martin Luther King Jr.'s 'Letter from a Birmingham Jail.'" As I returned home that evening, I regretted my amplification of Lather's exhortation and even considered sending a memo of apology. The following morning, I awoke to several emails from students who thanked me for my admonition and shared their appreciations of King's canonical letter. This canonical value for erudition is, I suppose, a mix of scholarship and pedagogy, but it is among the more shared values that Lather and I have. I admit that it is risky and certainly not above criticism. It is easily misunderstood, and the misunderstandings remind me of the bizarre pendulum between my aforementioned anti-intellectualism and outright and principled intellectual elitism. For Lather, I cannot know what she faces in that kind of erudition, but I am sure she could narrate it in terms that are frank.

At the same time, Lather's sense of canonical erudition is not reducible to a nostalgia for *Great Books*. She tracks a living and open canon with little mourning for the ideas left in the wake of contemporary thought. For whatever reason, I recall her reaction to Barack Obama winning the primary against Hillary Clinton. It went something like, "Well, I guess it is time to get to work for Obama." I don't think she ever took her Clinton bumper sticker off, but I also recall the matter-of-fact way in which she responded to the reality of the failed primary for her preferred candidate. This may not directly pertain to Lather's second sense of canonical erudition, but it does capture a sentiment of the phenomenon or, perhaps, a lack of sentimentalism in the face of change.

I recall protesting the speed of theoretical interventions in contemporary theory, arguing then, as I would now, that ideas take time and do not inject themselves into any vein of reality as directly or efficiently as some make it seem. Her response was instant. She exclaimed "Sometimes, Sam, concepts happen just like *that*!" Her emphatic reply was not so much a defense or apologia for theory so much as a sense of excitement that there is something at stake here and now. Real change can happen. There was a certain faith in intellectual work (using the word *certain* in a doubled fashion), a faith I continue to struggle to find. This faith was neither fideistic nor pious, and remained hopeful and open and ever-curious. I recall her open speculation on the fascinating possibility of trying to grasp the feminism of Sarah Palin, much to the chagrin of many in her class.

Perhaps it is this use of a faithful erudition—opposed to anti-intellectualism, committed to the pedagogical mastery of content, respectful of canons that are wide open and alive—that I wish to reflect upon and reconsider in Lather and, in a different way, myself.

The Ends

There is a useless sense of erudition that can overtake any sense of the ends of erudition. Theory is one of the sites where this kind of erudition for its own sake can take hold. When this happens, Lather's (1991) warning in *Getting Smart* rings clear: "Theory is too often used to protect us from the awesome complexity of the world" (p. 62). In this cautionary spirit, it is perhaps best to end by emphasizing that the uses of erudition for Lather do not include an aimlessness "getting lost." There is a worldliness and an affirmation of life that she puts to work in the service of a political and even moral purpose. I have focused on the pedagogical project here as her student, but now as I read her books and recall her teachings, I realize there is harmony to be found between the uses of erudition I have located within my own experience and the ones she deploys in her work. I am grateful for them. Here, in closing, are two more lasting lessons she taught me.

I returned to Ohio State to receive the dissertation award at a small ceremony of my peers and mentors. Lather always had a keen awareness of my nerves and the caring, blunt license to speak to me about them. Before I went up to receive my award, she leaned over and told me "just don't forget to say 'thank you.'" I minded my manners and began my remarks with a note of thanks, but I soon tilted at windmills and resorted to profanity to describe the awarded work's iconoclastic disposition. I knew that my antics had left the room in a state of some polite shock and sat back down next to her. She leaned over once again and said "Sam, there are two kinds of places in the world: places where you can and cannot say 'fuck.'" She was right, of course, even as it took me years to appreciate it.

References

Errante, A., Blount J., & Kimball, B. A. (2017). *Philosophy and history of education: Diverse perspectives on their value and relationship.* Routledge.

Lather, P. (1991). *Getting smart: Feminist research and pedagogy with/in the postmodern.* Routledge.

CHAPTER SEVEN

Talk French to Me: Rethinking the Qual/Quant Relationship: A Rendezvous with Patti Lather

ELIZABETH DE FREITAS, KATE O'BRIEN, AND NATHALIE SINCLAIR

DURING A VIBRANT SUMMER conference in Eugene, Oregon in 2014, where a group of people gathered to discuss the future of social research, a series of carefully curated small group conversations were organized. These involved clusters of four or five people brought together to address specific quandaries haunting the field of qualitative inquiry (Rosiek & Mazzei, 2014). One such cluster was inspired by Patti Lather's keen insight that digital media were changing the relationship between qualitative and quantitative research methods, and that new materialist philosophical paradigm shifts raised new questions about the ontological status of measurement (Barad, 2007; Coole & Frost, 2010; Kirby, 2011). In anticipation of that conversation, she expressed her excitement to learn what would feel quite foreign to her, and she said, with a laugh, "Come and talk French to me." The joke was that measurement and mathematics are rarely considered sensuous or seductive discourse, although often treated as a lingua franca! But Patti Lather knew better. Her interest in reimagining qual/quant entanglement was and continues to be part of an extremely important political project in the social sciences. The conversation we had that day was so rich that a special issue of *Cultural Studies↔Critical Methodologies* emerged in 2016, called *Alternative Ontologies of Number: Rethinking the Quantitative in Computational Culture* (de Freitas et al., 2016). More recent collaborations with Lather have led to our joint presentation at AERA on the quantum paradigm shift in the social sciences, where Patti focused on the need to rethink the image of science beyond classical Newtonian images of inquiry and towards new quantum formalizations of indeterminacy (Lather et al., 2022).

There are about 50 references to the word *quantitative* in the 2017 Routledge collection of essays by Patti Lather. In many of these instances, Lather reflects on her desire for *smart mixed methods research* that rises above the staid gesture of frequency counts—counts like the kind we have just made. Her critique during the 2000s of sloppy and simplistic applications of statistics in the social sciences sought a more sophisticated remixing of the quantitative and the qualitative. Her work pushed back at the positivism, scientism, and logical empiricism that came to dominate education research in the first half of the last century, but she was careful to show how the limits of the quantitative are tied to the limits of the qualitative: "Reading Kuhn and Foucault does not mean the end of quantitative methods but the historicizing and troubling of all paradigms as not innocent, with qualitative as dangerous as quantitative" (Lather, 2017, p. 146). And she invited a far more challenging critical discussion among qualitative researchers around the possibility of a "positive" disposition towards quantification (Lather, 2017, p. 146).

Her turn to science and technology studies (STS) helped to deepen our understanding of what is done more broadly in the name of science, inquiry, investigation, knowledge production, etc. Looking back at the *science wars*, it would be wise to note how easily the critics were branded *anti-science* when, as she explains, the target was not science but the impoverished philosophies of science that had taken hold of the *social* sciences. These philosophical framings of science focused on particular practices such as replication, refutability, generalizability, semantic incrementalism, etc., and produced an image of science derived largely from the work of analytic philosophers including Russell, Quine, Popper, and Putnam. Lather insisted that we consider alternative philosophical frameworks, and she always showed up with concrete suggestions; she reminded us that feminist philosophers of science and posthumanist thinkers in the 1980s had thoroughly contested the standard image of science, showing how it was a deeply situated and material practice—STS thinkers such as Donna Haraway, Evelyn Fox Keller, and Sandra Harding. These thinkers were not anti-science, but intent on showing how science actually achieved its aims, through on-the-ground alliances with the non-human, in a metamorphic onto-epistemic mixture, be it in the lab or in the field, and always as a political and economic affair. One of the key STS thinkers in this group, Bruno Latour (1987, 1993) argued that the conventional philosophies of science didn't accurately capture the material, political, and often horrifically destructive practices of science. In her essay "Methodology-21: What do we do in the Afterward?," Lather notes how the "quantitative imperialism" (Brady & Collier, 2004, as cited in Lather, 2013, p. 636) of random sampling methodologies had been shaken by STS and other critical projects, as was evident in the 2009 Spencer Foundation report on the preparation of researchers in education, and the call for better epistemological groundings across the paradigms (Lather, 2017, p. 322).

This chapter stays tuned to the challenge of thinking the quantitative with the qualitative in social inquiry. It is written in three voices—and three sections—by three authors who carry the torch that Lather set ablaze, determined to explore a "cultural studies of mathematics," as Lather once described it in conversation, whereby the very concepts associated with quantitative objectivity—number, measure, diagram, randomness—are shown to be far more lively and contingent than the power brokers would have us believe. Each section takes up and discusses Lather's work, showing how her words help us reclaim 'the quantitative' from those who marshal its power, in support of critical and inclusive projects across the social sciences.

The Incalculable
by Elizabeth de Freitas

The figure of the incalculable looms large in Lather's work. She evokes the incalculable as part of the promise of new materialist methodologies that enact "post-post" validity, a validity that would be "inexact, and yet rigorous, *incalculable*, flowing along the lines of Deleuzian transcendental empiricism" (Lather, 2017, p. 11–12, my italics). She also speaks of the "multiply-sited subject" characterized by "incalculable differences" (Lather, 2017, p. 103) and lauds the work of Elizabeth Povinelli whose postcolonial research method is described as "in excess of intersectionality" in its "attention to multi-directionalities, post-human bodies, intra-actional networks, contingency, non-mastery, and *incalculables*" (Lather, 2017, p. 326, my italics). The incalculable seems to ground the proposal for transformative methods: "We inherit and invent, each time anew, toward the something to come that is already at work, *incalculable*" (Lather, 2017, p. 311, my italics). Concerned with a delusional science that sees itself in terms of "protocols of calculation" (Lather, 2017, p. 289), she encourages new theoretical orientations and mixed methodologies that might attend to the "volatility beyond calculation" (Lather, 2017, p. 323). Indeed, she demands that we envision an "incalculable subject" that would run "counter to neoliberal and Big Data efforts to count and parse, capture, and model our every move, a subject outside the parameters of the algorithms" (Lather, 2017, p. 345).

In this section, I will relay my way through possible visions of the incalculable. Lather's trenchant critique of experimental or quasi-experimental protocols, and random-assignment experiments in the social sciences, draws attention to the ways in which *chance*—in all its unruly contingency—is tamed and quantified in such work. Her critique targeting the scientific harnessing of chance in the concept of *randomness* remains ever relevant, because I believe chance, contingency, randomness, and "getting lost" (Lather, 2007, p. 1) keep the incalculable afloat. In this section, I will continue Lather's attention to the incalculable, and link it to current concerns in software studies (Fuller & Weizman, 2021; Galloway, 2021; Parisi, 2017) about the incomputable or uncomputable. I realize I am shifting the register slightly and translating her incalculable to incomputable as I take up and grapple with the limits of software methodologies. In doing so, I hope to carry on her project of thinking about the quantitative as a moving target, as something that is imbricated with the qualitative differently in different media.

I learn from Lather that the future of qualitative and quantitative modes of engagement are themselves unscripted, as the two are re-assembled in different media over time. In other words, the conjoined in/calculable is itself an indeterminate and opaque conjunction, surfacing differently depending on our material conditions and our current mathematical practices. Today's digital media have to be examined for how they newly achieve that re-assembling, and how those fighting for liberty and inclusion might re-assemble this conjunction. Just as the qualitative and the quantitative are bound together, so are the computable and the incomputable. They are bound not in a rigid or fixed relation that never changes, but part of an undulating fold in the fabric of life, be it named digital or organic. The history of technology and media shows how delineations regarding the in/calculable and in/computable reshape the territory of life, labor, and learning. As a historical material practice, computation is a mode of *doing number* and can thrive or atrophy; domains come in and out of the realm of the computable. For instance, the 17th century saw the emergence of infinitary calculations while the last century has witnessed a global colonization through *digital* computing, as Turing's (1937) "universal machine" (p. 243) conceives of computation in terms of discrete-state machines.

Following Alexander Galloway (2021), I will explore three different claims that are made in the name of the incalculable or incomputable. Galloway (2021) uses the term "uncomputable" rather than incomputable. I have stuck with the latter term, as the word is nicely parallel to the term that Lather chose: the incalculable. His three claims are that the incomputable is found in: (a) analog life, (b) rational paradox, and (c) the practical material limits of calculation. All three of these answers offer some insight, as we try to navigate the new technical milieu.

The first answer correlates the incomputable with the concept of *analog* which refers to continuous media rather than discrete and digital media. The analog is said to be closer to the body and organic life; it is the flesh, the causal instinct, where intuition, affect, and aesthetic experience thrive. Accordingly, the body is ultimately incomputable, in all its unruly and unmastered contingency. This first answer helps us contrast the digital flux to the continuous flow, the binary truth value to the variegations of lived experience. But does this list of *flesh, affect* and *aesthetic experience* capture the incomputable and its correlate concept of incalculable? Not quite. We need to ask ourselves what is lost when we install a too simple binary between the fleshy body and the digital machine, or between the continuous and the discrete. Haraway's cyborg manifesto was meant to help us overcome this too simple binary. How might computability be something that transcends these distinctions? How might these distinctions actually hinder our ability to imagine the incalculable subject that Lather seeks?

Calculating involves a repeated ritual, an act of "forging a unit, then iterating the unit in series" (Galloway, 2021, p. 20), to be found, for instance, when weaving on a loom or programming a computer, or other situations where the conditions are ripe for such repetitious labor. The work of calculating is thus achieved through an iterative *multiplicity* of repeated actions, a cyclic ritual of rendering the next number, always another number in the count, as the ritual of counting forges a dis/ordered collective. Yes, calculation is an instrumental mode of governance and control, but counting is also a fundamental ritualistic participation in cultural and material collectivity (de Freitas & Sinclair, 2014, 2016). Numeracy and counting are important political acts that bring forth cultural and political multiplicity—as Hardt and Negri (2004) suggest, the socio-political multiplicity is always by necessity *numerous*. This approach suggests that our very understanding of the political, and even the possibility of the political, depends on a concept of number. Galloway (2021) cites Euclid's notion of arithmetic numbers as *plethos* (plethora) ($\pi\lambda\eta\theta\sigma\zeta$) which is often translated as *multiple* (p. 21).

The second answer is that the incomputable refers to the limits of Enlightenment reason due to inherent paradox or contradiction. This answer pertains to the positivist dream of a logical and axiomatic foundation on which science could be based, as articulated by highly influential mathematicians and logicians such as Gottlob Frege, Bertrand Russell, and David Hilbert in their work on mathematical logic and proof theory. The limits to such foundational projects were uncovered by various logicians and mathematicians in the early part of the 20th century, when the epistemic foundations of mathematics and science were shown to be inherently unstable and haunted by paradox. Kurt Gödel's (1931) incompleteness theorems demolished the dream, demonstrating how truth and provability were not always coupled, even in the simplest of arithmetic worlds. He showed the existence of the incalculable in mathematical formalisms, undermining the aim to offer absolute foundations for quantitative truth. This destabilizing of epistemic certainty pointed to the existence of truths that elided the rules of inference. Gödel showed that there would always be truths we could not prove, and that no consistent axiomatic system can prove its own consistency.

Poststructuralist theorists such as Jean Lyotard (1979) would take up Gödel's insight in *The Postmodern Condition: A Report on Knowledge*, to critique representation and correspondence theories of truth in the social sciences. In like manner, more recent theorists of the incomputable, including Beatrice Fazi, cite Gödel's incompleteness theorems along with Alan Turing's halting dilemma, to argue that the incomputable is always lurking in any attempt to calculate anything (Fazi, 2018). This affirms the persistence of incalculables. One can extend the claim that inherent incalculables haunt mathematics, and find numerous historical examples; irrational numbers were considered incalculable by ancient Greek geometers, for whom the world was assumed to be composed of commensurable proportions (*rational numbers*). Even then, the realm of the incalculable was dangerous—Hippasus was allegedly drowned for pointing out how the diagonal of a square could not be expressed as the ratio of two integers. And notably, the ancient Greek solution to their dilemma was a *differential theory of averages* that iteratively approximated the unruly irrational number, and gave them something they could work with, much like our current investment in neural network models of incremental computation. But it's important to know that Gödel's proof depends entirely on number theory in order to prove the weakness of logic! Number itself, for Gödel, was not the target of his destabilizing proof (Goldstein, 2005; Nagel & Newman, 2001).

The third answer that Galloway (2021) points to is the actual pragmatic limits of calculation and computation. This is because acts of counting and measuring are literal material practices that consume time and energy. Computing consumes energy, and calculating is labor. There are material limits to what can be calculated in any given time or place, as resources frame the conditions of the computable. The incomputable lies beyond those material limits. With relevance to our current context, note that large language models (LLMs) and various other kinds of neural network computational models require excessive amounts of energy (and data) to make even the most mundane inference. They are resource consumers, demanding a vast number of parameters and data points, and consuming lithium and rare earth minerals. The incomputable in this case points to the physical limits of our computing power and underscores the consequential destruction of the earth. Our best examples of AI today are considered wasteful and highly inefficient machines precisely because they require so many resources. Children learn to code faster and with more agility than do current machine learning models. Questions of resource depletion and the environmental cost of various computing practices have to become much more central in our debates about the limits of calculation and the uncomputable (Crawford, 2022).

Lather's critique in the early 2000s of random trial research and sloppy applications of statistics must be reframed today, as we witness the methodological absorption of a new kind of randomness. Her critique of classical parametric statistical models used in the social sciences hit the mark, but today algorithmic reason deploys the random variable in new ways. We have moved beyond Lather's original target of random control experiments and are working with an entirely different way of mobilizing the random. Lather herself asked her audience time and again to attend carefully to the new algorithmic conditions that were emerging. Past scientific paradigms saw 'the control' population as the calculable, and the random noise as that which muddied the clarity of inquiry, but our new algorithmic condition has internalized such noise (Parisi, 2019). Contingency and entropy have become the fuel of our current machine learning models (Parisi, 2017). Practices that are internal to algorithmic work—random vectors, noise modulation, error redistribution, generative hallucinations, etc.—have all become part of what we might call procedural randomness. As Galloway (2021) claims, "in a sense, randomness and contingency have become fully industrial. Today the computable is closely intertwined with the incomputable" (p. 20). In terms of methodological futures and the pursuit of what Lather called the incalculable subject, I agree with Galloway that there is no choice here between critique and computation. We must do both.

Diagrammatic Ruins
by Kate C. O'Brien

In this section of our three-way tango with Lather's oeuvre, I explore Patti's brazen insistence that we all *get lost*. Drawing on the early essays in Lather's (2007) compilation, *Getting Lost: Feminist Efforts Toward a Double(d) Science*, my investigation of quant/qual relations explores a rather esoteric subset of mathematical practices: weaving diagrams. Weaving is emblematic of a qual/quant mixture and is directly related to the history of computing. I use Lather's insistence that we dive into the ruins of knowledge—"knowledge that loses itself in the necessary blind spots of understanding" (Lather, 2007, p. vii)—to examine and experiment with weaving diagrams as carcasses of/for thought. Importantly, it is not the obscurity of these gridded images that makes weaving diagrams such fertile ruins. In fact, it is their lively implication in contemporary tensions between the quantitative and qualitative—a tension of which, in some sense, all diagrams partake—that make weaving diagrams such strangely productive sites of decay. As we will see in the examples that follow, it is the dense and growing network of connections between looms and computers that make these particular diagrams such playful sites to scram, vamoose, and skedaddle!

Weaving diagrams make an apt landscape for the work of getting lost because they are such disorienting images to begin with. Marshalled by rulers and organized into a tight grid of black and white, these diagrams have none of the romantic qualities of hand-made inscriptions. In Figure 1, showing four tones of a woven grayscale, the production of each shade of "gray" depends on a carefully patterned mixture of discrete elements. To make sense of the difference between the lightest and darkest tones in this field, I had to lean into the page and use a pencil point to carefully count squares. It turns out that the two central grays—in sharp contrast at the image's middle—are indeed *opposites*. The darkest color is made of a repeating pattern of one white box, then four black boxes, while the lightest tone inverses this. This central tone is constructed from rows of one black box followed by four white boxes.

Figure 7.1 This weaving diagram is from Birgit Schneider's (2007) *Textiles Prozessieren* [Textile Processing] (p. 23).

If one holds this diagram at a distance, however, the obviousness of these repeated patterns and their discrete elements disappears. Black boxes blur with white ones and create a series of gray square frames, which get lighter and lighter as they approach the graphic's outer edge. In fact, if you are reading this chapter on a computer screen, something similar is happening as your eyes take in the words on the page. It is a mixture of colored lights—or a vast array of pixels—that are processed by your senses as words. Historically, weaving and its attendant diagrammatic practices sit at the heart of this gaming of the discrete and continuous. The loom is the oldest human technology that uses quantitatively constructed patterns to generate qualities that feel absolutely unrelated to number.

Although we hardly notice it, something is getting lost in both the moments when I counted discrete squares with a pencil point—here, I no longer perceived the grays—and when I held the diagram at a distance to allow the grayscale to surface. At first, this loss feels like that of an optical illusion. In the case of the weaving diagram in Figure 7.1, it is also true that one perceives the same information in two strikingly different ways: You see the discrete; you see the continuous. You see the quantitative; you see the qualitative. However, this transformation is not like the sharp, disjunctive flip of these optical illusions. It is, instead, induced by a gradual shift in scale—e.g., leaning into the page or walking across the room. After moving back and forth, from the global perception of a paisley swirl and into the minutiae of its checkered pattern, one now stares in disbelief at the paisley's continuous sweep. In the weaving diagram, loss and lostness surface in this strange oscillation, where the diagram—even before we understand its relation to the weaving process—opens a hole in our sensorial capacities to distinguish between the smooth flow of a single gray tone and the jagged dance of individual black and white squares.

Perhaps this paradoxical fusion of the continuous and the discrete is not exactly what Lather (2001) has in mind when she enjoins us to "embrace the epistemological insufficiency" (p. 478) of contemporary science. But, when Lather's (2007) work sets out to explore "knowledge that loses itself in the necessary blind spots of understanding" (p. vii), it asserts that understanding always involves the generation of lacunae like these. She is interested in these holey bits—the detritus that is swept away or blinkered off in the process of creating something seeable, expressible, confident, and solid. Turning toward these blind spots—not to capture them or finally map the whole—Lather encourages us to wander, to loose ourselves, and lose ourselves in places that are difficult, if not impossible, to stand—places which we will not understand. In these places, it is knowledge *itself* that is doing the "losing"—not the "I" or "us" which ostensibly directs thinking. To explore "knowledge that loses *itself*" (Lather, 2007, p. vii, emphasis mine) implies a world of knowing in which mathematics, the quant/qual border, and science writ large, are all made and unmade in the processes of losing.

The etymology of loss implies a splitting of some kind, but how, when, and where this splitting action happens is productively confusing, remade again and again as we return to loss. In Lather's (2007) fifth plateau, "Loss and lost, lost, lost" (p. 11), she links the work of getting lost to mourning as a creative practice. Her ideas resonate with the complex way that Édouard Glissant (1997/1990) describes the experience of the *abyss* for Africans who lived through deportation to the Americas during the slave trade. Lather's (2007) list of losses includes the death of God, the loss of an innocent science, transparent theories of language, Enlightenment categories of rationality, individual autonomy. . . . Akin to Glissant's conceptualization of vertigo, she would agree that "this is not the vertigo preceding apocalypse and Babel's fall. It is the shiver of a beginning, confronted with extreme possibility" (Glissant, 1997/1990, p. 109). Lather herself suggests that dealing with loss "in ways other than nostalgia means accepting the disfigurations of language, loving what we do to ourselves with language (Cohen, 1998, p. 189) including the creative quality of loss" (Lather, 2007, p. 12).

Something quite similar could be said about the compromises we make in diagramming. As visuo-spatial attempts to capture a gesture "mid-flight" (Châtelet, 2000/1993, p. 10), diagrams both disfigure and liberate the elastic qualities of thought. For the neophyte, weaving diagrams seem to be made to mess with our certainty about the distinction between the discrete and continuous. But, for weavers, these diagrams are also graphic attempts to capture the wanton movements of yarn, to harness or understand how the entanglement of various lines of yarn produce color, pattern, and image. In this sense, weaving diagrams are allied with all mathematical diagrams, as places that can productively amplify the abstraction of mathematics by eluding the rationalizing force of even paraphrase, metaphor, or abbreviation (Châtelet, 2000/1993, p. 9). Cutting out, splitting, awakening the provocative virtualities of loom, line, and string, the weaver's diagram is a ruin primed for mourning the quant/qual divide.

One such ruinous realm might be found in *Pointed Twill Anomalies* (2018), a video piece made by Oregon-based artist and educator, Jovencio de la Paz. Soundlessly evoking a grainy TV connection (Figure 7.2), this video work derives from a research trip that de la Paz (who uses they/them pronouns) took to the archives of an Italian textile firm. After using their phone to document a series of weaving diagrams, de la Paz found that something strange had happened. In handling these images, their phone's sensory and processing devices had not generated the still reproductions that one might expect. Instead, the formerly still paper diagrams were reproduced as a flashing, vibrating frenzy of dancing diagonal twills. This collection of alien moirés might be considered a malfunction; de la Paz's phone, it seems, could not 'understand' the weaving diagrams enough to hold them still, or commit to a single interpretation. Untethered from the architecture of ink and paper, made by forces operating outside of de la Paz's control— yet somehow inside the algorithmic movement/quantitative actions of their phone—*Pointed Twill Anomalies* (2018) embraces the expansive unpredictability of digital sensation. While de la Paz describes this collaboration with self-generating parametric systems as employing "computational creativity" (de la Paz, 2024, para 2), Lather might also highlight its ruinous qualities as a computational enactment of getting lost.

Figure 7.2 Jovencio de la Paz, still from *Pointed Twill Anomalies (Weave Draft Aberrations)*, 2018.

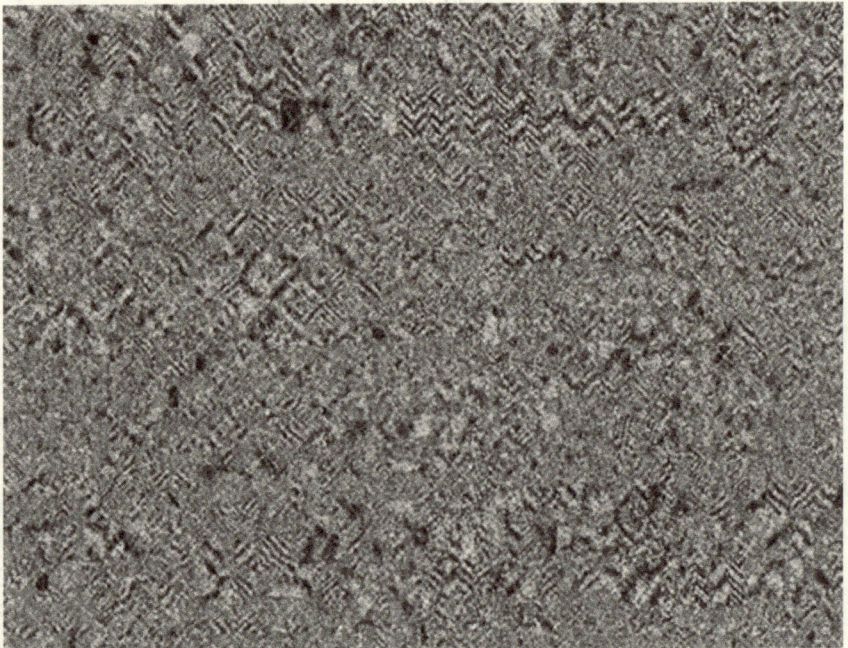

This kind of disorientation and confusion can also be felt in the *away from keyboard* space of a tapestry weaving workshop. As part of a master class for novice adolescent weavers, my student Winston quickly sensed an affinity between his devotion to digital art and weaving. In an uncanny reverse engineering of the digital—where the weaving diagram is both the (unknown) guide and *destination*—Winston drew the pixelated face of a "Creeper," the iconic, havoc-wreaking *mob* in the popular gaming world of Minecraft (Figure b) as his first weaving cartoon.

Figure 7.3 a) Winston's Creeper sketch, b) Screenshot of a Creeper inside Minecraft, c) Video still after Winston began a second experimental weaving in the workshop's second session.

While his diagram emerges from a seemingly arbitrary flow of pencil marks, the loom organizes and insists that movements and figures be produced in a more regimented way. To translate his drawing onto the loom, Winston touch-counts the eight squares along the bottom of his sketch and carefully aligns 16 corresponding warp strings on the left of his loom. Using these strings to weave a green yarn onto his loom, he slowly builds horizontal layers of yarn—over and under, over and under, line by line—while his eye and finger movements course horizontally across the bottom of his sketch. By working in proportional relation to his weaving diagram, Winston can read this diagram like a map. But in no time at all, he is lost in the aperspectival *vertigo* of the tangled yarn: In approaching the second row of pixelated squares in his diagram, which contains two distinct colors (green and white), it is as though Winston has lost hold of that intangible sense, from which he gathered together both the discrete and the continuous into the posthuman figure of the Creeper. In a moment of loss, Winston struggles to reorganize his thinking in conversation with friends and with a new series of weaving diagrams, which help him to explore how two discrete objects might touch. As Karen Barad (2012) highlights, "so much happens in a touch: an infinity of others—other beings, other spaces, other times—are aroused" (p. 206).

This is another example of how a weaving diagram enmeshes the doer in the strangely mobile quant/qual relations of material forms. Certain aspects of the diagram quickly yield information about the quantitative relations between pixels and warp strings. But other diagrammatic marks point to places where one finds oneself at an interpretive loss. In these moments, the weaver is overcome by the novel material demands of yarn and loom, but also drawn into new experiments that stretch them toward unfamiliar topological concepts related to the quality of contact between two differently colored or textured yarns: Do these yarns wrap around each other? Around which warp strings should they wind?

As the other sections of this chapter suggest, there is abundant space in mathematics for playing with uncomfortable conjunctions such as in/calculable, un/computable, un/thinkable, a/logonal, a/perspectival, all of which *live* in material-media practices, like algorithms, diagrams, textiles, and screens. In a certain sense, Lather's "getting lost" (2007, p. 1) is another way of engaging the mucky ontological realm of qual-quant intra-action. While the command to "get lost" suggests a useful image of dispersal, Lather's language is rather carefully not stated as a directive. She is for *getting* lost—a process that seems the proper mode of engagement when feeling our way through the vertigo of new qual/quant mixtures.

The Unthinkable
by Nathalie Sinclair

In this section, I bring Lather's work on validity into conversation with the concept of radical Pythagoreanism, articulated by mathematician Arkady Plotnitsky (2023). This conversation, in part, takes its cue from Elizabeth's attention to the incalculable, which she transforms into the incomputable and which I want to juxtapose with the unthinkable. The radical Pythagorean considers the unthinkable—or, to use Plotnitsky's neologism, the *alogonal*—not only possible within mathematics, but desirable and indeed necessary for mathematics to remain vibrant. Moreover, it's not just the unthinkable that matters, but the fact that the alogonal arises from a combination of geometry and number. Contrasted with logos, the alogon may evoke a binary of the thinkable *against* the unthinkable for some readers. However, Plotnitsky (2023) insists, "this thinking does not preclude, but, on the contrary, helps, the development of new concepts and theories. But it changes their nature, and in the first place, the nature of our thinking by making the unthinkable an irreducible part and thus the unavoidable concern of our thought" (p. 43).

This concept of the alogonal extends the insights of Lather's early essay "Fertile Obsession: Validity after Poststructuralism," first written in 1993, and then reprinted in her 2007 book *Getting Lost: Feminist Efforts Towards a Double(d) Science*. I had been working on an article in which I was trying out some methodological experiments of my own, which involve the use of re-enactments, and for which Lather's term *voluptuous validity* seemed particularly apt (Sinclair, 2024). In her essay, Lather writes that despite the postpositivist baggage associated with the word validity, she wants to continue using it: "I retain the term in order to both circulate and break with the signs that code it" (Lather, 2007, p. 118). It is precisely the working with-and-against that seems fertile, indeed, giving rise as it does to several different types of transgressive validities: ironic, neo-pragmatic, rhizomatic, and voluptuous. Lather (2007) seeks to reinscribe validity in a way that "uses the antifoundational problematic to loosen the master code of positivism that continues to shape even postpositivism" (p. 118). This is a validity that refuses a correspondence theory of truth. She announces her project as marking "a provisional space in which a different science might take form" (Lather, 2007, p. 117).

Plotnitsky juxtaposes the Pythagoreans and the Platonists in terms of how they want to handle the unthinkable, the alogonal. The latter thinkers want to get rid of it, see it as tainted by temporality and undesirable. The former thinkers see the alogonal as necessary and productive, not needing to be transformed into the thinkable. The Pythagoreans' discovery of incommensurable numbers (the so-called irrational numbers) is one of Plotnitsky's key examples. It exemplifies both the alogonal (that a length cannot be measured as a multiple of any other length) and its co-involvement with both number *and* geometry. The Pythagoreans were interested in numbers and their commensurable ratios (such as the ratios that produce harmonious sound), but when they encountered the diagonal of a square, no such commensurable ratios could be found. That diagonal has a length that is unthinkable . . . a diagonal is alogonal, atonal, abnormal . . . a thing that cannot be thought. While mathematicians eventually made the diagonal thinkable, by creating a new kind of number—finding a way to fit that unthinkable thing within a system that could connect to other, more thinkable numbers—there are still alogonals roaming around in that formidable edifice of mathematics.

Try to think of something that is neither finite nor infinite; neither continuous nor discontinuous (which is precisely what quantum theory demands). Plotnitsky insists that geometry ensures the ongoing fact of the alogonal in mathematics, as in the case of continuity: not only do we not know "how a continuous line, straight or curved [. . .] is constituted by its points" (Plotnitsky, 2023, p. 86), we *cannot* know. By this he means, "there may never be a rigorous mathematical concept of continuity, at least of a continuous set, that corresponds to our phenomenal intuition of continuity" (Plotnitsky, 2023, p. 86). The same is not true for discreteness. Perhaps the alogonal is the price of being able to mix geometry and number—a price that creates havoc, but also something new, something that cannot be read in terms of either number/algebra or geometry.

For Lather, validity is a problem to work on, not a solution to come up with—she avoids the solution that closes the door on the unthinkable. In her section, Elizabeth writes that Lather advocated for "smart mixed methods" which had to pursue a "more sophisticated remixing of the quantitative and the qualitative". In search of a kind of coherence between the quantitative view of the world and the qualitative view, such remixings must be understood as neither separate nor independent (Figure 7.4a). Remixings require smudging borders (Figure 7.4b), excisions and transplants (Figure 7.4c), and even new cuts altogether (Figure 7.4d), which generate the openings for the unthinkable. In all four types of Lather's transgressive validities, for which she provides specific examples, there are also interesting mixes at play. In one, there is the combination of words and image that create a "text that is dense with the absence of referential finalities . . . endlessly shifting the location of the unknowable and ironically using researcher power to undercut practices of representation" (Lather, 2007, p. 122). In another, there are interviews and peer debriefing and member checks, which are not used to check reality, but to produce a new one, upending the very codes that were originally used to analyze the interview data. The researcher ends up "unlearning her own privilege and . . . introducing dissensus into consensus" (Lather, 2007, p. 123). In a third, the research design literally invites the incommensurable by placing alongside each other various contestatory discourses and looking for discrepant data, attending to where "the facts unfit to fit categorical schemes" (Lather, 2007, p. 124).

Figure 7.4 a: Unmixed; b: Blurred; c: Excised and transplanted; d: A new cut.

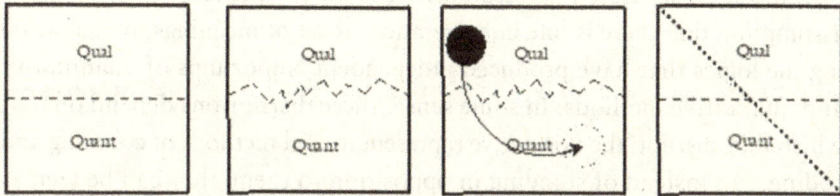

I see a parallel between Lather's comments and those of Plotnitsky, who views modern 20th century mathematics as arising from a shift away from reality, particularly in the sense of turning away from the need to represent reality. This liberating move is what makes modern mathematics seem abstract. Interestingly, it is also what allowed mathematics to be of use to quantum physics. This seems counter-intuitive—but when mathematics invents spaces, relations, and concepts that are not representing nature, these can be used to do different and even revolutionary work. In the case of quantum physics, the focus was less on finding a way to represent subatomic particles and their behaviors, and more on making predictions through the use of probabilistic methods. Importantly, for Plotnitsky's thesis about the alogonal, both the qualitative (read geometry) and the quantitative (read number) are at play, thus setting the stage for a reprise of radical Pythagoreanism. Similarly, quantum theory asks us to think of that which is neither continuous nor discontinuous. It is not asking us to engage in some Hegelian dialectic, which wants to do away with the unthinkable. It "places the ultimate nature of physical reality responsible for these discrete phenomena beyond representation or even conception" (Plotnitsky, 2023, p. 43).

Indeed, as the mathematician Weyl (1994/1928) asserted, "the conceptual world of mathematics is so foreign to what the intuitive continuum presents to us that the demand for coincidence between the two must be dismissed as absurd" (p.108). In response to Weyl, Plotnitsky (2023) ventures to say that while coincidence may not be possible, it "may be unavoidable, at least in so far as it is difficult to think of continuity, spatially or temporally, apart from our phenomenal intuition" (p. 85). It is indeed possible "to define the continuum algebraically, in a way more in accord with the idea of time" (Plotnitsky, 2023, p. 85), but the radical Pythagorean would rue any algebraic takeover in which geometry was hand-waved away.

Lather's four transgressive concepts of validity disrupt representation by refusing to separate the researcher from the researched, by rejecting the assumption that there is one interpretation or set of meanings, by questioning the logics that have produced independent emporiums of quantitative and qualitative methods. In some sense, these disruptions depend on that which they disrupt, the normative representational methods of counting and coding; but instead of standing in opposition to them, they can be seen as strategic geometric and diagrammatic reworkings of past validity measures, through inversions of inside/outside, reversals of subject/object, topplings of included/excluded, intrusions of context and affect as well as extrusions of leaky, unfit parts. We can read Lather's new validities in terms of the disruptive power of the geometrical alogonal—we can make sense of the political power of these new kinds of validity in terms of their spatial reconfiguring. Interestingly, the geometric carries the phenomenal intuition in mathematics and is precisely what allows for radical new spatial reconfigurations—it upsets (traditional methodological) assumptions about separateness, causality, representation. Lather's transgressions surface this spatial-geometric intuition and put it to work, reshaping our assumptions about belonging, proximity, and texture as we study complex relationality.

Lather's turn to quantum social science marks another intervention in debates on validity and measurement (Lather et al., 2022; Lather, 2024). Plotnitsky (2023) writes, "quantum measurement does not measure any property of the ultimate constitution of the reality responsible for quantum phenomena, which this constitution would be assumed to possess before, or even in, the act of observation" (p. 231). Quantum phenomena are alogonal; they cannot be separated enough to be measured, or known. Following Plotnitsky then, "Quantum phenomena may be telling us that the ultimate constitution of nature is alogonal and, as such, may not allow us to write its ultimate constitution in the language of mathematics or possibly in any language, or even to conceive of this constitution by any means, any logos, that is or will ever be available to us" (Plotnitsky, 2023, p. 50). While not being *writable* in mathematics, quantum phenomena have been creatively explored using modern mathematical theories, such as algebraic topology (see Manin, 1998). In fact, it was the very abstraction and non-representational nature of these theories that made them so useful to physics, engendering a new non-intuitive insight, that many social scientists have found intriguing and productive (i.e., Barad, 2007; da Silva, 2022; Wendt, 2015). While reality may not be writable in mathematics, Plotnitsky (2023) argues that certain kinds of mathematics enable us *"to relate to things* in nature and mind which are . . . beyond the reach of phenomenal thinking or all other thinking, including mathematical thinking" (p. 229, *my emphasis*). So, while social scientists have been leaning on quantum theory for new onto-epistemologies, it is not surprising to see some of them turn to mathematics as well, as in da Silva's (2022) fractal thinking and de Freitas et al.'s (2022) experiments with geometric inversion. Relating to nature through modern, alogonal mathematics seems an ironic move if ever there was one—the discipline that prides itself on reason can nonetheless relate unreasonably to reality!

Lather (2007) writes that "the human sciences are in search of a discourse to help chart the journey from the present to the future" (p. 117). In light of the discussion of the quantum in this piece, and its reworking of time (and space), it is tempting to suggest that there is no such journey—not a linear one at least. The time-as-arrow thinking that vectors from the past, through the present, to the future, has been shattered by quantum theory, which, among other things, tells us that there is no such thing as the (shared) present and that the future can affect the past.

Perhaps what Lather is in search of is a kind of quantum journey that does more than travel upward and onward from present to future. This could involve traveling back to unearth the ways in which representational research methods of the past are teeming with unfits, lurking within the schemes and codes, carefully covered, or smoothed over by desires for determinacy. Now that we affirm ironic, neo-pragmatic, rhizomatic, and voluptuous validity in post-qualitative research (in Lather, 1993 or 2007 or 2024), we will surely find these in/validities also in research methods of the past. In other words, to play with Latour's (1993) refrain ("we have never been modern") we might also say: research has never been positivist.

References

Barad, K. (2007). *Meeting the universe halfway: Quantum physics and the entanglement of matter and meaning.* Duke University Press.

Barad, K. (2012). On touching—the inhuman that therefore I am. *Differences: A Journal of Feminist Cultural Studies,* 23(3), 206–223. https://doi.org/10.1215/10407391-1892943

Châtelet, G. (2000). *Figuring space: Philosophy, mathematics and physics.* (R. Patton & M. Zagha, Trans.). Kluwer. https://doi.org/10.1007/978-94-017-1554-6 (Original work published 1993).

Cohen, T. (1998). *Ideology and inscription: "cultural studies" after Benhamin, de Man, and Baktin.* Cambridge University Press.

Coole, D., & Frost, S. (2010). *New materialisms: Ontology, agency, and politics.* Duke University Press.

Crawford, K. (2022). *Atlas of AI: Power, politics and the planetary costs of artificial intelligence.* Yale University Press.

de Freitas, E., & Sinclair, N. (2014). *Mathematics and the body: Material entanglements in the classroom.* Cambridge University Press.

de Freitas, E., & Sinclair, N. (2016). The cognitive labour of mathematics dis/ability: Neurocognitive approaches to number sense. *International Journal of Education Research, 79,* 220–230.

de Freitas, E., Dixon-Román, E., Lather, P. (2016). (Eds.). Alternative ontologies of number: Rethinking the quantitative in computational culture. *Cultural Studies↔Critical Methodologies, 16*(5). https://doi.org/10.1177/1532708616665575

de Freitas, E., Sinclair, N., le Roux, K., Solares-Rojas, A., Coles, A., & Ng, O. (2022). New spatial imaginaries for international curriculum projects: Creative diagrams, Mapping experiments, and critical cartography, *Qualitative Inquiry, 28*(5), 507–521.

da Silva, D.F. (2022). *Fractal sensing/thinking on a planetary scale.* https://planetarysensing.com/fractal-sensing-thinking-on-a-planetary-scale/

de la Paz, J. (2018). *Artist statement.* https://www.jovenciodelapaz.net/text

Fazi, B. (2018). *Contingent computation: Abstraction, experience, and indeterminacy in computational aesthetics.* Rowman & Littlefield.

Fuller, M. (Ed.). (2008). *Software studies: A lexicon.* The MIT Press.

Fuller, M., & Weizman, E. (2021). *Investigative aesthetics: Conflicts and commons in the politics of truth.* Verso.

Galloway, A. (2021). *The uncomputable: Play and politics in the long digital age.* Verso Books.

Galloway, A. R., & Thacker, E. (2007). *The exploit: A theory of networks.* University of Minnesota Press.

Glissant, E. (1997). *Poetics of relation* (B. Wing, Trans.). The University of Michigan Press. (Original work published in 1990).

Gödel, K. (1931). "Über formal unentscheidbare Sätze der Principia Mathematica und verwandter Systeme, I", Monatshefte für Mathematik und Physik, v. 38 n. 1, pp. 173–198. doi:10.1007/BF01700692

Goldstein, R. (2005). *Incompleteness: The proof and paradox of Kurt Gödel.* W.W. Norton & Company.

Hardt, M., & Negri, A. (2004). *Multiplicity: War and democracy in the age of empire.* Penguin Books.

Kirby, V. (2011). *Quantum anthropologies: Life at large.* Duke University Press.

Lather, P. (1993). Fertile obsession: Validity after poststructuralism. *The Sociological Quarterly, 34*(4), 673–693.

Lather, P. (2001). Postmodernism, post-structuralism and post(critical) ethnography. In P. Atkinson, A. Coffey, S. Delamont, J. Lofland, & L. Lofland (Eds.). *Handbook of ethnography* (pp. 477–492). Sage. https://doi.org/10.4135/9781848608337

Lather, P. (2007). *Getting lost: Feminist efforts toward a double(d) science*. State University of New York Press. https://doi.org/10.4135/9781848608337

Lather, P. (2013). Methodology-21: What do we do in the afterward?. *International journal of qualitative studies in education, 26*(6), 634–645.

Lather, P. (2017). *(Post)Critical methodologies: The science possible after the critiques*. Routledge.

Lather, P. (2024). *Quantizing research in education: Post qualitative, post quantitative?* [Conference keynote]. International Congress of Qualitative Inquiry, Urbana-Champagne.

Lather, P., de Freitas, E., Rosiek, J. Sinclair, N. (2022). *Toward a quantum social science: New paradigms for educational inquiry* [Panel for the Critical Issues in Curriculum and Cultural Studies SIG]. Annual Meeting for the American Education Research Association, San Diego.

Latour, B. (1987). *Science in action: How to follow scientists and engineers through society*. Harvard University Press.

Latour, B. (1993). *We have never been modern* (C. Porter, Trans.). Harvard University Press.

Lyotard, J. (1979). *The postmodern condition: A report on knowledge*. Manchester University Press.

Manin, Y. (1998). Interrelations between mathematics and physics. In M. Audin (Ed.), *Matériaux pour l'histoire des mathématiques au XXe siècle Actes du colloque à la mémoire de Jean Dieudonné* (pp. 157–168). Société Mathématique Française.

Nagel, E., & Newman, J.R. (2001). *Gödel's proof: Revised edition*. New York University Press.

Parisi, L. (2017). Computational logic and ecological rationality. In E. Hörl (Ed.), *General ecology: The new ecological paradigm* (pp. 75–100). Bloomsbury.

Parisi, L. (2019). Media ontology and transcendental instrumentality. *Theory, Culture, Society, 36*(6), 95–124.

Plotnitsky, A. (2023). *Logos and alogon: Thinkable and the unthinkable in mathematics, from the Pythagoreans to the Moderns*. Springer.

Rosiek, J., & Mazzei, L. (2014). Beyond reflexivity and advocacy: Exploring the ontological turn in educational research [Conference paper]. Conference funded by the American Education Research Association, University of Oregon.

Schneider, B. (2007). *Textiles prozessieren: Eine Mediengeschichte der Lochkartenweberei*. [Textile processing: A media history of punch-card weaving]. Diaphanes.

Silva, D. F. da. (2022). *Unpayable debt*. Sternberg Press.

Sinclair, N. (2024). Knowing as remembering: Methodological experiments in embodied experiences of number. *Digital Experiences in Mathematics, 10*(1), 29–46.

Turing, A. M. (1937). On computable numbers, with an application to the entscheidungsproblem. *Proceedings of the London Mathematical Society, 42*(1) 230–265.

Wendt, A. (2015). *Quantum mind and social science: Unifying physical and social ontology* (3rd ed.). Cambridge University Press.

Wendt, A. (2023). *Quantum Boot Camp*. https://www.youtube.com/watch?v=tLHgn4PIGj4

Weyl, H. (1994), *The continuum: A critical examination of the foundation of analysis*. (S. Pollard & T. Bole, Trans.). Dover. (Original work published 1928).

CHAPTER EIGHT

Between the No Longer and the Not Yet: Patti Lather's Contribution to (Post) Qualitative Research Methodology

MAGGIE MacLURE

Between the no longer and the not yet lies the possibility of what was impossible under traditional regimes of truth in the social sciences.

Patti Lather, *Getting Smart* (1991)

Introduction and Summary

THIS CHAPTER EXAMINES PATTI Lather's distinctive contribution to the development of theoretically informed (post)qualitative research methodology. I discuss some continuities and transitions in her methodological writings in key texts from the late 1980s onwards, as she navigates through and circles among feminist research, critical theory, ethnography, poststructuralism, and the array of post-foundational approaches that have emerged as part of the *ontological turn* in Western thought. I trace the ways in which she has rethought and reworked qualitative inquiry, first in response to poststructuralism's crisis of representation, and subsequently to the immanent and speculative ontologies of posthumanism and the new materialisms. The aim is not to document a linear narrative,[1] but to focus rather on Lather's transformations of the conceptual architecture and the ethical obligations of qualitative research.

I show how her process has been one of insistently tapping into the intellectual currents of the surrounding milieu. This has not only strengthened the theoretical underpinnings of a field that has often organized itself through common sense and watered-down scientism, but has also, crucially, opened an interstitial *space of indetermination* where research might "take us beyond ourselves" (Lather, 1991, p. 2). I suggest that by registering the subterranean perturbations running through the field and amplifying their potential to spark new thought and epistemic *trouble* (one of her favourite terms), Lather has operated both as a seismographer and a sorcerer for the field of qualitative research. Toward the end of the chapter, I pursue some questions that Lather's work has crystallized for me, concerning relationality and incommensurability in postfoundational research.

The success and reach of Lather's interventions into the body of qualitative research can be seen in the rapid spread of the term *post-qualitative* itself. First coined by her close collaborator Elizabeth St. Pierre (2011), Lather, in her own writing and in collaboration with St. Pierre and others, has fleshed out the approach in a range of journal special issues and key articles. The success of this project is evident in the fact that the term has now become detached from names and has entered general usage. There is now a degree of consensus over the defining characteristics of post-qualitative or postfoundational inquiry (see for instance Lather's own [2016] "top ten+ list").[2] However, *post-qualitative* remains somewhat of a *catachresis*—a term without a stable referent. It is the task of contemporary and future scholars to further flesh out its meaning and import. Taking my lead from Lather and others, I use it in alternation with other words that occupy the space of research in the ontological turn: posthuman, postfoundational, Deleuzian, etc. . . .

Poststructuralism and Deconstruction

In Lather's (1991) renowned *Getting Smart*, she brings feminism and critical theory into a productively unsettling encounter with poststructuralism/postmodernism[3] in an attempt to fashion an emancipatory pedagogy and praxis. She saw emancipatory potential in poststructuralism's decentering of the human subject, viewing this as a resource for resisting the mono-lithic *master narratives* of Enlightenment humanism with their heroic imag-inaries of the centered subject, equipped to produce knowledge and master the world through the exercise of reason. She was especially troubled by the persistence of this self-assured subject in the neo-Marxist critical pedagogy of the time. In its mission to expose the illusions of ideology, critical peda-gogy disparaged local knowledge and culture, and granted the self-avowed, "(largely male) architects of critical pedagogy" entitlement to speak on behalf of the marginalized subjects of their research (Lather, 1991, p. 48). However, Lather (1991) also detected "the dead hand of ideological sound-ness" in dogmatic feminisms, when these betrayed a similar colonial impulse to speak for, and in place of, research participants (p. 29). In both cases, un-assailable certainties and built-in asymmetries of power-knowledge worked against the prospects of emancipatory action.

Lather's intention was not to abandon her commitments to feminism or neo-Marxism by simply replacing them with poststructuralism. Nor did she aspire to produce a "spurious synthesis" (Lather, 1991, p. 49). Quoting Spi-vak, she positioned them rather as "persistent interruptions of each other" (Lather, 1991, p. 31). Out of the clash of incommensurable approaches, Lather sought to open a space of difference within pedagogy and research where intellectuals might divest themselves of their privilege so that diverse subjects and unforeseen possibilities for action might emerge. While her the-oretical influences (her "theory girl- and boyfriends": [Lather, 2017, p. 315]) have changed over the years, it is notable that Lather has always turned to theories with the potential to take us "beyond ourselves" (see for example Lather, 1991, p. 2). She has always been drawn to that which resists con-tainment within boundaries and evades representation: to the unintelligible, the undecidable, the incalculable, the incommensurable.

Lather was also acutely aware of the risks inherent in the encounter with postmodernism. The challenge was to mobilize it in the attempt to shake up a complacent social science without being contaminated by its "ir-redeemable political ambivalence" (Lather, 1991, p. 31). In common with many feminist scholars at the time, she saw dangers of nihilism and polit-ical paralysis in postmodernism—for instance in the proposition that re-alities are multiple and discursively constructed. The project of dismantling the centered subject of humanism was—as it continues to be—contentious when many are still fighting to have their humanity recognized.

At the time of writing *Getting Smart,* Lather (1991) still hoped to protect the political and emancipatory projects of feminism and critical practice by discriminating between the good and the bad postmodernisms, as it
were. She rejected a postmodernism of indifference and advocated, quoting
Huyssen and Hutcheon, "a cultural and adversarial postmodernism, a postmodernism of resistance" (Lather, 1991, p. 1). However, by the time of her
book *Getting Lost* (Lather, 2007), she expressed serious doubts about
that vision of an emancipatory postmodernism. She detected the lingering
presence of an Enlightenment "faith in the knowledge that will set us free"
in the very title of *Getting Smart* (Lather, 2007, p. vii). Announcing *Getting
Lost* as "a more disabused text" (Lather, 2007, p. vii) she envisaged a deconstructive praxis that was

> grounded in a shift from totalities to noncontainment, a principle of excess
> and infinite proliferation where a rigorous praxis refuses much in an effort to
> "stop thinking straight" . . . practices that are in excess of subjects presumed
> to know about subjects presumed to be unknowable. (Lather, 2007, p. 108)[4]

This formulation of praxis, under the influence of Derridean deconstruction, looks for excess and proliferation in the failures of modernity
and humanism. It seeks places where boundaries can be breached, and binary oppositions—good/bad, self/other, etc.—can be pressed to reveal their
internal fissures. In common with other feminist poststructuralist scholars
at the time (cf. chapters in St. Pierre & Pillow, 2000), Lather (2007) used
and developed a poststructural/Derridean lexicon of *loss, ruins, haunting,
rupture, mourning, messiness, not knowing, stuck places,* and *trouble.*[5] The
task, she wrote, "was to situate the experience of impossibility as an en-
abling site for working through aporias" (Lather, 2007, p. 15). She developed a deconstructive praxis that would work the tensions in these spaces of
impasse and ruin, where there was no chance of escape to the high ground
of conceptual purity or the underground of foundations. Well aware that
deconstruction could, to use Derrida's terminology, be both a poison and
a remedy, Lather practiced a *doubled science* of writing/researching *under erasure*—that is, simultaneously using and troubling concepts that are
problematic, but without which it is impossible to think. For instance, in
one of her most influential articles, "Fertile Obsession: Validity After Poststructuralism" (Lather, 1993), she pursued the question of the legitimation of

knowledge in anti- or post-foundational research, without however abandoning the term *validity* itself. The term, and the search for watertight legitimation procedures, had been a thorn in the side of qualitative method, so she transformed the perplexities contained in that contested status into four *framings* of validity after post-structuralism: ironic, paralogic, rhizomatic, and voluptuous. Drawing concepts from Baudrillard, Lyotard, Derrida/Deleuze, and Irigaray respectively, the four frames offered different resources for resisting the closures of conventional method and opening research onto new ways of knowing and doing. The transgressions offered by the four framings included: proliferating simulacra to defeat the codes of normal science; fostering "difference and heterogeneity" (Lather, 1993, p. 686) through the use of paradox and discontinuities; unsettling from within by playing with the excess of meaning that resists capture by categories; and embracing excessive, embodied, and "leaky" practices that go "too far" and so unsettle the etiquette of method (Lather, 1993, p. 686).

Lather had developed her work on transgressive validity during her poststructural ethnography, undertaken with Chris Smithies, of women living with HIV/AIDS, published as *Troubling the Angels* (Lather & Smithies, 1997). For instance, the issue of voice was challenging. As Lather (2007) pointed out, poststructuralism is suspicious of voice when this is understood as the innocent and uncomplicated expression of the humanist subject's inner thoughts and experiences. And yet, the imperative for these women's voices to be heard was absolute. She found herself caught between "wanting to get in the way and interrupt the romance of voice and . . . wanting to get out of the way and let the power of voice go forward" (Lather, 2007, p. 26). The solution was to attempt a self-deconstructing text in which the authorial voice could honor the women's stories without smoothing or suppressing their complexity into confessional tales or ethnographic "data," while simultaneously undermining the authority of the authorial voice itself.

Troubling the Angels (1997), in common with other poststructural research writing at the time, was an experimental text that intentionally breached the generic conventions of academic and narrative texts.[6] It was written as a nonlinear *hypertext* of fragments and unconventional layouts—an assemblage of excerpts of the women's stories, the authors' own interpretations and personal reminiscences, images, references to art and philosophy, ethnographic detail, and contemporary accounts of the AIDS crisis. Unusual and uncomfortable affects circulated in the text, manifesting as uncertainty, dissent (including between the authors), hurt feelings, high spirits, disappointment, affection.

Looking back, Lather felt that the mode of writing of *Troubling the Angels* (1997) had been successful in partially disabling the authorial voice and allowing the text to become something that was not fully within the authors' control or intentions. Significantly, she attributed this success to the opening of their writing to *chance and contingency*:

> Here, quite open to chance, connections, many of which align or resonate with one another, are made under contingent circumstances. Judith Butler . . . speaks of a writing "which precedes and mobilizes the one who writes, connecting the one who writes with a language which 'writes' the one". Chris and I both knew and did not know what we were doing, both intentional agents and vessels of history writing us in ways we did not and do not always understand. (Lather, 2007, p. 110)

This account succinctly captures the logic of writing under erasure, where the writer is both knowing and unknowing, intentional agent, and vessel of history. Interestingly, in its recognition of the importance of chance, it also resonates with the direction that Lather subsequently took as she began to register the perturbations of the new materialisms and the *ontological turn* in continental theory, and to pursue their implications for qualitative research.

Post-Qualitative Inquiry and the Ontological "Turn"

Lather has shown an unwavering commitment to the power of "not-knowing"—to that which exceeds meaning and, as noted, holds the potential to take us *beyond ourselves*. This commitment received new impetus with the incursion of speculative, post-humanist, and new materialist philosophies into the humanities and social sciences, and particularly with the publication of Karen Barad's (2007) ground-breaking *Meeting the Universe Halfway*. Lather's seismograph (see below) soon registered the potential of Barad's feminist materialism to bring forth a decolonizing methodology that would deny the individual knower/researcher the privilege of interpreting the world on behalf of others. Attuned to the queer logics of quantum mechanics, Barad's agential realism posits a relational, material, and more-than-human ontology, in which knowers, knowledge, matter, affect, and agency do not pre-exist the entanglements out of which they emerge. In the ontological turn, science does not stand opposed to the social, and the researcher's ingenuity does not predate or predict events, but instead is part of their formation. In the work of Barad and other thinkers, Lather (2017) found resources that might allow us to "unhinge one's own understandings" (p. 324, after Lenz-Taguchi) and disabuse ourselves of the presumption that we are the owners and sources of our own decisions—that they are born within us and are uncomplicatedly ours.

The radical openness of the realist ontologies of Barad and other philosophers of immanence offered a more affirmative, mobile, and vital form of "not-knowing" than the melancholic jouissance inhering in the mournings, hauntings, and impasses of Derridean deconstruction. It promised to free the energies of invention from the backward drag of critique. A "different canon" was now driving Lather's methodological thinking, comprising Barad, Deleuze, DeLanda, and Haraway among others (Lather, 2017, p. 345). As well as contributing to the developing corpus of post-foundational research in the social sciences through her own writing, she has introduced readers to exemplary ethnographic and empirical studies by others and gathered a productively unruly field loosely together through journal special issues and participation in conferences and seminars.[7]

The Necessary Dilemmas of Working Between the No Longer and the Not Yet

Postfoundational research cannot rely on preexisting models to trace its path and guarantee its truths. Working within an immanent ontology, we are obliged to grope towards, in Lather's (2017) words, "a research imaginary that finds shape and standards in what we are making in its name" (p. 337). Current work necessarily proceeds, she notes, by "fits and starts," always liable to "reinscribe what we are trying to get over" (Lather, 2017, p. 338). She identifies some instances of such reinscriptions in post-qualitative studies, where what is announced as "new" carries the traces of what it disavows. She points out, for instance, that "angst" or the expression of feelings during fieldwork is not new. Experimental writing likewise has, she reminds us, a long history, as does the recognition of the limits of our own knowing (Lather, 2017, p. 338).

It is not that such concerns—about feelings, epistemic violence against the "other," the limits of individual knowledge, or the need to disrupt conventional genres—are now irrelevant. But they would need to take on a new onto-ethical status to avoid replaying some of the tropes of Enlightenment humanism. Lather (2017) notes that one tendency is for the intact phenomenological self of the researcher-subject to covertly enter the "vacuum" left by the reticence about representing others (p. 338). Another is a misrecognition of the workings of affect, an important concept in posthuman theory. Lather (2017) notes that affect often gets domesticated into a "liberal investment in emotional authenticity" (p. 338). She draws on Berlant's (2011) critique of *affective inflation* to argue for a *deflationary aesthetic* that would restore feeling to a position as "just one nodal point among many" (Lather, 2017, p. 338).

Lather's observations chime with some of my own thoughts on the difficulties of imagining and fabricating a new architecture for qualitative inquiry while still inhabiting the foundations of the old. They also invite me to take them further. I do think it is difficult to sit with the impersonality of affect, in the Deleuzian sense of intensities that connect and disconnect prior to their partial capture as discrete feelings or "affections," resulting in a kind of affective "inertia" (Colebrook, 2013, p. 1). It is difficult to reimagine one's obligations towards more-than-human agents without reactivating a stance of reflexivity—a self-searching that repeats the old colonial gesture that Lather critiqued in her earlier work, of supposedly empowering others without really redistributing the privileges that accrue to the researcher-self or considering what inhuman relationality might be.

Some of the most provocative and promising work in postfoundational research has come, in my view, from mobilizing art and craft practices as ways of affirming the importance of embodiment, sensation, movement, relationality, and matter in the unfolding (and closing off) of the world. The turn to art has a powerful appeal as a way of releasing possibilities beyond the constraints of rationality and the straitjacket of language; but I wonder if sometimes it licenses notions of artistic "play" as unfettered or undirected creativity. The same could be said of arguments to the effect that, because postfoundational research prioritizes inventiveness, there is no place for method, or that method is essentially a matter of "making it up." I would argue, drawing on Deleuze (2000), that postfoundational research needs to be open both to the play of chance and the constraints of necessity. It demands an encounter that in Deleuze's terms "forces us to think" (MacLure, 2024a, p. 244).

Perhaps the most pressing dilemma is that academic posthumanism replays the ethico-political offences of poststructuralism: namely, dismantling the human in the face of ongoing struggles by many for recognition as full members of a "humanity" policed by Western interests. The wound is possibly deeper in the case of posthumanism as there is a particular colonial arrogance in work that announces itself as "new" without acknowledging the prior existence of posthuman ontologies in the Indigenous, dispossessed and formerly enslaved societies subjugated by Western imperialism (e.g., Jackson, 2013; Todd, 2016). Pasley et al. (2024) argue that "ancient ways of knowing/being/relating [such as non-human agency] that had been condemned as ignorant and 'savage' reappear white-washed and made digestible to Western thought/rationality" (p. 25). They mock the political indifference that they see in Western posthumanism, and the failure of academics to examine the colonial orthodoxies built into their education systems.

> Instead of theorising the different ways tenured professors are no different from trees, rocks, animals, water, and the cosmos, a term like "posthumanism" might be recalibrated toward the hopeful possibility of a humanity that dislodges the settler logics of progress and development. (Pasley et al., 2024, p. 26)

Lather has frequently expressed the debt owed to research involving Indigenous communities. She has often chosen instances of Indigenous practice or methodologies to exemplify significant developments in the field.[8] Invited to address the question, "What new sensibility, configuration or 'dominant' logic now for educational theory?" for a journal special issue, she responded:

> I'd put my money on some non-hegemonic multiple that includes 'trans' and Afro-pessimism/futurism and queer and feminist and indigeneity and decolonization in an assemblage weighted differently in different contexts and made paradoxical by the insistences of a post-humanism driven by the quantum physics that interrupts it all. (Lather, 2019, p. 1602)

Relationality and the Incommensurable

Nevertheless, posthuman and postfoundational researchers continue to face very real challenges to avoid an extractive or superficial relationship to Indigenous and anti-colonial thought and practice. It is a dilemma that

I emphatically fail to resolve here. However, Lather's writing does help me, or perhaps force me, to think further on the question of relationality and incommensurability. She has wrestled with relationality across her oeuvre, always returning to the question of what would be an ethical, useful, and socially just relation toward those others that are drawn into the ambit of the research—the participants, their communities, their knowledge, and belief systems. She has struggled with, and at the same time tried to channel, the potential energies of seemingly incommensurable values and worldviews.

Alison Jones and Kuni Jenkins (2008) raise the question of incommensurable realities in their *post-interpretive* account of a key moment in early contact between Māori people and British settlers in Aotearoa New Zealand: the arrival by boat in 1814 of British settlers and two subsequent events on the shore, described in the archives as a sermon from the missionary Samuel Marsden and a "sham fight" (p. 126) by the Māori. Jones and Jenkins (2008) "materialize" (p. 128) another, unwritten scene based on Māori recognition (including that of Jenkins) of the contours of the two depicted events, in which there is no sermon led by Marsden and no mock fight. There is a political meeting led by the Māori chief Ruatara, and a *pōwhiri*, a choreographed and ritualized welcome and assimilation of the newcomers into local structures. Jones and Jenkins (2008) resist a constructivist or interpretive account of the two scenes as alternate readings, arguing that they are two different, simultaneous, real events: "there was a fight and there was no fight; there was a sermon and there was no sermon" (p. 131). Lather (2017) notes that Jones and Jenkins "make something politically powerful happen," (p. 307) in which new forms of agency surface. It is no longer a matter of harnessing difficult knowledge in order to fuel new intellectual challenges, but "a provocation toward the discovery of a different real, ontological trouble" (Lather, 2017, p. 307). Claire Colebrook (2019) is critical of what she terms the "fetishization" of relationality in posthuman theories, to a point where it has become another "grand narrative" (p. 189). She sees colonial violence in the imaginary of an all-encompassing relationality that erases the alterity and the specificity of Indigenous and nomadic societies as the price of their admission into a global and undifferentiated "humanity". As many Indigenous and anti-colonial scholars have noted, this supposedly universal "humanity" is far from undifferentiated and is indeed precisely the version of humanity that emerged with slavery, plantation capitalism, and settler colonialism.

Many societies have no vision of themselves in empathetic relation to this tarnished globe as members of a one-world, "filiative humanity" that emerged at a time when "[t]erritorial conquest and scientific discovery" were interchangeable (Glissant, quoted in Colebrook, 2019, p. 190). After Tuck and Yang (2012), who propose an "ethics of incommensurability" that refuses the settler promise of inclusion, Colebrook argues for a radical cut in relationality. "Rather than grounding ethics in the proliferation of relations and movements and aiming for an intuition of an ever-varying dynamic whole, one might think of *a severed and disruptive elsewhere*" (Colebrook, 2019, p. 186, emphasis added). The worlds opened up by such a cut would be, in Deleuzian terms, "incompossible"—not alternate versions, or a bouquet assembled from diverse spheres, but a non-communicating, "incommensurable simultaneity" (Colebrook, 2019, p. 191).

Seismographer, Sorcerer

At the end of her volume of selected works, Lather (2017) states: "I have long thought of my feminist qualitative work as seismograph, an index of the kind of work that remains possible in the AFTER" (p. 353). Indeed, references to the seismograph crop up across her writing. At the start of *Getting Lost*, she writes: "In this book, feminist ethnography is situated as a seismograph of sorts, an index of a more general tension in the human sciences" (Lather, 2007 p. viii). Later in that book, she characterizes herself and her co-writer of *Troubling the Angels* (Lather & Smithies, 1997) as a seismograph: "whatever our authorial intentions, we were, as writers, also a registering apparatus, a kind of seismograph, an ensemble, an aggregate of registrations" (Lather, 2007, p. 111). She forages among diverse fields, not only in search of concepts to strengthen the underpinnings of feminist ethnography or qualitative inquiry—though she certainly has accomplished this. Her aim as seismograph is also to sense the perturbations at the weak spots where the edifice of normal science and the certainties of positivist method might be put under pressure.

The seismograph *registers*—it does not *know*. After describing herself and her co-author, Chris Smithies, as "a registering apparatus" Lather (2007, p. 111), in an excerpt already discussed, spells out how these registrations operate according to an uncanny logic of writing/being written, knowing/not knowing: "Chris and I both knew and did not know what we were doing, both intentional agents and vessels of history writing us in ways we did not and do not always understand" (Lather, 2007, p. 110).

There is something divinatory about this depiction of the seismograph, as an opening of the self to forces that one does not fully comprehend or control. Lather had invoked this kind of divinatory impulse as early as 1991 with the publication of *Getting Smart*.

> Both my desire for and experience of writing this book have been to amplify a discourse already much up in the air, to tap into a Zeitgeist that is suffusing academic thought and practice, *to open myself so that it can come through me*. While this may be overstating the passivity and receptivity in the act of writing which is this book, there has been a sort of "channelling" experience at play here. (Lather, 1991, p. xx; emphasis added)

This quasi-divinatory practice, in which the writer-researcher is a vessel or channel for ideas that come from elsewhere, runs through Lather's oeuvre, across the manifest changes in her theoretical allegiances. Her citational practice can also be understood in quasi-divinatory terms. Her writing is a dense, intertextual fabric of citations across a broad spectrum of approaches and genres—feminism, methodology, personal anecdote, high theory, and the occasional hit of low humor. I read this, not as a muting of her own voice (far from it), or a conventional bolstering of arguments through an appeal to other "authorities," but as a strategy of refusal to settle and spell out, in order to summon something less tangible. The multiple "voices" in her writing are not deployed, it seems to me, because they are all saying "the same thing" in a superficial sense. They seem rather to "channel" more occluded lines of thought or sense that cannot easily be put into words—but can be put to work.

Looking back over her work, Lather (2017) describes herself as "a kind of science outlaw" whose goal was "always changing the social imaginary about research" (p. 353). I would suggest that she has also been a kind of sorcerer, tapping into the intensities and currents running through the intellectual milieu and amplifying them for us so that we might put them to work in the hope of "inventing practices that do not yet exist" (Lather, 2017, p. 315). The sorcerer was an important figure of the posthuman for Deleuze and Guattari (e.g., 1987).

Standing apart from the social order and inclined to form alliances with non-human entities, the sorcerer was attuned to the hidden forces of the cosmos that exceeded capture by normative knowledge systems (see Ramey, 2012, on the "hermetic" strain in postfoundational philosophy). Skonieczny (2017) argues for a politics of sorcery in contemporary life. The sorcerer is not, he asserts, a social isolate, but "a finely-tuned receiving device, who . . . can attune him- or herself to something which is 'not yet conscious' for society as a whole, and yet permeates it and pushes from underneath" (Skonieczny, 2017, p. 976). In my view, this aptly describes the service (albeit only one of many) that Patti Lather has performed for the intersecting communities of feminists, methodologists, empirical researchers, policymakers, and social activists who have been energized by her work.

Epilogue

I chose to write this chapter in a rather formal, impersonal style. I kind of wish I hadn't, but it's too late now. So I want to end a second time by expressing my personal debt to Patti Lather and her work. I tried this once before in a conference presentation, subsequently published (MacLure, 2024b), and it bears repeating. Patti had invited me to be part of a panel on Bad Girl Theory and Practice: Qualitative Research in Post-Truth Times. My paper expressed some reservations about the figure of the academic bad girl, so I prefaced it with this.

> It is important to start by asserting that the field of educational research is indebted to the insubordinate critique, the intransigent thought, and the political activism of generations of outstandingly good bad girls who are also exceedingly good scholars. I have felt their impact profoundly, not only from reading and being incurably infected by their writing, but also by experiencing the affective charge of their presence at conferences and events. I vividly recall the first of many such experiences: a packed conference symposium decades ago whose headline presenters were Patti herself and Deborah Britzman. . . . I remember the spiky hair, the Doc Martens, the biker jackets; women standing in every spare space, and sitting in the aisles, bodies almost piled on top of one another. It was powerful magic, and everyone there felt it. It would be impossible to over-state the difference their work, and their presence, has made. (MacLure, 2024b, p. 631)

Patti's presentation at that packed AERA Annual Meeting in 1989 had without doubt the strongest impact on me among the countless ones I have attended throughout my career (runner up: Ivan Illich). She showed us how to take theory and philosophy seriously and purposefully in qualitative research without abandoning the commitment to empirical research designed to effect positive change in the world. She taught us to do it with generosity towards the work of others, and to do it with style, energy, brio, and a dash of humor.

I have also enjoyed all the wine and bourbon consumed in conference bars, and an utterly unforgettable road trip in 2018 through Patti's home state of South Dakota.

Notes

1. Lather (2017) has provided thoughtful and entertaining reflections on her own intellectual trajectory.

2. It is possible that the term "post-qualitative" is becoming less favored than other terms such as "postfoundational" (e.g., Mazzei & Jackson, 2024) and "posthuman" (Rosiek et al., 2024).

3. I follow Lather in using both post-structuralism and postmodernism as closely related terms, though I use poststructuralism more frequently. Lather (2007) provisionally describes the difference between them thus: "Postmodernism generally refers to the material and historical shifts of the global uprising of the marginalised, the revolution in communications technology and the fissures of global multinational hyper-capitalism . . . Poststructuralism refers more narrowly to a sense of the limits of Enlightenment rationality . . . the limits of consciousness and intentionality and totalizing explanatory frameworks" (p. 5).

4. Lather is paraphrasing the arguments here of Bill Havers.

5. In *Troubling the Angels*, her co-authored poststructural ethnography of women living with HIV/AIDS, Lather writes that "troubling became my code word for deconstruction" (Lather & Smithies, 1997) as a more accessible word outside the rarified atmosphere of the academy.

6. Unlike other poststructural works at the time, the authors wanted *Troubling the Angels* to break out of the academic world and be accessible to a far wider lay audience, hoping to publish it as a trade book. Lather (2007) later described this attempt as largely unsuccessful, due to the structures of publishing, the stranglehold of academic genre, and resistance to unconventional texts.

7. With Elizabeth St. Pierre, she co-edited an influential special issue on post-qualitative research to represent and consolidate emerging work (Lather & St. Pierre, 2013). She has also become interested in postfoundational work on computational cultures, algorithmic thought, and new ontologies of number—work which promises to render the divide between quantitative and qualitative method irrelevant, and to radically reconfigure the empirical (de Freitas et al., 2016).

8. This includes work by Linda Tuhiwai Smith, Alison Jones and Kuni Jenkins, Elizabeth Povinelli, and Margaret Somerville and her colleagues.

References

Barad, K. (2007). *Meeting the universe halfway: Quantum physics and the entanglement of matter and meaning.* Duke University Press.

Berlant, L. (2011). *Cruel optimism.* Duke University Press.

Colebrook, C. (2013). Hypo-hyper-hapto-neuro- mysticism. *Parrhesia, 18,* 1–10.

Colebrook, C. (2019) A cut in relationality, *Angelaki,* 24(3), 175–195.

de Freitas, E., Dixon-Román, E., & Lather, P. (2016). Alternative ontologies of number: Rethinking the quantitative in computational culture. *Cultural Studies ↔ Critical Methodologies, 16*(5), 431–434.

Deleuze, G. (2000). *Proust and Signs.* Continuum.

Deleuze, G., & Guattari, F. (1987). *A thousand plateaus: Capitalism and schizophrenia* (B. Massumi, Trans.). University of Minnesota Press.

Jackson, Z.I. (2013). Animal: New directions in the theorization of race and posthumanism. *Feminist Studies, 39*(3), pp. 669–685.

Jones, A., & Jenkins, K. (2008). Indigenous discourses and "the material". *International Review of Qualitative Research, 1*(2), pp. 125–144.

Lather, P. (1991). *Getting Smart: Feminist research and pedagogy with/in the postmodern.* Routledge.

Lather, P. (1993). Fertile obsession: Validity after poststructuralism. *The Sociological Quarterly, 34*(3), 673–693.

Lather, P. (2007) *Getting lost: Feminist efforts toward a doubled science.* SUNY Press.

Lather, P. (2016). Top ten+ list: (Re)thinking ontology in (post)qualitative research. *Cultural Studies ↔ Critical Methodologies, 16*(2), 125–131.

Lather, P. (2017). *(Post)critical methodologies: The science possible after the critiques.* The selected works of Patti Lather. Routledge.

Lather, P. (2019). What new sensibility, configuration or 'dominant' logic now for educational theory? *Educational Philosophy and Theory, (50)*14, 1602–1603.

Lather, P., & Smithies, C. (1997). *Troubling the angels: Women living with HIV/AIDS.* Westview Press.

Lather, P., & St. Pierre, E.A. (2013). Post-qualitative research. *International Journal of Qualitative Studies in Education, 26*(6), 629–633.

MacLure, M. (2024a). Transversal inquiry: The "adventure of the involuntary". In L.A. Mazzei & A.Y. Jackson (Eds.), *Postfoundational approaches to qualitative inquiry* (pp. 243–255). Routledge.

MacLure, M. (2024b). Resistance, desistance: Bad girls of post-qualitative inquiry. *International Journal of Qualitative Studies in Education, 37*(3), 631–641.

Mazzei, L.A., & Jackson, A.Y. (Eds.) (2024). *Postfoundational approaches to qualitative inquiry.* Routledge.

Pasley, A., Jaramillo-Aristizabal, A., & Romero, N. (2024). Gratuitous posthumanism in education: 'There is no thought not yet thought'. In J.A. Bustillos Morales & S. Zarabadi (Eds.), *Towards posthumanism in education: Theoretical entanglements and pedagogical mappings.* Routledge.

Ramey, J. (2012). *The hermetic Deleuze: Philosophy and spiritual ordeal.* Duke University Press.

Rosiek, J., Adkins-Cartee, M., Donley, K., & Pratt, A. (2024). A review of posthumanist education research: Expanded conceptions of research possibility and responsibility. *Review of Research in Education,* 48(1), pp. 220–247.

Skonieczny, K. (2017). To think as sorcerer: An exercise in political imagination. *Theory & Event,* 20(4), pp. 973–988.

St. Pierre, E.A. (2011). Post-qualitative research: The critique and the coming-after. In N. Denzin & Y. Lincoln (Eds.), *The handbook of qualitative research* (4th ed.) (pp. 611–625). Sage.

St. Pierre, E.A., & Pillow, W.S. (2000). *Working the ruins: Feminist poststructural theory and methods in education.* Routledge.

Todd, Z. (2016). An Indigenous feminist's take on the ontological turn: Ontology is just another word for colonialism. *Journal of Historical Sociology,* 29(1), pp. 4–22.

Tuck, E., & Yang, K.W. (2012) Decolonization is not a metaphor. *Decolonization: Indigeneity, Education and Society,* 1(1), pp. 1–40.

CHAPTER NINE

First Interlude: An Affective Temporality for 'Grappling with the (Im)possibility of Anti-Violence: Jiu-Jitsu as an Embodied Praxis of Mattering(,) Differently'

ELISSA BRYANT

THIS STORY OF RE-MEMBERING (Lather, 2016) traces the history of the grappling-based martial art known today as Jiu-Jitsu as it developed materially in struggles between the oppressed and empire. As I grapple with the symbolic implications of Jiu-Jitsu as a relational ontology of anti-violent liberation that has always already been, I apply my own "matterphorical" (Barad & Gandorfer, 2021) Jiu-Jitsu practice towards engaging with the (im)possibilities of enacting anti-racist, anti/de-colonial work as a white settler-scholar, explored as praxis which "takes incommensurability seriously" (Lather, 2007, p. 339). In this way, I intend to offer Jiu-Jitsu as one embodied answer to Lather's (2016) challenge to enact a "narration of methodology" (Markussen, 2005) which might "move us away from the theories and practices whose grip on us we are trying to break" (Lather, 2007, p. 339).

Rolling With the Text

The text to which this piece is the first interlude does not make itself legible in written form, but is instead *becoming* itself, in the Deleuzian sense, as a *text*, in the Derridean sense, in the relational ontology of anti-violence located in and on, with and through, by and to, the bodies that 'roll'[1] with my body on the mats. The written counterparts presented here and elsewhere should therefore be understood as interludes, offering a contextually relevant exploration of the text as a 'lost' praxis of somatic inquiry invoked by Lather's (2013) call toward work which might "produce different knowledge and produce knowledge differently" (p. 635).

In these interludes, I explore Jiu-Jitsu as an iteration of what Barad and Gandorfer (2021) have called "matterphorics," an "aesth-ethics of thought", which calls for both "sense-making" and "sensing in the making", with a heightened attentiveness to the intra-action of onto-epistemological and ethical concerns regarding the violence(s) already inherent in representation (p. 2). I consider how the origins of Jiu-Jitsu might be contextualized alongside the embodied and intra-actionary practices of Lather's (2007) call for staying 'lost' in (post)qualitative inquiry that engages a matterphorical praxis for liberatory work that matters(,) differently (Barad & Gandorfer, 2021).

Inspired by Lather's and Smithies' (1997) *Troubling the Angels*, and as a textual enactment of Jiu-Jitsu, there are multiple ways for readers to move through and around these interludes. The historical context relating to Jiu-Jitsu as a martial art is presented in text boxes numbered #1 through #8. Readers who would like to read these in a chronotypical linear timeline can do so by finding them in numerical order, either before or after engaging with the rest of the content. As they are presented here, I instead apply Rifkin's (2017) Indigenous temporal heterogeneity, unsettling settler-oriented understandings of time and historicity by acknowledging coexisting temporal multiplicities in opposition to colonial linear temporal structures, with the intent to enact what Indigenous scholar Dian Million (Tanana Athabascan) (2013) calls an "affectively informed Indigenous conceptual frame" (p. 50). Interrupting colonial modes of chrononormativity in this way is intended to open potential for a Derridean reading of Jiu-Jitsu as an Indigenous temporal phenomenon which has always already been enacting prophetic continuities toward "potentially political manifestations of peoplehood" (Rifkin, 2017, p. 186).

My own personal reflections are also offered in text boxes throughout, called "Afterwords," again inspired by Lather (1997; 2017b), to temporally locate these practices of looking back as a "matter of meaning-matter making" (Barad & Gandorfer, 2021, p. 25) in response to the double-bind (Spivak, 2012) of my own whiteness in anti-racist, anti/de-colonial work. They are not arranged numerically and can be read either as they are presented, in any order, or omitted entirely, inviting readers to determine for themselves whether or not my reflections on whiteness are a necessary contribution, and in response to Hunter and van der Westhuizen's (2021) challenge for white scholars to enact anti-racist work *through* whiteness that does not become *about* whiteness.

Afterwords

Grappling with the (im)possibilities of my own liberation from white-supremacist logics in my doctoral studies, it wasn't until the final semester, in a course taught by Gabriel Huddleston devoted specifically to Patti Lather's work, that the act of meaning-making began to re-emerge for me as a thinkable, if aporetic, (im)possibility. I have most recently noticed Lather's work coming for me again to change the trajectory of my life and work on the mats of a dojo,[2] where I unsuspectingly enrolled my six-year-old son in a Jiu-Jitsu class, watching him take on an embodied practice of 'keeping it moving' as he began to develop a seemingly counter-intuitive newfound self-assurance rooted in his repeated failure. I started to recognize something profoundly philosophical was happening in this game that I needed to pay closer attention to, and before I knew it, I had signed up for an adult class. Within weeks of my doctoral graduation in December of 2023, I had decided to move to my own dojo to train more intensively.

I want to make it abundantly clear from the outset that what I am suggesting in this work is not about grasping for some self-assured physical safety or heroism. To the extent that I am suggesting Jiu-Jitsu as an intervention in the material sense (to which there is certainly also a theoretical counterpart), I mean to represent it as an embodied intervention in the form of an *aesthetic re-education* (Spivak, 2012) for my own whiteness-as-embodied-violence, and a challenge to my own allegedly individual consciousness, with and through an "ethical relationality" (Tuck & Gaztambide-Fernández, 2013) to and by the 'other' on the mats.

The "Gentle Art" of Anti-Violence

A Visual Introduction to Gracie Jiu-Jitsu by Rener Gracie:

Figure 9.1[3]
(Note: For those without 28 minutes for the full video, watch minutes 4–6, then 24–28.)

Jiu-Jitsu is an aporia in itself, as a form of combat described by some as "dangerous cuddling" (Chiu, 2019), where practitioners skillfully apply techniques intended to redirect their partner's energy towards their *submission*,[4] primarily skeletal leverage and torsion. A submission is accomplished when a participant either taps their partner's body or the mat two times, says the word "tap" aloud, or loses consciousness due to a vascular neck restraint called a "choke."[5] Most people who start Jiu-Jitsu quickly stop coming back, but not because they get hurt or are physically incapable. Above the door of the dojo where I train are the words "Submit Your Ego," the feature of Jiu-Jitsu which practitioners warn is often the most difficult (Ellis, 2024).

Jiu-Jitsu techniques rely on the neutralization of strength and size as sources of power to instead privilege the equanimity of mind, which is a central feature of Buddhism (Hardes & Hogeveen, 2018; Benesch, 2020). Kinnon (2024) notes that he finds "it's those 'good athletes' that walk in the door that you never see again" (p. 34) whereas the smaller and weaker people tend to stick with it. He explains:

I will never forget my first official class in which a 15-year-old girl choked me repeatedly for 6 minutes. For some men, this would be devastating to

their manhood [. . .] Jiu-Jitsu forces the individual to examine their mistakes and their skill level, and to accept that they will be beaten hundreds
of times before they start to win on their own. [. . .] The fact that a small
teenager could take hold of a grown man with fighting experience opened
my eyes. The last 3 years of consistent training have helped me understand
how my ego works and how I adapt to loss. [. . .] For me, it is the closest
I feel to a higher power. In the chaos, I find peace. (Kinnon, 2024, p. 34)

Re-Memberance #1: Before 527 C.E.

Jiu-Jitsu's Contested Origins Among Buddhist Monks

Traditional Japanese Jujutsu ("gentle art") is a grappling-based
martial art with a long and contested history (Rouse, 2017). Most historians agree that it was used in Japan by the Samurai[6] (Turnbull, 2013),
after having originated far earlier in either Ancient Greece, India, China, or among the Indigenous (Jōmon) peoples of Japan (Condé, 2022).
It is most widely believed that the techniques were first brought to the
Buddhist monks of northern India in 527 C.E. as a dharma ("path of
rightness") teaching, known then as "Shuai Chiao," from the warrior
monks of the Shaolin temple of China, to enable their defense against
the constant attacks they endured at the time without violating the moral values of Buddhism, which prohibits doing harm to others (Griffiths,
2023; Silva, 2024). The Buddhist concept of 'upāya-kauśalya,' or "skillful metapraxis" (Schroeder, 2011; Conze, 1954; Kasulis, 1992), as well
as Indigenous scholarship on storywork (Archibald, 1997; 2008; 2012;
Sandelowski, 1991; TallBear, 2014) and felt theory (Million, 2009), all
affirm Lather's (2007) assertion that a story does not have to *be* true
to *reveal* truth. In the absence of consensus among historians, this origin story of Jiu-Jitsu becomes all-at-once: factual, mythical, theopoetic,[7]
political, and racialized.[8] Yet, this is the story in which I locate the matterphorical (Barad & Gandorfer, 2021) truth of Jiu-Jitsu I draw upon in
this work. I intend to carefully represent that story here as *iterative* in
my own experience, and not as epistemologically appropriative (Davis,
2018) nor as conclusive or representative of the complex and contested
philosophical, cultural, and historical origins of Jiu-Jitsu itself.

Re-Memberance #2: 1906–1917

Maeda Develops His Vale Tudo Techniques in Brazil

At 5'4" and 145 pounds, Maeda was a small fighter who grew his notoriety by publicly challenging much larger opponents from a wide variety of other martial arts. Reportedly, Maeda was defeated only twice in over 2,000 "Vale Tudo" ("anything goes") matches throughout Mexico, Cuba, Costa Rica, and Brazil (Gatling & Svinth, 2021).

Afterwords

In my first 'roll' as a white-belt,[9] I was utterly shocked to find myself flipped together into some relational "data as enactment assemblage" (Lather, 2016, p. 7) as I quickly realized I had no clue at any moment what choices my body would make next. Yet somehow, the black-belt 'other' predicted my every move, subverting my intentions before I could even discern them. This aporetic 'inter' undercut my own allegedly individual subjective awareness, as I was caught up by an utterly bizarre dissociative feeling. My own body felt completely unknowable to me, yet entirely understood by the 'other.' This instantly gave way to a realization that all possibilities available for the 'self' to consciously direct the movement of our assemblage had been foreclosed. Suddenly, there was a pause in the dialogue, and only three choices remained: "tap, snap, or nap," as they say, by which they mean that I could either submit and be released, injure myself by continuing to move, or lose consciousness. I tapped.

Rolling with Anti-Violence

For Derrida, foreclosure of possibility is the definition of violence (1967/ 1978). Derrida critiques discourses that approach the concept of 'non-violence' as antithetical to, free from, or purified of violence as ultimately forms of the colonial spatial violence of exteriority/alterity. Because he also considers discourse itself, whether speaking, writing, or acting, to be inseparable from the spatial, as articulation always occurs in a time and place, violence is similarly fundamental to discourse for Derrida (1967). He writes, "There is war only after the opening of discourse, and war dies out only at the end of discourse" (Derrida, 1967, p. 117). Thus, in the Derridean sense, peace only becomes possible *as violence* itself, as the end of a discourse, as the death of every possibility except peace. This is what I mean when I use the term *anti-violent*, rather than *non-violent*, in considering Jiu-Jitsu as an anti-violent discourse.

Re-Memberance #4: 1917–1941

Maeda Learns Techniques from Afro-Brazilian Capoeira

In Brazil, Maeda found particular inspiration in an Afro-Brazilian martial art with a liberatory history, which had by then been practiced in Brazil for over a century, called Capoeira.[10] Capoeira was developed by the enslaved Africans who were held captive in Brazil and likely originates from N'Golo (Desch-Obi & Thomas, 2008). The (im)possible challenge for Capoeiristas was not a commitment to doing no harm as in Jiu-Jitsu, but in avoiding detection during training while developing techniques that could produce tremendous, potentially lethal force without any apparent escalation (Santos, 2023). Capoeira is thus an explosive fighting technique, cleverly disguised as a dance. Practitioners gather in a circle, playing instruments which are themselves weapons, as two players enter the center of the circle to perform a highly responsive acrobatic dialogue with their bodies, each attempting to gain the perceived advantage according to the group (Ferreira & Beatriz, 2014).

Re-Memberance #7: 1950s

Waldemar Santana Teaches Capoeira to the Gracies in Brazil

Santana was an accomplished Capoeirista from Bahia, Brazil. In the early 1950s, Santana moved to Rio to train with the Gracies, who had opened their own school teaching what they had learned from Maeda. Santana became a highly influential instructor at the school, weaving insights from Capoeira into the Gracie techniques (Cairus, 2013). Until recently, the significance of Santana's historical influence as a Black man on modern Jiu-Jitsu has remained largely unacknowledged (Santos, 2015). Santana was one of only two people to ever win a Vale Tudo match against Hélio Gracie, the other being Japanese judoka Masahiko Kimura (Santos, 2015).

Figure 9.4[11] Photo: Valdemar Santana "The Black Panther" Source: Wikimedia Commons

Afterwords

As I have written elsewhere (Bryant, 2023), Hunter and van der Westhuizen (2021) draw on Puar's (2007) concept of "queer assemblages" in calling for a decolonial analysis of whiteness in which "the deconstructionist impulse must translate into an onto-epistemic struggle," asserting that there are no "White people," but only people who have been racialized as "White" (p. 2). However, as Vice (2021) clarifies, while race is indeed a social construction, it is also not a merely incidental feature in our present society, but is "morally relevant and identity-constituting, whether one likes it or not" (p. 317). Further, as Morales (2022) explains, a white-supremacist culture is itself an epistemological barrier between white people and an understanding of the mechanisms of whiteness, such that anti-racist endeavors to de-center whiteness must engage authentically with BIPOC scholarship, leaving white scholars "constantly brushing up against epistemic appropriation" as yet another enactment of white-supremacy (p. 709).

Morales (2022) says this aporia leaves many white scholars feeling "theoretically bereft," and as other scholars have noted, ultimately draws out a re-centering of whiteness that focuses the work towards "where do I fit" and "what about me" (Spivak, 2012; Tuck & Gaztambide-Fernández, 2013; Patel, 2021). Vice (2021) explains that this struggle to engage in anti-racist work while white challenges one's ability to maintain integrity and self-respect alongside an awareness of the responsibility to resist. According to Hunter and van der Westhuizen (2021), this is the angst that underlies the "White hand-wringing" among progressives more broadly, and leads to a whiteness that enacts itself as "a political and even ontological dead-end that obviates any possibility for ethical existence or inter-racial solidarities that pursue anti-racism," which is itself yet another re-entrenchment of race thinking (p. 18). Whiteness is anything but fragile.

Lather (2001) notes that for Visweswaran (1994), the practice of failure is central to feminist inquiry. In this "self-wounding laboratory," researchers tasked with "thinking the limit" must embrace "reflexivities of discomfort" (Pillow, 2004, p. 175) in the field. Lather (2001) writes:

> The task becomes to throw ourselves against the stubborn materiality of others, willing to risk loss, relishing the power of others to constrain our interpretive 'will to know,' saving us from narcissism and its melancholy through the very positivities that cannot be exhausted by us, the otherness that always exceeds us. (p. 202)

Rolling seriously with Patti Lather's (2007) work involves grappling with these aporetic joint-locks. As she often states regarding encounters with our limits of knowing, "the task is to meet the limit, to open to it as the very vitality and force that propels the change to come" (Lather, 2007, p. 37).

Similarly, Barad and Gandorfer (2021) challenge scholars seeking to enact *matterphorical* scholarship, which "encounter[s] what is unrecognizable and imperceptible, yet sensible and constructive of sense without separating it from the physical world" (p. 20), noting what Indigenous knowledges have maintained for time immemorial (Tuck & Yang, 2012; Todd, 2016), that matter and meaning, ontology, epistemology, and ethics are inseparable: "Mattering (and the double entendre is crucial here) is a matter of meaning-matter making" (Barad & Gandorfer, 2021, p. 25).

White-Belts Roll with Black-Belts

While Jiu-Jitsu techniques are specifically designed to minimize physical risk for both victims and assailants, injuries are very possible if the techniques are not executed properly. This is most common among white belts, who have not yet developed an embodied awareness of the risks and appropriate responses integrated into a state of 'flow' (Hardes & Hogeveen, 2018) with their training partners. White belts have a reputation for being somewhat irresponsible, whether out of ignorance, overconfidence, aggression, or a combination of these. For this reason, it is a steadfast rule at every dojo I have visited that new white belts should begin their Jiu-Jitsu training by rolling with black belts.

A significant part of building a Jiu-Jitsu strategy is learning when to *tap out*, as this develops a very specific sense for when the limit of understanding has been reached. For example, white belts often attempt to muscle through a technique that is impossible, failing to notice that a necessary body part has been immobilized until trying to move it, which can lead to unintended twisting, falling, or excessive pressure on joints. However, there is far less possibility to work outside the limitations of white belt ability when rolling with black belts, due to their ability to anticipate these mistakes and either redirect the movement or stop the roll entirely to offer instruction.

Learning to *tap out* serves as a method of 'giving up' that is counter-intuitively essential to developing the ability to persevere in Jiu-Jitsu. What truth could this narrative provide for researchers pushing the boundaries of our own understandings toward Lather's (2016) framing of the (post) qualitative, wherein she notes that the present moment "feels to me like the moment of attachment and detachment when those of us trained in ideology critique moved into deconstruction. What had to be let go of? Of what could we/would we not let go?" (p. 349). How could practices that are ethically *safe* for both participants and researchers be better approached through accountability to black belt mentorship rather than the institutional standards of those more interested in individualistic competition than collective anti-violence?

Re-Memberance #5: 1920s

Capoeira "Safely" Re-introduced as Sport

Capoeira had been outlawed in Brazil since 1789, but the unique terrain in Brazil's mountainous rainforests had enabled Capoeiristas to practice in secret. Capoeira was only again deemed permissible when it was reintroduced as a standardized game with a points-based ranking system in the early 1920s, and many believe this is also the origin of modern breakdancing. However, in the 1940s, *Mestre* Vicente Ferreira Pastinha opened a school seeking to return to the cultural and philosophical origins of Capoeira as a form of self-defense, and this style is known as Capoeira Angola today (Varela, 2017).

Figure 9.6[12] Photo: Ricky Malandro Lawson
Source: Instagram @mrmalandro

Re-Memberance #3: 1912–1940s

Jujutsu Under Government Control in Japan and Racism in the West

In 1912, Japan began implementing a standardized and highly controlled martial arts curriculum in public schools, overseen by the government (Power, 1998; Benesch, 2020). By the 1930s, martial arts instruction in Japan had become a fountainhead of official governmental propaganda in support of the war (Power, 1998), adding instruction in fencing, rifle marksmanship, grenade throwing, and more (Benesch, 2020).

During the same timeframe, attitudes in the West began to turn sharply against the Japanese, portraying Traditional Jujutsu techniques as underhanded rather than clever, representing "the physical embodiment of the Yellow Peril" (Rouse, 2017, p. 2). Traditional Jujutsu quickly fell out of vogue among white elites and military cadets, replaced by more 'honorable' combat sports such as boxing (Rouse, 2017).

Re-Memberance #8: 1990s

The Ultimate Fighting Championships (UFC) Shock the West

Carlos and Hélio Gracie set out to breed,[13] and train from birth, an enormous family of Jiu-Jitsu practitioners, having 30 children and hundreds of grandchildren between the two of them, as they continued developing their techniques in Vale Tudo fights for decades (Gracie & Maguire, 2021). Meanwhile, the American occupation of Japan had placed even more limits on martial arts training there. This limited exposure to Traditional Jujutsu, driven by racism, nationalism, and militarism, enabled the Gracies to shock the world when they came on the American martial arts scene in the 1990s. Empowered by the entertainment industry and the advertising made possible by the televised Ultimate Fighting Championship matches they helped create, the Gracie family quickly became ubiquitously associated with Jiu-Jitsu around the world (Gracie & Maguire, 2021).

Lather (2016) describes the present moment of grappling toward the (post)qualitative in research and theory as a collective attempt to move against "the 'qualitative positivist' dominant unleashed by 'best practices'" (p. 337) among educational and research-oriented institutions. These institutions enforce practices that, despite their stated intentions to protect participants and hold researchers accountable, actually function to prioritize potential for monetization, add potential harms, and limit possibility. Lather's (2007, 2016) work encourages researchers to consider how institutions such as the National Science Foundation, seemingly recognizing some impending danger in the possibility for the (post)qualitative to go *too far*, have no other capacity to resist its momentum than to apply their regulatory power to prescribe and enforce 'best practices,' ensuring that (post)qualitative research remains unfunded and unpublished unless it first agrees to behave itself.

Afterwords

Sitting in the car about to go into training, I realized I was sweating profusely, and my heart was racing. I couldn't understand why I was feeling this way. My coach and I are almost always the only two women in the room. I am 5'2" and around 125 lbs., with no previous martial arts experience. No one in the dojo expects me to be good at this. I don't even expect *myself* to be good at this. I also know failure is part of the learning process. I trust everyone at my dojo to help me stay physically safe during training. So, what could possibly be causing me to panic. The answer came to my mind immediately: "I'm afraid that if I don't get it right, that will prove to everyone that I don't belong with them, and that I'm not the kind of person who can ever learn to do this." I knew this feeling well. This is the same ontological panic I feel when I confront my own embodied aporia of white anti-racist work. I suddenly realized why I had felt so drawn to Jiu-Jitsu in the first place. I reminded myself that 'belonging' is innate, but 'proficiency' requires showing up consistently, ready to "submit your ego" and learn from the embodied knowledge of the 'other'. The willingness to fully engage with that commitment to re-lational accountability as a *process*, not an achievement, is what keeps everyone safe to keep trying, in both Jiu-Jitsu and in anti-racist, anti/decolonial work. I finally composed myself and walked in the door, con-fident that this Jiu-Jitsu practice was offering me a medicine, however unpleasant, for the wounds of white supremacy and colonialism that can only be attended to in and through my own body, just as it is.

It is important to remember, when considering a Derridean application of anti-violence, that the refusal to foreclose possibility is *itself* a foreclosure of possibility, a death of the outcomes that would have proliferated as a re-sult of being *open to foreclosure*. There is no way around it. Violence moves through our collectively conscious enactments, as consciousness can *itself* be described, in the very material sense of quantum mechanics, as a foreclosure of possibility for the particle-as-wave (Wendt, 2015). Learning to 'roll' with violent possibilities is always already a process of *becoming* which must re-main "on guard against itself" (Lather, 2007, p. 104).

Response-Able Anti-Violent Movement

For Lather (2001), response-ability is about recognizing the intra-action between observers and theorizers and is an endeavor towards remaining "ethically in touch with the other," rather than "pretending to theorize from the outside," which she recognizes as violence (p. 24).

> Rather than some angst of displacement, this might be the effacement that I have been trying to track across Derrida for years. This is a demastering: a work without force, a work that would have to work at renouncing force, its own force, a work that would have to work at failure, and thus at mourning and getting over force, a work working at its own unproductivity, absolutely, working to absolve or to absolve itself of whatever might be absolute about 'force' (Derrida in Lather, 2001, p.144).

The fundamental principles that make Jiu-Jitsu so effective against larger and stronger opponents rely on an intuitive reciprocity of movement and distance management between opposing forces that is itself recognizably Derridean. In the simplest terms, this means that every unit of physical exertion contributed by one partner amounts to an equal unit of physical rest for the other partner. Someone who tries to submit a more technically skillful partner using physical strength will quickly exhaust themselves, becoming increasingly likely to make technical mistakes, while their partner rests waiting for an opportunity to apply a more skillful technique.

This strategy was integral in Traditional Jujutsu, Capoeira, and later the Vale Tudo matches fought by Maeda, Santana, and the Gracies in Brazil, and greatly contributed to the fact that the historic 1955 match between Santana and Hélio Gracie lasted almost four hours (Banjoko & Gracie, 2004). However, as this Vale Tudo form of Jiu-Jitsu was further commodified and commercialized, rules were deemed necessary for participant 'safety,' and while many techniques were prohibited for having the potential to cause severe injury or severe pain, many others were prohibited simply for being less entertaining to audiences (Andreasson & Johansson, 2019). In modern competitive contexts, a technique frequently utilized by both Hélio and Santana in the aforementioned historic match is now called "stalling the clinch," which is a violation of the rules, as are other forms of "failing to advance position," like repeatedly backing away, staying in a neutral or defensive position, or repeatedly dropping to the ground, which can all lead to penalties, referee intervention to require a standing fight, and eventually disqualification (Sánchez-García & Malcolm, 2010). Even "timidity," which is explicitly defined by the UFC to include "avoiding eye-contact with an opponent" is considered one such violation (UFC, 2024). Of course, such a requirement would introduce an *additional* safety concern for participants outside of a sportive context wherein eye-gouging is also deemed impermissible. Thus, concerns over 'safety' were the means through which 'the rules' enabled centuries of anti-violent strategies from Traditional Jujutsu and Capoeira to be co-opted and subsumed into the $12 billion industry known today as the UFC, which is ironically anything but anti-violent (Sánchez-García & Malcolm, 2010).

However, Gracie Jiu-Jitsu demonstrates that the perceived power differential between objects always only exists to the extent that subjects can be compelled by the force of *the rules*. The reason a Jiu-Jitsu practitioner would not deliver a standing strike is thus not for a lack of striking capability, but an awareness that this unskilled violence offers an outstretched arm as the most obvious of many new potential sites for proliferation of opportunities for skillful anti-violent strategy and technique (Gracie, 2024). Pain-based techniques are also considered risky in Jiu-Jitsu for a different reason, based on the same principle of reciprocal energy between opposing forces, as animals instinctively react to acute pain with uncontrolled force via a neurological phenomenon known as the *amygdala hijack*, dramatically increasing the intensity of the situation in ways that are impossible to anticipate, and redirecting the strategic advantage (Gracie, 2024).

Re-Memberance #6: 1930s

Carlos Gracie Teaches Hélio Gracie Jiu-Jitsu

Carlos Gracie's younger brother, Hélio, suffered severe vertigo and other health issues which limited his ability to participate in training with Maeda (Gracie & Maguire, 2021). However, Hélio spent years developing a new approach while training with Carlos, adapting the traditional judo position of *guard* to enable him to not only protect himself defensively but also to submit opponents offensively through skeletal leverage with very little strength, successfully engaging the traditional Jiu-Jitsu chokes and joint locks, all while lying on his back. This approach is known today as "Gracie Jiu-Jitsu" (Gracie & Maguire, 2021).

The reciprocal nature of Jiu-Jitsu techniques applies not only to the exchange of energy, but also to the positional relationship in proximity to the 'other.' This means that the more vulnerable the position appears subjective-ly, the more objective potential there is for a powerful return technique (Gracie, 2024). There are many examples of this, but one of the most ex-treme can be viewed via the QR code below, to allow readers to visualize the mechanisms of action, and to reiterate the importance of Capoeira in developing Jiu-Jitsu as an anti-violent strategy, as this is not a Traditional Jiujutsu technique. What is important in considering the *Martelo de Nega-tiva* as a *word* in an anti-violent *dialogue*, in the Derridean sense, is that it only becomes available to a person who is on the ground in a defensive posi-tion, looking up at an opponent who is standing. In a non-sportive context, this technique therefore represents what could be the last opportunity for the person on the ground to anti-violently *say* which life *matters*, effectively.

Figure 9.7[14, 15]

Queer (Dis)Crit scholar, Mia Mingus (2013), writes that repairing harm must move beyond granting individualized *access* and *representation*, es-pecially for the multiply-marginalized. Instead, it must enact interdepen-dent work which "disrupts power disparities within deliberative spaces by explicitly articulating and subverting these arrangements" (Annamma & Handy, 2021, p. 45). Hélio Gracie's story demonstrates the ways that Jiu-Jitsu can be adapted responsively to subvert the dynamics of power in this way. A quick search on Reddit for "Jiu-Jitsu and Disabilities" reveals that many Jiu-Jitsu practitioners consider (dis)abilities to be an advantage on the mats, as (dis)abled practitioners develop strategies that are embodied in unexpected ways for those who habitually only roll with normatively able bodies. Reflecting on a partner with an amputated leg, user *Shillandorbot* shares that, though initially nervous to hold onto an empty pant leg, they found that "it's a blast rolling with him because so much of Brazilian Jiu-Jit-su just doesn't work (half guard, De La Riva, etc. just don't exist) and you have to improvise" (Reddit, 2023).

Relational Accountability: 'All the Way In, or All the Way Out'

To conclude this interlude as truly *Latherian*, I can offer no tidy recommendations for moving forward. I can, however, apply Jiu-Jitsu to my own foreclosure of thought toward the proliferation of possibilities in one particular direction, as I anticipate my own work will move there next. Returning to the strategy of 'distance management' which is fundamental to Jiu-Jitsu, and as readers can recall from/revisit in the introductory video, practitioners must first learn to remain either "all the way in, or all the way out" during a roll, as the space between partners could place them within striking distance of each other, often called the *red zone*, thereby proliferating options for the physical strength and pain-based techniques which privilege the unskilled violence of institutions.

Afterwords

My own struggle as a white woman attempting to enact emancipatory work continues to be a whirlwind of upheaval and change. I have often preferred to forget where I started this process, yet I know that if I keep growing as I intend to, I'll someday look back at the present version of myself and want to roll my eyes just as hard. In fact, I'm doing it already. In the introduction of this interlude, I clarified for readers that my interest in Jiu-Jitsu is not about attaining some self-assured or heroic sense of physical safety. Now that I have more fully explored what I meant by this sentiment, I realize that it isn't true. However, I've elected not to go back to remove or reframe it, because I think the untruth reveals more truth than I had intended. While the philosophical and theoretical applications had initially felt more relevant to me, I now think the truth of that statement has more to do with my own relationship to fear than Jiu-Jitsu. I'm a classic people-pleaser, but much to my chagrin, I've realized that this is not a virtue, as I can see clearly now that inaction is itself an action.

It is also true that just a few months ago, a viral social media trend revealed that many women claim that they would rather encounter a bear while hiking in the woods than an unknown man (Encinas, 2024), and I agreed. Far too many men responded to this information, not with self-reflection, but with rage, unironically implying that these women

deserved to be mauled by bears to show them how much more dangerous bears are than men, proving the point which escaped them entirely
(Iqbal, 2024). In this social and cultural context, my fears about physical safety are entirely legitimate, and these fears are of course exponen-
tially compounded for the multiply-marginalized, many of whom do
not have the privilege(s) of people-pleasing toward safety.

My people-pleasing self would much prefer to respond to the (im)
possibility of my embodiment in emancipatory work by simply ignoring
my fears and instead putting myself out there for extrinsic validation.
But I now notice that this is a suspiciously disembodied, strength- and
point-based strategy that makes a lot of (white-feminist-adjacent) assumptions about the existence of 'rules' and 'referees,' and I remember
that simply 'showing up' with fear as a white woman has often been
weaponized against the multiply-marginalized.

Black feminism reminds me that a collective win by 'submis-
sion-only' utilizes mechanisms learned and enacted through relational accountability to black-belt mentorship. When there are no rules,
when the liberatory results are intrinsic to the anti-violent techniques
themselves, fear is one of many insights through which I must learn the
techniques and establish the pace that allows me to become the 'other'
in *perpetual* engagement toward anti-violent enactment. As Prentis
Hemphill (2024) writes in *What it Takes to Heal: How Transforming
Ourselves Can Change the World*:

> The courage we need is the courage to fail and stay. The courage to reimag-
> ine every aspect of our social relations. The courage to relinquish grasping
> what was and build piece by piece a new structure for how and what we
> produce. The courage to exit the safety of our dying delusions. The courage
> to reach for one another. (p. 187)

A few weeks ago, I attended a women-only Jiu-Jitsu retreat led
by Professora Nathalie Ribeiro, recently named the 2024 Women's
BJJ World Champion (IBJJF, 2024). As I worked through what was,
without a doubt, the most physically and emotionally exhausting week
of my life, I also witnessed how women move differently through the
world when the threat of physical violence is lifted, when their personal

boundaries are real and enforceable. Between training sessions, as we hiked along a remote trail and climbed down to an isolated beach area to look for abalone shells, we laughed about the viral 'man vs. bear in the woods' debate, and dreamed about a Queer/femme "Choose the Man" Jiu-Jitsu club with a bear mascot.[16]

"Love Has Come for Me"
by Raine Hamilton (2022)[17]

It's the heavy-lifting of the soul,
it's when to rock and when to roll.
All the senses here combine to tell me:
To pay attention to the news,
to talk-show headlines with the clues
of how to be (and how to stay) courageous.
Tell me, 'oh, Night has come'.

And Love has come for me! [repeating]

To all the parts that kept me safe,
to all that led me to the place
where I can let it go, and let it lie:
I thank you,
by my Maker's hand,
knowing what I did not know,
that I might stand here willing to receive it
when the Night has come.

And Love has come for me! [repeating]

And I know this face.
Oh, I've walked these floors.
and I know that I should name it,
beholding so spectacular a thing.
I see that I can hold it all.
It comes to fill the space that I'm within.

IG: @tatawribeiro

IG: @cyberjiujiteira

IG: @junes_mom &
June (age 11!)

IG: @naked_growth

IG: @shobasantosh

IG: @molly.4645

IG: @esseewhy

IG: @66longlegs

And what if I could hold you there?
An uncomfort to your trite, unloving heart,
    that will come to know the difference.
            The points of light
                that amplify,
                that resonate,
        as *sympathetic thought*,
the kind of thing that tears the walls down
        when the Night has come.
        And, Oh! The Night has come!

And Love has come for me! [repeating]

IG:@linesofflights (L)   IG:@cute_rapscallion   IG: @mddod
& @ngespinolina (R)

Notes

1. A "roll" is a Jiu-Jitsu match between two participants.

2. A dojo is a gym where martial arts training occurs.

3. QR Code URL: https://tinyurl.com/yckdzyev "I survived my first Brazilian Jiu-Jitsu class with Rener Gracie" (Full Length, 28:42)

4. A "submission" is a win accomplished in Jiu-Jitsu when one participant either taps their opponent's body or the mat three times, says the word "tap" aloud, or loses consciousness due to a vascular neck restraint.

5. Contrary to what the name implies, a sportive "choke" does not compromise the airway and has been thoroughly researched and demonstrated to be safe, with < 0.05% of practitioners (N=4421), of whom 33.5% report receiving a sportive choke > 500 times over decades of training, reporting any ongoing symptoms (Stellpflug et al., 2020).

6. In the late-nineteenth century, the Japanese government romanticized the Samurai as scholar-warriors in order to construct an 'honorable' masculinized national identity, mirroring the Western romanticization of European knighthood and boxing around the same time (Rouse, 2017; Akihiko & Pih, 2010).

7. See Caputo, J. D., & Keller, C. (2007).

8. The romanticized notion of the Samurai (see earlier endnote) promoted by the Japanese government, alongside the Orientalism (Said, 1978/2010) of Eastern culture in the West

in the early twentieth century, led to the exoticization and appropriation of Traditional Jujutsu among Western elites (Rouse, 2017; Akihiko & Pih, 2010).

9. The Jiu-Jitsu belt ranking progression starts with white (beginner), then blue (intermediate), purple (advanced), brown (expert), and black (professor) (IBJJF, 2012).

10. QR Code URL: https://tinyurl.com/2s4jtu75 "Capoeira—A journey to the roots of this Afro-Brazilian martial art" (Full Length, 52:02).

11. QR Code URL: https://tinyurl.com/4vehw4p7 "Capoeira Master Rates 9 Capoeira Scenes in Movies and TV" (Full Length, 14:44).

12. QR Code URL: https://tinyurl.com/5ey3fxt4 "Can Capoeira Work for Street Self Defense?" (Full Video, 20:37).

13. It is important to note that it is no exaggeration to say that this generation of Gracies believed women existed solely for reproduction, and that their misogyny took the predictable trajectory to homophobia (*Playboy*, 2001). Notably, Rener Gracie, largely due to the influence of his wife, Eve Torres-Gracie, has recently taken on the task of redirecting the Hélio Gracie's lineage toward bullying intervention, women's empowerment, police de-escalation training, and other more socially-conscious endeavors (Gracie University, 2024b; c; d).

14. QR Code URL: https://tinyurl.com/yc4z8m67 "What is the strongest kick? Karate, Capoeira, MMA, Taekwondo" (Full length, 5:10).

15. It is important to note that this video was produced for entertainment purposes, and clearly not with a suitable research design. Its inclusion here should be considered as a demonstration of the technique, not an assertion about their 'findings.'

16. Pictures and Instagram usernames of the retreat participants are included with their permission.

17. QR Code URL: https://www.youtube.com/watch?v=OBl6zkKIVCk

18. QR Code URL: www.edaffect.com/jiujitsu

References

Akihiko, H., & Pih, K. K. (2010). Men who strike and men who submit: Hegemonic and marginalized masculinities in mixed martial arts. *Men and Masculinities, 13*(2), 190–209.

Andreasson, J., & Johansson, T. (2019). Negotiating violence: Mixed martial arts as a spectacle and sport. *Sport in Society, 22*(7), 1183–1197. https://doi.org/10.1080/17430437.2018.1505868

Annamma, S. A., & Handy, T. (2021). Sharpening justice through DisCrit: A contrapuntal analysis of education. *Educational Researcher, 50*(1), 41–50. https://doi.org/10.3102/0013189X20953838

Archibald, J. (1997). *Coyote learns to make a storybasket: The place of First Nations stories in education* [Unpublished doctoral dissertation]. Simon Fraser University.

Archibald, J. (2008). *Indigenous storywork: Educating the heart, mind, body and spirit.* University of British Columbia Press.

Archibald, J. (2012). An Indigenous storywork methodology. In J.G. Knowles & A. L. Cole (Eds.), *Handbook of the arts in qualitative research: Perspectives, methodologies, examples, and issues* (pp. 371–385). SAGE Publications.

Banjoko, A. & Gracie, R. (2004). *Interview with Royce Gracie*. On the mat. http://onthemat. com/interview-with-royce-gracie/

Barad, K. (2007). *Meeting the universe halfway: Quantum physics and the entanglement of matter and meaning*. Duke University Press.

Barad, K., & Gandorfer, D. (2021). Political desirings: Yearnings for mattering (,) differently. *Theory and Event*, 24(1), 14–66. https://dx.doi.org/10.1353/tae.2021.0002.

Benesch, O. (2020). Olympic Samurai: Japanese martial arts between sports and self-cultivation. *Sport in History*, 40(3), 328–355. https://doi.org/10.1080/17460263.2020.17 39739

Bryant, E. (2023). *"Synaesthography" as a felt method of currere: Mutually causative art-based storytelling and emergent inquiry for collective care among K–12 public school teachers imagining otherwise* [Unpublished doctoral dissertation]. Texas Christian University.

Cairus, J. (2013). The Gracie clan and the making of Brazilian jiu-jitsu: National identity, culture and performance, 1905–2003 (Publication No. 9780499001627) [Doctoral dissertation, York University]. Pro Quest.

Caputo, J. D., & Keller, C. (2007). Theopoetic/theopolitic. *Cross Currents*, 56(4), 105–111.

Chiu, M. (2019). *'You've got to trust me not to kill you' Brazilian Jiu-Jitsu: Grappling with trust and feminisms on the mats* [Master's thesis]. Goldsmiths University of London.

Condé, R. (2022). Brazilian Jiu Jitsu: A historiographical fraud. Russian Journal of Physical Education and Sport 17(3), pp. 88–90. https://doi.org/10.14526/2070-4798-2022-17-3-107-109

Conze, E. (1954). *Buddhist texts through the ages*. Philosophical Library.

Davis, E. (2018). On epistemic appropriation. *Ethics*, 128(4), 702–727. https://doi.org/10. 1086/697490.

Derrida, J. (1967/1978). *Writing and difference*. University of Chicago Press.

Derrida, J. (2001). *The work of mourning*. University of Chicago Press.

Desch-Obi, M., & Thomas, J. (2008). *Fighting for honor: The history of African martial art traditions in the Atlantic world*. University of South Carolina Press.

Ellis, R. ([The Art of Skill]. 2024, Jan 19). *Jiu Jitsu is for people that like to do hard things* [Video]. YouTube. https://www.youtube.com/watch?v=ZNarK-u9u7w

Encinas, A. (2024, April). Man or bear? Hypothetical question sparks conversation about women's safety. *USA Today*. https://www.usatoday.com/story/tech/news/2024/04/30/man-bear-tiktok-debate-explainer/73519921007/

Ferreira, M. B. R., & Beatriz, M. (2014). Indigenous games: A struggle between past and present. *Journal of Sport Science and Physical Education*, 67, 48–54.

Gatling, T. A., & Svinth, J. R. (Eds.). (2010). *Martial arts of the world: An encyclopedia of history and innovation*. ABC-CLIO.

Gracie B., (2024). *We are Gracie Barra*. https://graciebarra.com/we-are-gracie-barra/

Gracie, R., & Maguire, P. (2021). *Breathe: A life in flow*. Dey Street Books.

Gracie, R., & Volponi, P (2023). *The 32 principles: Harnessing the power of jiu-jitsu to succeed in business, relationships, and life*. BenBella Books.

Gracie University. (2024). *Explore the Gracie Jiu-Jitsu programs*. https://www.gracieuniversity.com/

Gracie University. (2024b). *Gracie SafeWrap lateral restraint system*. https://www.gracieuniversity.com/pages/public/information?enc=%2bxsl1oejgkW4nRqsGofJdA%3d%3d

Gracie University. (2024c). *Gracie Bullyproof*. https://www.gracieuniversity.com/Pages/Public/Information?enc=5ruAJc3RhhlwP%2bWe1ep5rQ%3d%3d

Gracie University [GracieBreakdown]. (2018, April 25). *Man vs. woman, strength vs. technique: A jiu-jitsu experiment* [Video]. YouTube. https://www.youtube.com/watch?v=-FUMcJltEXQ&t=71s

Griffiths, A. (2023). *Bodhidharma and the beginnings of Kung Fu*. The History of Fighting. https://www.historyoffighting.com/bodhidharma.php

Hamilton, R. (2022). *Love has come for me* [Video]. YouTube. https://www.youtube.com/watch?v=OBl6zkKIVCk

Hand, C. A., Hankes, J., & House, T. (2012). Restorative justice: The Indigenous justice system. *Contemporary Justice Review, 15*(4), 449–467. doi:10.1080/10282580.2012.734576

Hardes, J., & Hogeveen, B. (2018). Flow, skilled coping, and the sovereign subject: Toward an ethics of being-with in sport. In G. Breivik (Ed.), *Skills, knowledge, and expertise in sport* (1st ed.). Routledge.

Hemphill, P. (2024). *What it takes to heal: How transforming ourselves can change the world*. Randomhouse.

Huddleston, G. (2015). An awkward stance: On Gayatri Spivak and double binds. *Journal of Critical Literacy: Theories & Practices, 9*(1).

Hunter, S., & van der Westhuizen, C. (Eds.). (2021). *Routledge handbook of critical studies in whiteness* (1st ed.). Routledge. https://doi-org.ezproxy.tcu.edu/10.4324/9780429355769

International Brazilian Jiu-Jitsu Federation (IBJJF). (2012). *Graduation System*. https://ibjjf.com/graduation-system

International Brazilian Jiu-Jitsu Federation (IBJJF). (2024). *World IBJJF jiu-jitsu championship 2024*. https://www.ibjjfdb.com/ChampionshipResults/2465/PublicResults

Iqbal, S. (2024). *The way some men are reacting to the bear debate on TikTok reinforces why women choose the bear*. Pedestrian. https://www.pedestrian.tv/news/man-vs-bear-debate-reactions/

Kasulis, T. P. (1992). Philosophy as metapraxis. In R. Reynolds & D. Tracy (Eds.), *Discourse and practice* (pp. 169–198). State University of New York Press.

Kinnon, C. (2024). *Intersection of warriors and addicts: An approach to harm reduction integrating Brazilian Jiu-Jitsu* [Unpublished doctoral dissertation]. Pacifica Graduate Institute.

Lather, P. (2001). Postbook: Working the ruins of feminist ethnography. *Signs: Journal of Women in Culture and Society, 27*(1), 199–227. https://doi.org/10.1086/495677

Lather, P. (2004). This IS your father's paradigm: Government intrusion and the case of qualitative research in education. *Qualitative Inquiry, 10,* 15–34. https://doi.org/10.1177/1077800403256154.

Lather, P. (2006). Paradigm proliferation as a good thing to think with: Teaching research in education as a wild profusion. *International Journal of Qualitative Studies in Education.* https://doi.org/o.1080/09518390500450144.

Lather, P. (2007). *Getting lost: Feminist efforts toward a double(d) science.* SUNY Press.

Lather, P. (2010). What kind of science for what kind of politics?: Feminist (post)critical policy analysis and the democratization of knowledge. *Counterpoints, 345,* 73–88. http://www.jstor.org/stable/42980485

Lather, P. (2013). Methodology-21: What do we do in the afterward?. *International Journal of Qualitative Studies in Education, 26*(6), 634–645.

Lather, P. (2016). Top ten+ list: (Re)thinking ontology in (post)qualitative research. *Cultural Studies ↔ Critical Methodologies, 16*(2), 125–131. 10.1177/1532708616634734

Lather, P. (2017a). From research as praxis to praxis in the ruins. In H. Malone, S. Rincón-Gallardo, & K. Krew (Eds.), *Future directions of educational change: Social justice, professional capital, and systems change* (pp. 71–85). Routledge.

Lather, P. (2017b). The work of thought and the politics of research: (Post)qualitative research. In P. Lather (Ed.), *(Post)Critical methodologies: The science possible after the critiques* (1st ed.) (pp. 331–343). Routledge. https://doi.org/10.4324/9781315619538-28

Lather, P. (2018). *Against proper objects: Toward the diversely qualitative* [Keynote Presentation]. Summer institute in qualitative research, Manchester Metropolitan University.

Lather, P., & Smithies, C. (1997). *Troubling the angels: Women living with HIV/AIDS.* Westview Press.

Markussen, T. (2005). Practising performativity: Transformative moments in research. *European Journal of Women's Studies, 12*(3), 329–344.

Million, D. (2009). Felt theory: An Indigenous feminist approach to affect and history. *Native Feminism, 24*(2), 53–76. https://www.jstor.org/stable/40587781

Million, D. (2013). *Therapeutic nations: Healing in an age of Indigenous human rights.* University of Arizona Press.

Mingus, M. (2011, Feb 12). Changing the framework: Disability justice. *WordPress.* https://leavingevidence.wordpress.com/2011/02/12/changing-the-framework-disability-justice/

Mingus, M [Equitable Education]. (2013, Nov. 30). *Mia Mingus on disability justice* [Video]. YouTube. https://www.youtube.com/watch?v=3cJkUazW-jw

Morales, S. (2022). Locating the "white" in critical whiteness studies: Considerations for white scholars seeking to dismantle whiteness within educational research. *International Journal of Qualitative Studies in Education, 35*(7), 703–710. doi: 10.1080/09518398.2022.2061731

Patel, L. (2021). *No study without struggle: Confronting settler colonialism in higher education.* Beacon Press.

Pillow, W. (2004). *Unfit subjects: Educational policy and the teen mother.* Routledge.

Playboy. (2001). Interview with Hélio Gracie. *Playboy Magazine*. https://www.global-training-report.com/hélio2.htm

Power, G. H. (1998). *Budo in Japanese and U.S. policies*. San Jose State University.

Puar, J. K. (2007). *Terrorist assemblages: Homonationalism in queer times*. Duke University Press.

Reddit. (2023). Jiu-Jitsu and disabilities. *Reddit*. https://www.reddit.com/r/bjj/comments/12dmy87/jiu_jitsu_and_disabilities/

Rifkin, M. (2017). *Beyond settler time: Temporal sovereignty and Indigenous self-determination*. Duke University Press. https://doi.org/10.2307/j.ctv11smrwm

Rouse, W. L. (2017). *Her own hero: The origins of the women's self-defense movement*. NYU Press. https://www.jstor.org/stable/j.ctt1gk091g.6

Said, E. W. (1978/2003). *Orientalism*. Penguin Classics.

Sánchez-García, R., & Malcolm, D. (2010). Decivilizing, civilizing, or informalizing? The international development of mixed martial arts. *International Review for the Sociology of Sport, 45*(1), 39–58. https://doi.org/10.1177/1012690209352392

Sandelowski, M. (1991). Telling stories: Narrative stories in qualitative research. *Journal of Nursing Scholarship, 23*(3).

Santos, J. R. (2015). *Saber do negro, Rio de Janeiro*. Pallas.

Schroeder, J. (2011). Truth, deception, and skillful means in the Lotus Sutra. *Asian Philosophy, 21*(1), 35–52.

Silva, A. (2024). *Silva BJJ Association*. https://silvabjj.com/history/

Spivak, G. C. (1988). *Can the subaltern speak?* Macmillan.

Spivak, G. C. (2012). *An aesthetic education in the era of globalization*. Harvard University Press.

Stellpflug, S. J., Schindler, B. R., Corry, J. J., Menton, T. R., & LeFevere, R. C. (2020). The safety of sportive chokes: A cross-sectional survey-based study. *Physician and Sports Medicine, 48*(4), 473–479. https://doi.org/10.1080/00913847.2020.1754734

TallBear, K. (2014). Standing with and speaking as faith: A feminist-Indigenous approach to inquiry. *Journal of Research Practice, 10*(2).

Todd, Z. (2016). An Indigenous feminist's take on the ontological turn: 'Ontology' is just another word for colonialism. *Journal of Historical Sociology, 29*(1). https://doi.org/10.1111/johs.12124

Tuck, E., & Gaztambide-Fernández, R. A. (2013). Curriculum, replacement, and settler futurity. *Journal of Curriculum Theorizing, 29*(1).

Tuck, E., & Yang, K. W. (2012). Decolonization is not a metaphor. *Decolonization: Indigeneity, education & society, 1*(1).

Turnbull, S. (2013). *The Samurai: a military history*. Routledge.

Ultimate Fighting Championship (UFC). (2024). *Unified rules of mixed martial arts*. https://www.ufc.com/unified-rules-mixed-martial-arts

Valdemar Santana. (2023, May 6). *Wikimedia Commons*. https://commons.wikimedia.org/w/index.php?title=File:Valdemar_Santana.jpg&oldid=760325637.

Varela, S. G. (2017). *Power in practice: The pragmatic anthropology of Afro-Brazilian ca-poeira*. Berghahn Books.

Vice, S. (2021). Integrity, self-respect, and white privilege. In S. Hunter & C. van der West-huizen (Eds.), *Routledge handbook of critical studies in whiteness* (1st ed.). Routledge. https://doi-org.ezproxy.tcu.edu/10.4324/9780429355769-26

Visweswaran, K. (1994). *Fictions of feminist ethnography*. University of Minnesota Press. http://www.jstor.org/stable/10.5749/j.ctttf31

Wendt, A. (2015). *Quantum mind and social science: Unifying physical and social ontology*. Cambridge University Press.

CHAPTER TEN

Latherian Theorizing: A Post-Intentional Phenomenological Analytic Process Inspired by *Getting Lost* with Patti Lather

SARA K. STERNER

It is not a matter of looking harder or more closely, but of seeing what frames our seeing-spaces of constructed visibility and incitements to see which constitute power/knowledge.

Patti Lather (2007, p. 119)

Introduction

IN THIS CHAPTER, I share the development of Latherian theorizing, an analytic process that was inspired by the writing of Patti Lather (1993, 2007) and evolved from the research processes of a post-intentional phenomenological (Vagle 2014, 2015, 2018) research study. To set the context of the chapter, I provide an overview of post-intentional phenomenology, a snapshot of the larger study, and a discussion of the three-part analysis process the method employs, with an emphasis on thinking with theory (Jackson & Mazzei, 2012). The chapter continues with a further exploration of Latherian theorizing. I highlight how it developed as an analytic process rooted in post-intentional phenomenology and use direct examples from the study to illuminate the value and possibility of Latherian theorizing in other qualitative research studies. Woven throughout the chapter are explorations of the development process that illuminate the different ways that Lather's work inspired this analytic process.

Initial Connections: A Journey of Voice through Multilayered Writing

My first exposure to Patti Lather's work was through a narrative inquiry course completed during my doctoral studies. Lather's (1997) essay about creating multilayered texts was shared as an exemplar of a multivocal approach and style of narrative representation in academic writing. Engagement with this piece and her multilayered texts was pivotal for me, offering a scholarly space where I first felt truly at home as a writer in academia. This format of academic writing pushes the boundaries of traditional texts with different formatting styles, split pages, footnotes, and endnotes used as narrative and analytical devices, and other means to engage in meaning-making and writing as praxis.

Lather's writing as productive disruption is most salient in the multilayered prose crafted for *Troubling the Angels: Women Living with HIV/AIDS* (Lather & Smithies, 1997). "The textual and interpretive practices [of creating multilayered texts] work toward a multiplicity and complexity of layers that unfold an event which exceeds our frames of reference, evolving insight into what not knowing means" (Lather, 1997, p. 254). This expansive understanding emphasizes that it is *both* the text that is created and the process of writing the text that are important to this assemblage. Engaging with Lather's method of crafting a multilayered text allowed me an iterative praxis in both the writing process and the research that I had not experienced before. In the act of writing and in the texts that are produced, the crafted compilation of words becomes an explicit textual assemblage and an embodied way to capture the elusive lines of flight that emerge through the process.

Exploring multilayered writing was transformational for me as a scholar, and I eventually developed a form of multilayered writing based on Lather's work (Sterner & Fisher, 2020). In my writing experimentation with the form, my layered texts have included a purposeful interplay of images with captions (visual vignettes), sidebars, footnotes, and/or endnotes. When I am writing a multilayered text, I do not write sequentially but move throughout the layers, shifting between them in a multilayered process of thinking and writing. In many respects, each layer is always in a process of becoming—being made and unmade as I move between them, following the lines of flight (Deleuze & Guattari, 1987) of my writing. As one line of flight leaks into another, I try to follow it where it will take me. Latherian theorizing was born out of this engagement with the complexities and polyphonous aspects of Lather's multilayered writing.

Contextualizing Latherian Theorizing in the Theoretical-Methodological Framework of Post-Intentional Phenomenology

Phenomenology as a qualitative research method has many different branches, which can be used as both a theoretical lens and a methodological process to engage with phenomena as they are experienced. Phenomenology, at its core, is the study of phenomena and how they are manifested in the world. Current theoretical understandings of phenomenology are grounded in the philosophical teachings of Edmund Husserl and Martin Heidegger[1] (Dahlberg, et al., 2008; Sokolowski, 2000; Vagle, 2014; 2015; 2018). However, contemporary phenomenologists (Dahlberg et al., 2008; Dahlberg & Dahlberg, 2020; Giorgi, 1985, 2005; van Manen, 2016; van Manen & van Manen, 2021) have developed beyond the initial philosophical understandings of the field into current-day theoretical and qualitative research methodologies. The strength of the philosophical origins and the early methods of Husserl and Heidegger vary in modern methods depending on the type of phenomenology framing the theoretical orientation of the study. As different expressions of phenomenology continue to develop as qualitative research methods, it is important to be aware of the distinctive onto-epistemological and philosophical characteristics that are core to the conceptual frameworks for each.

Post-Intentional Phenomenology: A Brief Overview

In addition to originating from the larger tradition of phenomenology, post-intentional phenomenology is also grounded in post-structuralism, Deleuzoguattarian (Deleuze & Guattari, 1987) concepts of the rhizome and lines of flight, and has some components that are directly connected to Lather's work. Vagle (2018) points scholars to Lather's work, adding this exact quote (from the original 1993) to his discussion of post-reflexivity, to emphasize the need for post-intentional phenomenologists to "see what frames our seeing" (p. 32) as part of this approach. By signifying the *post* aspect of the theory, this framework recognizes that there is no one set way of knowing phenomena because they are "partial, situated, endlessly deferred and circulating through relations" (Vagle, 2014, pp. 111–112). This focus on "post-ness" also regards knowledge, ways of being, and identity as fluid, always complex, and multiple in its manifestations. This particular method, because of the way it endeavors to find the productions and provocations of a phenomenon (Vagle, 2015; 2018) and its distinctive methodological components, opened up the opportunity for Latherian theorizing.

Central to this branch of phenomenology is a recognition that phenomena are produced in varied and multiple contexts and are constantly fluctuating, being both made and unmade in the process. With the influence of the French philosophers Deleuze and Guattari, post-intentional phenomenology engages closely with their concept of lines of flight (1987) as one approach to conceive the many, partial, and tentative multiplicities of phenomena (Vagle, 2014; 2015; 2018). For Deleuze and Guattari, lines of flight are intricately linked to the idea of assemblage, or the layered and entangled aspects of the lifeworld. Following the possible lines of flight allows the post-intentional phenomenologist to consider the productions and provocations of phenomena as they take shape, "flee, elude, flow, and leak" (Vagle, 2015, p. 11). The move to consider lines of flight expands considerations of phenomena beyond Husserl and Heidegger, acknowledging their elusive nature. With this understanding, the post-intentional phenomenologist recognizes that we are always entering the middle (Vagle, 2014; 2018) of the entangled and partial productions and provocations of phenomena under study.

Also central to post-intentional phenomenology is the role that poststructural studies plays in the understanding of intentionality, a core concept in phenomenology. In post-intentional phenomenology, a single intentionality no longer exists, and intentionality must become plural. Post-intentional phenomenologists bring intentionalities to the table to see the connections that are manifest through the assemblages and lines of flight of the phenomenon as it is experienced by real, fleshed, bodily people living in the world. Embracing intentionalities also creates opportunities to glimpse the phenomena as they are being experienced (Vagle & Hofsess, 2016), even though that glimpse is tentative, partial, elusive, and multi-directional.

Post-intentional phenomenology seeks to "see what the phenomenon might become" (Vagle, 2018, p. 136) by noticing how a "post-intentional phenomenon is produced and produces, is provoked and provokes—through social relations in the world" (Vagle, 2018, p. 140). It recognizes that phenomena are constantly being made and unmade and thus are ever-evolving, multiple and partial, sometimes concretely expressed, at other times elusive to grasp. The assumptions and philosophical grounding of post-intentional phenomenology offer a pathway to "contemplate and theorize the various ways things manifest and appear in and through our being in the world" (Vagle, 2018, p. 23), while also providing a tangible means to explore phenomena as they take shape, in their multiple/partial/varied/complex manifestations, productions, and provocations.

The methodology of post-intentional phenomenology.

To make the shift from philosophical theory to a concrete methodology, Vagle has created a methodological process that is both philosophically grounded and provides a practical means to engage with phenomena under study. The method of research consists of five components:

1. Identify a post-intentional phenomenon in context(s), around a social issue;

2. Devise a clear yet flexible process for gathering phenomenological material appropriate for the phenomenon under investigation;

3. Make a post-reflexive plan;

4. Explore the post-intentional phenomenon using theory, phenomenological material, and post-reflexions;

5. Craft a text that engages in the productions and provocations of the post-intentional phenomenon in context(s), around a social issue. (Vagle, 2018, p. 139)

Additionally, Vagle recognizes that post-intentional phenomenology as qualitative research has the dual characteristics of Method (philosophy/theory) and method (a five-component process). The convergence of the Method of post-intentional phenomenology's founding understandings of phenomena (rooted in post-structuralism and philosophy) combined with the method, create a clearly delineated yet still flexible means to explore the multiplicities of the phenomena. Each of these aspects of post-intentional phenomenology served as the foundation for the development of Latherian theorizing, especially the analytic process I followed in component four of the method.

Post-intentional phenomenology: Methodological assemblage.

Another important contextual component of post-intentional phenomenology, central to the development of Latherian theorizing, is that it both allows *and* encourages the weaving of other methodologies into the research process, especially if those methods help to illuminate the phenomenon as it manifests in the moment of study (Vagle, 2014; 2018). Thus, in my post-intentional phenomenological research, I include narrative inquiry (Clandinin & Connelly, 2000; Connelly & Clandinin, 2006) to "explode beyond tradition" and craft at least some part of the story of the phenomenon in an artful manner (Vagle, 2014, p. 136). It is in this aspect of post-intentional phenomenology where I bring in the Lather-inspired multilayered texts. The creation of such complex texts to share my findings allowed me to engage deeply in the complexities and multivocality of the phenomenon I studied.

Through the process of crafting the different layers of multilayered texts, I create opportunities to both reflect upon, and illuminate how, the phenomenon is lived out in the world and in the phenomenological materials explored in the study. This layered approach to writing about and through complex phenomena allows an opportunity to engage in "the textual possibilities for telling stories that situate researchers not so much as experts 'saying what things mean' in terms of 'data,'. . . . [Instead] the researcher is situated as witness giving testimony to the lives of others" (Lather, 2007, p. 41), in my case the productions and provocations of the phenomenon. It is in the process of crafting the layers, or the art of the narrative format, where phenomena begin to open up for me and Lather's influence in my writing is evident. The layering, and the process of layered writing, gives me a different access point to consider any given exploration of a phenomenon, and this writing is a locus of praxis (Lather, 2007). Together, with the study focus, each of these aspects of writing, post-intentional phenomenological M/method, and the layered assemblage of the iterative research process created a rich space for me to engage with Lather's influence on a more analytic level.

A Context for Latherian Theorizing: A Study of Reading Whitely

Latherian theorizing originated within the context of my work on a larger post-intentional phenomenological study of the dominant reading experiences that shape readers, a phenomenon I characterize as reading whitely (Sterner, 2019a, 2019b, 2023). In addition to the theoretical commitments of post-intentional phenomenology, the study is grounded at the theoretical nexus of teacher education (Davey, 2013; Darling-Hammond & Bransford, 2005), children's and adolescent literature (Bishop, 1990; Derman-Sparks, 2013; Thomas, 2016), culturally relevant pedagogy (Ladson-Billings, 1995, 2006, 2014; Gay, 2000, 2002a, 2002b), and second-wave white teacher identity studies (Jupp et al., 2016; Jupp & Lensmire, 2016). Using the five-component method noted earlier and taking up these theoretical framings, I investigated productions and provocations of reading whitely in the lived experiences of the study participants, many among them preservice teachers.

Based on the theoretical framing, I conceptualized reading whitely as a phenomenon that takes shape in reading experiences produced and provoked in contexts where regularized understandings of normalcy and discourses of influence are steeped in the hegemony of white cultural norms and white supremacy. Reading whitely is a phenomenon that often works in the background; thus, it is an adverse and pernicious influence that is often overlooked. A crucial objective of the study was to begin to reveal how reading whitely takes shape and consider what it means to read whitely. In being able to grasp, even if momentarily, a deeper understanding of the phenomenon, it served as an initial step for its disruption.

The study was conducted with an undergraduate children's literature course focused on developing knowledge of diversity of formats, genres, and representation in literatures for young people. Situated in the macro context of the field of children's literature and education and the micro context of the collective experiences of the course's students and instructor, the participants' lived experiences of reading whitely guided the study. The phenomenological materials generated from the study include course design and planning, instructional pedagogies, course materials, completed assignments, classroom interactions, and focal student interviews. The analytic process, using the three-part method of post-intentional phenomenological analysis (Vagle, 2018), engaged with the productions and provocations of reading whitely to explore the intensities of the phenomenon and its vivid illuminations. This analytical shift provided a means to consider the phenomenon in intricate and multifaceted ways and opened up a context for the development of Latherian theorizing as one method of analysis.

Process for Data Analysis and the Value of Thinking with Theory

To continue to unpack how Latherian theorizing developed in my work, it is crucial to further explain the process for analysis in post-intentional phenomenology. While it uses the traditional whole-part-whole analysis process that is common to phenomenology, it has additional components that guide philosophically oriented considerations of the phenomenon. Vagle's (2018) iteration of the methodology brings together a three-part analysis process (Component 4): deconstruct the wholes of the phenomenological materials; think with theory (Vagle employs Jackson & Mazzei's 2012 conceptualization of formally thinking with theory as a plugging-in process for this stage of analysis); and analyze post-reflexions. While these exist as individual and seemingly linear elements of analysis, in practice they are taken up in a rhizomatic manner that ebbs and flows, builds on intensities, and follows the intertangled path of openness, wonder, and inquiry (Vagle, 2018) that is foundational to this method.

As post-intentional phenomenological analysis methods have evolved with each iteration of the M/method (Vagle 2014; 2018), the addition of the methodological process of thinking with theory (Jackson & Mazzei, 2012) as a formal part of the analysis has made an indispensable impact on the research process. Bringing theory to the next layer of analysis flows into an exploration of the phenomenological materials that illuminates the productions and provocations of a phenomenon. Thinking with theory allows a post-intentional phenomenologist to step outside of themselves and purposefully think with a powerful theoretical concept or theorist. This process provides a path for deeper exploration of the phenomenon and how it is being shaped and manifested in the phenomenological materials. In the next section of the chapter, I explore how I was able to "engage plugging in as a *process* rather than a concept, something [I] could put to work" (Jackson & Mazzei, 2012, p. 1, emphasis original) and embrace multiple theoretical concepts to "incite the provocations to be found in a plugging of theory into data into theory" (Jackson & Mazzei, 2012, p. 10). In this case, I shift from thinking with theory to thinking with a theorist, Patti Lather.

Phenomonological Material Under Analysis: The Readerography

To engage with reading whitely in this study, I selected a single course assignment, the Readerography, as my focal phenomenological material. The Readerography is a reading biography that asks students to explore their identity as readers and consider which books have been important in their reading lives. With an emphasis on consciousness raising, after sharing their book lists with one another, students are subsequently asked to analyze the titles on their list, shifting from discussing their Readerography titles to critically analyzing them. I have characterized this moment as the pivot because the tenor of the room often takes a radical shift in that moment. Throughout the analysis process, I considered the Readerography through different lenses, selecting four specific elements of the assignment that would be most beneficial to reveal the productions and provocations of reading whitely: assignment, list, pivot, and response. Through this shifting of focus, I recognize the Readerography as one large cohesive whole that is a collection of smaller wholes vibrating with meaning.

Latherian Theorizing: Getting Lost in the Phenomenon and Finding New Ways of Knowing

Texts that do justice to the complexity of what we know and understand include the tales not told, the words not written or transcribed, the words thought but not uttered, the unconscious: all that gets lost in the telling and the representing. My argument is that a stance of "getting lost" might both produce different knowledge and produced knowledge differently. . . .

—Patti Lather (2007, p. 13)

During the study of reading whitely, as I was collecting phenomenological material, post-reflexing, and beginning the process of analysis, I read Lather's *Getting Lost: Feminist Efforts Toward a Double(d) Science* (2007) as a pathway for theorizing my work. At the time I was struggling with what theory to think with as I analyzed the final component of the Readerography, the response. With relative ease, I had been able to find powerful theories to think with for the other components of the Readerography. Yet, in engaging with the participants' responses to the Readerography assignment I continued to be unable to find a theory that would help illuminate this especially complex and tangled provocation of reading whitely. Throughout my post-reflexive journal, there were starts and stops as I attempted plugging in with one potential theory or another. I felt lost.

Where It Started: The Development of Latherian Theorizing

Returning to Lather's writing in this moment was both a comfort and a challenge. This particular text guided me to attempt to engage in a "useful practice of getting lost as a fertile space for shifting imaginaries in the human sciences" (Lather, 2007, p. xii). Recognizing that one component of writing as praxis and attempting to shift the imaginaries of my exploration of reading whitely was to engage with Lather's book in a multilayered manner. To guide that process, I created a note-taking routine as an attempt to "do justice to the complexity" (Lather, 2007, p. 13) of knowing, telling, and representing the fleeting, shifting, wispiness of reading whitely. In creating a structured but flexible means to interact with each chapter, I was able to consider the methodological openings that Lather suggests. The process revealed an iterative space for praxis-making. It was my first step toward "thinking with Lather" and allowing myself to embrace getting lost along the way.

The original Latherian thinking process: Notes on Getting Lost.

To craft these multilayered notes, I set up my post-reflective notebook in a specific way each time I read a different chapter of *Getting Lost* (Lather, 2007). Knowing that representing the lines of flight of my thinking processes would be incomplete, I attempted to work toward a Lather-informed Deleuzean "stumbling" practice (Lather, 2007, p. 13) while I read. It was important for me to have space on the paper for this process, so I opened my post-reflexive notebook to a two-page spread. On the left-side page, I created three columns with headings (quotes, revisit/theoretical pulls, and ideas/intensities), and I left the right-side page blank to give space to "produce knowledge differently" (see Figure 1: Original Latherian Thinking Process). The juxtaposition of a more bounded and defined space on the left and the open rhizomatic space on the right allowed a surrender to the complexity.

Figure 10.1 Original Latherian Thinking Process

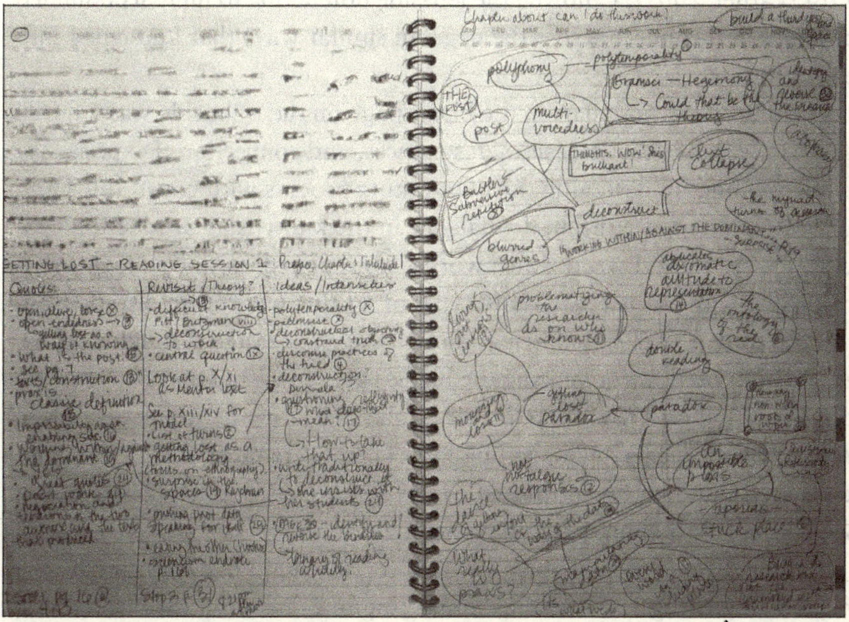

It is compelling to see the visual representation of the multiplicities at play in this noticing/noting process that captured a moment in time. While there is a messiness in the handwritten and interlacing play of what I have written, it powerfully captures my rhizomatic experience of sense-making. It is a starting place in which I am attempting to engage in "a 'field of representation' (producing different knowledge, resisting table meaning)" (Jackson & Mazzei, 2012, p. 2) and begin to do justice to the representation of that process. Part of the approach I used was grounded in the known, using some of my regular note-taking practices of work organized in a linear fashion, capturing resonant quotes and information through a bulleted style list on the left side. Holding on to this component of familiarity started as a signpost to guide me into the praxis of writing. It is important to recognize that the unspoken voice of how unbounded I felt is not actually represented on the page. I was fighting being lost, rather than embracing its potential.

In drawing the three columns, an initial anchoring space was generated on the page, and I was able to release some of what was holding me back. At first, I reveled in the bound linearity of this information-gathering space on the page. Eventually, though, as I settled into my engagement with *Getting Lost* (Lather, 2007), I allowed the left-side notetaking to jump its bounded columns and connect across the page, in similar ways that I designed into the right side.

Without any boundaries, the blank page on the right side was a fertile space to lean into the intensities, resonances, and connections I experienced while reading. In designing the note-taking process with constrained and unconstrained space, I found a balance in the knowledge production process. On the right, I wrote down words, concepts, ideas, and thoughts that resonated with me as I read. Both types of writing were taken directly from the text and as swells of information that were generated through reading. As I felt no need for organizing the blank page, I was not concentrating on the formatted representation, rather on the free flow of my experience as a reader deeply engaged with getting lost. There were times when I felt compelled to bound off my jottings in circles and boxes as part of this process, which gave me a glimpse into the potential for analysis.

After reading each chapter, I would revisit what I had captured on the page, recognizing and drawing connecting lines between the resonances, which would further my thinking. Employing this twofold noting activity allowed me to chase multiple lines of flight as I read. It also built a powerful crescendo of my thinking, reading, and theorizing to produce new knowledge. Upon reflection of this generative form of writing as praxis, I realized it had the potential to be used for analysis of the final component of studying reading whitely as it was produced and provoked in participant reactions to the Readerography.

Theory at Work: Latherian Theorizing

In the culminating exploration of reading whitely and the analysis of the reactions of my participants, I shifted from Jackson and Mazzei's (2012) thinking with theory to thinking with Lather (2007), expanding on the way I took up Latherian thinking (just detailed). To enact the Latherian theorizing technique, I used two aspects of bringing Lather to work: employing Lather's scholarship about validity in qualitative research and using it as a meaning-making path and the thinking/writing/production process that evolved from getting lost with and engaging in her writing. This theoretical focus opened up a generative path to consider how reading whitely has taken shape in the participant responses to the Readerography and the pivot. Making the shift from noting to Latherian theorizing allowed the provocations of reading whitely to explode and be revealed in the phenomenological materials and the knowledge production process itself.

To adapt my thinking from a note-taking knowledge generation process to analysis, I used a similar format with three-bounded columns on the left and the open page on the right for intensities and explosions that flow out of the deconstruction/reconstruction analysis. (See Figure 10.2: Latherian Theorizing Process.) To fit the phenomenological material of the response and the post-intentional phenomenological focus of this study, I altered the bounded left-side headings in the first two columns. Changing from the focus I used in notetaking (quotes and revisit/theoretical pulls) helped me engage in a more analytic stance, with a new focus on noticings/questions that emerge and ideas/intensities. It also brought the previous knowledge development from the phenomenological materials, post-reflexive journaling, and analytic theorizing to bear (Vagle, 2018) in the process. The final column on the left side remains the same, as a space for capturing ideas and intensities. The right side of the notebook functions in the same way as my original Latherian thinking process, serving as a space to capture the resonances that materialize from the analysis. To enhance the analysis, I included another layer into the "plugging in" (Jackson & Mazzei, 2012; Vagle, 2018) process and color-coded the different phenomenological materials under review (general participant responses, focal participant responses, and researcher responses). In the interplay of each of these components of Latherian theorizing, I captured something that might be lost in another text or in another theorization and meaning-making production.

Latherian theorizing in this manner was dynamic and generative. It evolved and resonated more as I engaged with the phenomenological materials, while remaining rooted in the original design of thinking with a theorist. As seen in Figure 10.2, I was able to chase lines of flight while capturing them visually on a page (as much as it is possible to represent such ephemeral tendrils of meaning in any textual capturing). Through this analysis, I was able to note the identities of each phenomenological material and allow myself to jump into the production of knowledge in unexpected ways. It was also a vibrant way to engage with an embodied post-structural meaning-making and the chasing of lines of flight that underpins post-intentional phenomenology. Latherian theorizing created a space to analyze differently

Figure 10.2 Latherian Theorizing Process

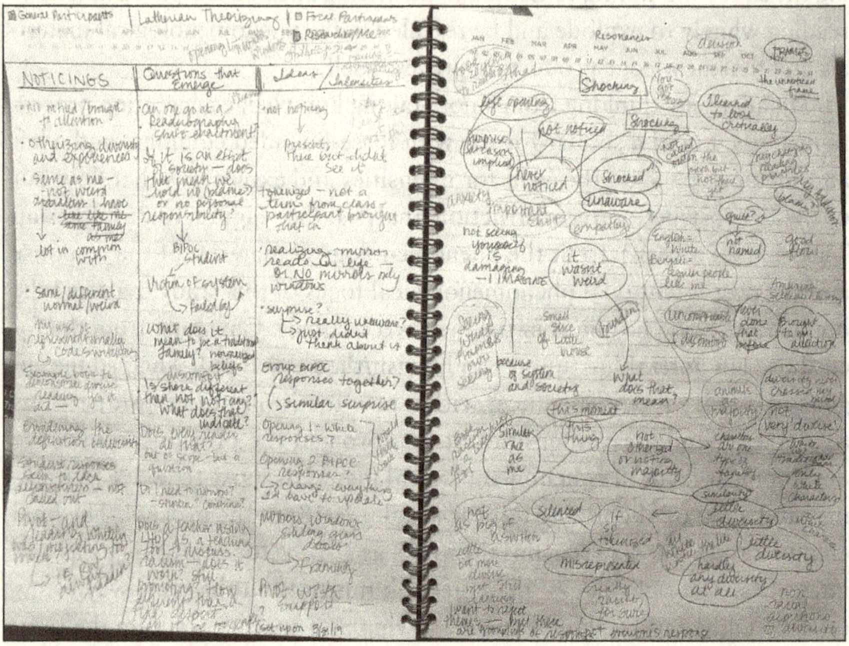

—to assume an analysis as a rhizomatic entanglement that ebbs and flows, builds on intensities, and follows a path of openness, wonder, and inquiry (Vagle, 2018). It captured the progression of getting lost in and through the analysis and led to a greater depth in my understanding that would not have been achieved without the undertaking.

Productions of Getting Lost Through Latherian Theorizing

In sharing how Latherian theorizing developed in and through my research, I hope to encourage other researchers to explore the methodological possibilities for its use in their work. In closing, I forward two aspects of Latherian theorizing that I feel are deeply valuable from a qualitative analysis perspective. I have argued that it is an analytic pathway that has the potential for enacting "a stance of 'getting lost' [that] might both produce different knowledge and produced knowledge differently" (Lather, 2007, p. 13). Bringing methodologically intriguing analysis is a crucial component of the expansion of qualitative research.

Seeing the Frame: A Revelatory Nature of Latherian Theorizing

Latherian theorizing opens one way to glimpse the unseen and the partially seen manifestations of phenomena through analysis. Taking up this process to explore reading whitely created a meaning-making path to see how it was *taking* shape (explicitly and implicitly) in the responses to the Readerography and the pivot. Seeing what frames our seeing, as researchers, is a recognition that we as subjects are always products of the internal and external structures that consciously and unconsciously impact our meaning-making processes. The way we speak and act in the world is framed by the multiplicities of our identities, social interactions, systems of power, oppressive structures, and the collected realities of our lived experiences. It is a polyphonic conglomeration of our ways of being and knowing in the world. Just as a window frame may fade into the background as we gaze through the glass, these influences become the normalized structure that is often no longer seen. Unlike a window, though, systems of power and oppressive structures, especially for those in the dominant culture, might have never been seen in the first place. It is important to shift our gaze and look more closely at that which has been rendered invisible.

Iterative journeys of Latherian theorizing.

The use of Latherian theorizing also allowed for an iterative journey that led to a crafted text. Taking up the focal elements of the phenomenological materials when plugged into Latherian theorizing produced more knowledge about reading whitely, exposing productions of the phenomenon that needed further illumination. Informed by the productions that emerged from the Latherian theorizing process, I crafted a poem that represented participant responses in a multilayered text (Sterner, 2019a). Getting lost in this journey to theory allowed me to consider how reading whitely was provoked in the participant responses and then radiated intensities that took shape as I crafted them into the poetic construction. The intensities and explosions of the phenomenon that I captured on the right side of the Latherian theorizing process reverberated with similar pulses, and connections were revealed as I worked to deconstruct the wholes of the responses and take them up theoretically. This is a powerful outgrowth of both the Latherian theorizing process and the process/product of the poetic construction itself.

Conclusion: Engaging in the Complexity

My previous life as an elementary school teacher was deeply steeped in the complex and intermingled narratives of the field. Always present were the voices of children, challenges and joys of teaching, rhetoric of what it means to be an elementary school teacher, and forces of the system of education ebbing and flowing in the work. In my graduate studies, my knowledge as an elementary educator were not always valued as a form of knowing. Furthermore, this background of knowingness was often minimized by the scholarly demands expected of the academy. Through the lens of Lather's multilayered writing, I felt a deep place of knowing. Finding this representation of the multiplicities of experience and voice was a scholarly home that beckoned to me. Having that home place evolve into a process for analysis and expansion of my research as a post-intentional phenomenologist was extremely powerful for me as a scholar.

Latherian theorizing, as I have applied it, is a different approach to engage with theory that creates a pathway for *getting lost* in the analysis process. It served as a framing to "produce different knowledge and produce knowledge differently" while thinking with Lather (2007, p. 13). It also embodies the lived theorizing that emerged during my study of reading whitely.

Throughout this chapter, I have shared multiple ways in which thinking with a theorist and Latherian theorizing was a place of synthesis. It allowed a convergence of the theoretical and conceptual framing that shaped my study and also expanded beyond synthesis into a generative production. Moreover, I share Latherian theorizing as a recognition of how Patti Lather has played a role in my academic life as a scholarly foremother. I am ever grateful for how her writing allowed me to both be found in the academy and get beautifully lost in the work.

Note

1. I note this philosophical lineage here as a tracing of the Western philosophical roots of phenomenology. I also recognize that Heidegger's association with, and membership in, the Nazi party is absolutely indefensible. His work is tainted because of that reality. I continue to further interrogate this history and to consider how best to engage with these roots of the philosophy that acknowledge and respond to the tensions of its foundations in productive and disruptive ways.

References

Bishop, R. S. (1990). Mirrors, windows, and sliding glass doors. *Perspectives: Choosing and Using Books for the Classroom, 6*(3), ix–xi.

Clandinin, D. J., & Connelly, F. M. (2000). *Narrative inquiry: Experience and story in qualitative research.* Jossey-Bass.

Connelly, F. M., & Clandinin, D. J. (2006). Narrative inquiry. In J. Green, G. Camilli, & P. Elmore (Eds.), *Handbook of complementary method in education research* (pp. 477–488). Lawrence Erlbaum Associates.

Dahlberg, H., & Dahlberg, K. (2020). Phenomenology of science and the art of radical questioning. *Qualitative Inquiry, 26*(7), 889–896. https://doi.org/10.1177/1077800419897702

Dahlberg, K., Dahlberg, H., & Nystrom, M. (2008). *Reflective lifeworld research* (2nd ed.). Studentlitteratur.

Darling-Hammond, L., & Bransford, J. (Eds.). (2005). *Preparing teachers for a changing world: What teachers should learn and be able to do.* John Wiley & Sons.

Davey, R. (2013). *The professional identity of teacher educators: Career on the cusp?* Routledge.

Deleuze, G., & Guattari, F. (1987). *A thousand plateaus; Capitalism and schizophrenia.* (B. Massumi, Trans.). University of Minnesota Press.

Derman-Sparks, L. (2013). Guide for selecting anti-bias children's books. Teaching for Change. [Weblog]. http://www.teachingforchange.org/selecting-anti-bias-books

Gay, G. (2000). *Culturally responsive teaching: Theory, research, & practice.* Teachers College, Columbia University.

Gay, G. (2002a). Preparing for culturally responsive teaching. *Journal of Teacher Education, 53*(2), 106–116. doi:10.1177/0022487102053002003

Gay, G. (2002b). Culturally responsive teaching in special education for ethnically diverse students: Setting the stage. *Qualitative Studies in Education, 15*(6), 613–629. doi:10.1080/0951839022000014349"

Giorgi, A. (1985). *Phenomenology and psychological research.* Duquesne University Press.

Giorgi, A. (2005). The phenomenological movement and research in the human sciences. *Nursing Science Quarterly, 18*(1), 75–82.

Jackson, A. Y., & Mazzei, L. (2012). *Thinking with theory in qualitative research: Viewing data across multiple perspectives* (1st ed.). Routledge.

Jupp, J. C., & Lensmire, T. J. (2016). Second-wave white teacher identity studies: Toward complexity and reflexivity in the racial conscientization of white teachers. *International Journal of Qualitative Studies in Education, 29*(8), 985–988. doi:10.1080/09518398.2016.1189621

Jupp, J. C., Berry, T. R., & Lensmire, T. J. (2016). Second-wave white teacher identity studies. *Review of Educational Research, 86*(4), 1151–1191. doi:10.3102/0034654316629798

Ladson-Billings, G. (1995). Toward a theory of culturally relevant pedagogy. *American Educational Research Journal, 32*(3), 465–491. doi:10.2307/1163321

Ladson-Billings, G. (2006). "Yes, but how do we do it?": Practicing culturally relevant pedagogy. In J. Landsman & C. W. Lewis, (Eds.), *White teachers, diverse classrooms:*

A guide to building inclusive schools, promoting high expectations, and eliminating racism (pp. 29–42). Stylus.

Ladson-Billings, G. (2014). Culturally relevant pedagogy 2.0: Aka the remix. *Harvard Educational Review, 84*(1), 74–84.

Lather, P. (1993). Fertile obsession: Validity after poststructuralism. *The Sociological Quarterly, 34*(4), 673–693.

Lather, P. (1997). Creating a multilayered text: Women, AIDS, and angels. In W. G. Tierney & Y. S. Lincoln (Eds.), *Representation and the text: Re-framing the narrative voice.* (pp. 233–258). State University of New York Press.

Lather, P. (2007). *Getting lost: Feminist efforts toward a double(d) science* (SUNY series, second thoughts). State University of New York Press.

Lather, P., & Smithies, C. (1997). *Troubling the angels: Women living with HIV/AIDS.* Westview Press.

Sokolowski, R. (2000). *Introduction to phenomenology.* Cambridge University Press.

Sterner, S. K. (2019a). *A post-intentional phenomenological exploration of reading whitely* (Order No. 13902840) [Doctoral dissertation, University of Minnesota Twin Cities]. ProQuest Dissertations & Theses Global. https://www.proquest.com/dissertations-theses/post-intentional-phenomenological-exploration/docview/2624891362

Sterner, S. K. (2019b). The phenomenon of reading whitely: A post-intentional phenomenological exploration. CLA Research Award Précis. *Journal of Children's Literature, 45*(1), pp. 64–67.

Sterner, S. K. (2023). Chasing lines of flight: Using post-intentional phenomenology for educational research. In J. DeHart (Ed.), *Phenomenological studies in education* (pp. 1–21). IGI Global. https://doi.org/10.4018/978-1-6684-8276-6.ch001

Sterner, S. K., & Fisher, L. C. (2020). Expanding academic writing: A multilayered exploration of what it means to belong. *Taboo: The Journal of Culture and Education, 19*(5). https://digitalscholarship.unlv.edu/taboo/vol19/iss5/5

Thomas, E. E. (2016). Stories still matter: Rethinking the role of diverse children's literature today. *Language Arts, 94*(2), 112.

Vagle, M. D. (2014). *Crafting phenomenological research* (1st ed.). Left Coast Press.

Vagle, M. D. (2015). Curriculum as post-intentional phenomenological text: Working along the edges and margins of phenomenology using post-structuralist ideas. *Journal of Curriculum Studies, 47*(5), 594–612.

Vagle, M. D. (2018). *Crafting phenomenological research* (2nd ed.). Routledge.

Vagle, M. D., & Hofsess, B. (2016). Entangling a post-reflexivity through post-intentional phenomenology. *Qualitative Inquiry, 22*(5), 334–344

van Manen, M. (2016). *Writing in the dark: Phenomenological studies in interpretive inquiry* (1st ed.). Routledge. https://doi.org/10.4324/9781315415574

van Manen, M., & van Manen, M. (2021). Doing phenomenological research and writing. *Qualitative Health Research, 31*(6), 1069–1082. https://doi.org/10.1177/10497323211003058

CHAPTER ELEVEN

Notes on Research as an Occasion for Education

Deborah P. Britzman

Research no longer merely seeks successful comprehension. It returns to things that it cannot understand. It measures what it loses by fortifying its needs and methods.

Michel de Certeau (1988, p. 39)

Let us appreciate Patti Lather's research for its involvement in blending the language of time, place, and space with keen theoretical ideas, and further, for rethinking the ways a story unfolds as its education. Lather's significant contributions begin with relating the human sciences and their contentions of life's conditions with their methods of study. By this, I refer to the ability to treat research as situation, as subject to concern for its problems, methods, theories, and fields of data, and as an object of its interventions. It is human science as its education; research that reads itself reading. From my psychoanalytic vantage point, this polymorphous research presents its emotional situation as affected by the course of its studies, by what it does not know, and by what can push against its practices.

Lather possesses the rare talent of working between the cracks of practice and its theoretical lines, treating qualitative research and data as a strange conductor. Her research constellation comprises feminism, Marxism, critical theory, poststructuralism, postmodernism, deconstruction, new materialism, and post-truth. It also bears witness to the conflicts of late 20th century education: human rights, birth control, sexual freedom, intellectual adventure, and open-mindedness. These theoretical frames and the urgencies they meet and create serve as placeholders for elusive objects of study. To name just a few of Lather's research objects: Angels, Walter Benjamin, HIV-AIDS, Foucault, and Haraway (Lather & Smithies, 1997). Here, high theory entangles with popular culture, revealing the contentions of method, politics, policy, and science with issues of desire. Lather's (1986) groundbreaking paper, "Research as Praxis" used politics to unearth what methods of objectivity attempted to bury. Lather's (1991) first book—*Getting Smart*—opened the crypt of education with a question that can also be read as a manual for research on-demand: how to challenge relations of domination through pedagogy and research. For me, the key signifier in her early titled study belongs to the reach of 'getting' as in, 'getting to know,' and as unsettling procedures for experience on the move. It must be said that research against all odds is a working through of resistance and its defenses of stupefying arguments. It is research as a refocusing of attention, attitude, ideas, and interpretation.

Of course, Lather is not alone in these endeavors. Along with others who made it their work to freely associate with the problems of our time, Lather pressed the idea that there is more than one science. And she is in good company. Isabelle Stengers (2018), for example, writes in *Another Science is Possible*, a manifesto of 'slow science.' In thinking alongside Bruno Latour's frame of "matters of concern," Stengers (2018) proposes "there are situations that concern us before they become objects of preoccupation or choice, situations which, in order to be appropriately characterized, demand that 'we feel concern'" (p. 3). The felt concern is within the encounter, places where we live and meet practices of science. The felt concern is that in whatever form science takes, the abnormal, the anomaly, the accident, and the error set the structure going and implode its assumptions and prescriptions.

Another example of a science capable of critiquing the possibilities and obstacles to its limits of knowledge belongs to the work of Thomas Kuhn (1970) and his analysis of science textbooks. Textbooks are that other community of agreement over method, observation, and rules of conduct. Kuhn sees the conflicts of science as emerging in the education of the field and argued that as taught, normal science mainly seeks a puzzle that can be solved. Social science, he writes, considers unsolvable problems, anomalies, and the stuff that resists prevailing frames. Human science, such as invested practices of subjectivity like medicine, law, education, and social work, however, is different. Its field of humanity may be where we study not only the breakdown of meaning and the crisis of signification but also what we forget. Human science would be a problem of learning and what Freud noticed as a science of 'the impossible professions' (Britzman, 2009). Human sciences and its helping professions have as their conditions of possibility their obstacles to relationality. They are the playground of desire, transference, transformation, and resistance—places we live, work, imagine and, at times, suffer and so challenge what research can even mean.

Kuhn (1970) presented the field of education with the idea of its methods as *paradigm wars*. I want to note that his orientation was in the study of scientific communities of agreement and disagreement as founded by the education of the next generation and as found between the lines of the little textbook. And in this sense, Lather is known for entering the fray and, with commentary, makes room for others through her generous citations and interests in the wide world of theory. With *Getting Smart* (1991), and its companion or punctuation text *Getting Lost* (2009), Lather takes on the researcher's battles with form, style, argument, theory, language, and problems of communication. In any of her books, one will find fields of theory in search of open-ended phenomena and the obstacles met along the way. She invites readers to open the crypt of their education, so that all of us may wrest practices away from the pretense of mastery, measurement, omnipotence, and yes, normal science. The puzzle, she argues, has missing pieces. But because researchers work in their ruins, or in the fragments left over from experience, and because there are gaps, empty spaces, and loss, there is no whole story to recover.

My readings of Lather's work take the long view, thinking with pieces of our shared history and scenes of our uneven development to make a case for the study of the uncertainties and the chances we live. My frame in thinking with Lather is part nostalgia, part clinical in concern, and part affection for friendship. This constellation is driven by reading with *negative capabilities*, a clinical concept presented in the psychoanalytic work of Wilfred Bion (1994), known for his concern for the difficulties of thinking one's thoughts, the difficulties of tolerating uncertainty, and for thinking within the trouble made when linking together fragments of disparate themes with the conflicts they emit. Bion described this intimate difficulty through the tenders of emotional attitudes, created in everyday encounters with the unknown whenever people meet. And what is most unknown is the field of experience, or what Bion simply referred to as frustration. It is a different way of approaching the hazards of coming to know without the advance of understanding. Bion argued that thinking one's thoughts is a process of getting to know emotional experience and doing so by symbolizing frustration, doubt, paradox, uncertainty, and irony without reaching for quick solutions. Negative capabilities are cultivated because research has the double problem of finding and losing experience, or what Lather (2007) has termed as "getting lost." In my review of our friendship, I am after the return of felt experiences, or areas of shared concern that, while urgent at the time of their unfolding, still trouble our contemporary constructions, whether admitted or not.

Another lens into what has happened to research belongs to Certeau's (1993) case analysis of the Freudian novel. And it is true that one of the early drafts of one of Freud's (1939) last works, *Moses and Monotheism*, carried the subtitle, 'a Historical Novel.' Freud's last social study was a grand speculation on the nature of Jewish origin where a story of history is woven from the psychical dynamics of memory that involves forgetting, repression, and working through. As read by Certeau, 'The Freudian novel' emerges with the unease of knowledge and is oriented by their studies of incompleteness and their tendency toward disruption. Certeau (1993) wrote on the possibilities and improbabilities of knowledge in our age of great philosophical contradictions, where science cannot unify, where disunity is admitted, where limits are the defining feature of any paradigm, where communities of agreement dissolve onto conflict and change, where transference is ever present and transformative, and where the articulations of our exploratory frames are affected by and meet with the contingencies of history. This affected research into the uncertainties of our time carries debates on the status of otherness, exclusion, difference, and systematization. These uncertainties are embroiled in our theory and method wars.

Lather's writing against totality emerges from the cracks of narrative and the fertilities sown by praxis, an odd combination of theory and activity. The work is to think beyond the general appeal of critique and the splitting of the object from intersubjective life. The work is to take apart (deconstruct) the stalemate of words and consider their soft underbelly of discourse (and, here I am thinking of Lather's (2010) deconstruction of voice, empathy, and validity, for example). Room is created for our contentious discussions that focus the vulnerabilities and limits of our research frames.

In Lather's work, we find the wherewithal to undo what has been done, to bring into view the fractures of knowledge and do this with strong metaphors such as: fragility, incompleteness, fertile obsessions, validity, and getting lost. Here one can find populations of angels, bad girls, and the play of deconstruction that Lather described as "troubling."

Research can do the work of troubling clarity, troubling angels, troubling troubling, and troubling "the politics of accessible language" (Lather, 2010). Along with the melancholic science of Walter Benjamin (1999), Lather (1999) named this exploration as "working the ruins" and even later than that, could acknowledge the mess of research as tied to policy, pedagogy, governmentality, psychology, and professional conferences (Lather, 2009). Most noteworthy are dedicated questions such as: What is research for? What ends can be served by the study of method and interminability of research? And what is the work of theory, high and low?

I am a reader, fellow traveler, seeker, friend, and witness in Lather's wild world of research. It must be wild in the sense that research opens onto free association with an interest in bringing disparate themes into tension. In 2017, sponsored by my research chair in pedagogy and psychosocial transformations, Lather gave a talk at York University in Toronto. I had ambitions that included creating novel research with studies of *difficult knowledge* and proposed education and its research as an emotional situation always subject to transference, affect, anxiety, regression, the unconscious, and phantasies (Britzman, 2024). I wished to join clinical knowledge of psychoanalysis to literary scenes, aesthetics, and arguments over the possibilities of assuming a subjective position in a world compelled by flattening reality to a mode of virtual compliance with belief in symbolic equations.

Along with Lather, I, too, am after a different logic, one that involves psychical life with methods that construct, deconstruct, and elaborate a way of conceptualizing what the world is like and what the phenomenology of communicating the corners of our human conditions may open. Such concerns are elegantly described by Certeau (1988): "Psychoanalysis takes up the definition given to fiction as being knowledge jeopardized and wounded by its otherness (the affect, etc.) or a statement that the speaking subject's utterance deprives of its 'sérieux.' In the analytic field, this discourse is effective because it is "touched" or wounded by the affect (p. 27). Certeau was referencing absence and the losses of foundations, reliability, seriousness, consciousness, intentionality, completion, and self-agreement. Such study does emerge from the Freudian novel that privileges illusions, errors, mishearing, parapraxis, and dreams dedicated to the transference and the contingencies of its after-effects. It is this transitional space of culture and psychical life that research finds itself in and, as Lather (2007) has written, this is our way of getting lost, or our ticket to *Science without Foundations*. Certeau (1988) would put the problem as one of representation and not only as repeating an injury of realism: "Representation thus disguises the praxis that organizes it" (p. 203). Ten years later Gillian Rose (1996) would link representation to the dynamics of learning. "Learning in this sense mediates the social and the political: it works precisely by making mistakes, by taking the risk of action, and then by reflecting on its unintended consequences, and then taking the risk, yet again" (Rose, 1996, p. 38). Then, too, there would be unrepresented states, a noted shift that the psychoanalyst Gail Reed et al. (2018) described as situations of vulnerability, weakness, and danger created in the shifts "from a universe of presences to a universe of absences" (p. 3).

Lather and I did not write together, although many of our papers sit side by side as did our presentations, books, years of students, and of course our research conversations. We met at the crossroad of research, the heart of what, looking back, began as Method and Theory Wars—over critical pedagogy, ethnography, poststructuralism, postmodernism, feminism, and queer theory—signs of life that respond to the lockstep of quantitative methods where it could feel as if results, normativity, and generalizations too hastily overturn contingency, plurality, uneven development, and singularity. It was a time where the education of researchers foreclosed awareness of its investments in subjectivity, desire, and wild analysis. The American Educational Research Association (AERA) was one example of the foreclosure of wild research through its insistence that any proposal must first define data, reliability, validity, and outcomes. Of course, quantitative measurement was not the only game in town, and there was deep concern for studies of the quality of life inside and beyond the gates of education.

Around 1994, I sat next to Lather in a big AERA panel titled, Yes, But is it research? When each presenter was asked their hopes for the future of research, I recall stating in my most Foucauldian voice, "I hope research can become unintelligible to itself." That may have been my best projection. A few years later, in another AERA meeting, I was with Lather when we tried to discuss Derrida's study on mourning Marxism. At that time, we were accused of ruining Marxism with deconstruction.

One of the enigmatic panel proposals organized by Lather in 2019 had the title, Bad Girl Theory and Practice: Qualitative Research in Post-Truth Times. I sat there with Lather, Janet Miller, Lisa Weems, and Maggie Mac-Lure. We each had about 15 minutes to address the situation of *data*. From my view, data proposed a psychoanalytic situation, always already subject to interpreting the contingencies of dreamwork: the ways ideas assume their reversals, condensation, deferrals, substitutions, their limits of representation, and their undoing. After over 20 years of sending in American Educational Research Association proposals and attempting to stuff my work into their narrow template, after being subject to the pretense of blind referees and the frustration of significant rejections with the paltry sentence "no one would be interested," and, after being assigned to the tiniest presentation rooms, this 2019 panel would be our last in-person session before the fallout of the COVID-19 pandemic closed national borders, schools, universities, in-person public talks, and, of course, sent AERA into a tiny virtual and untenable space.

Five years earlier, around 2014, I submitted my lone proposal to an AERA poster session. I felt there could be informal exchange. Even then, the AERA template for proposal submission felt punitive, and because it was also a blind review, I did not cite my work. The proposal was accepted, but one reviewer warned that I should have cited Britzman. Indeed. Lest it seem like a carnival of complaints, along with Lather, these emotional situations behind the scenes of communicating research should suggest there is a conflict between education and freedom played out in the strictures of professional organizations and in normative conceptions of research. And these conflicts are encountered again through the ways the research story can be told. The working through is found when history returns (Britzman, 2024).

So one can now say the temple of data had deep roots in the frame imposed on our graduate education, where instead of asking, what is your situation and what are your areas of concern, we had to go find data, quantify its objects, verify its truth value, worry about the null hypothesis, and then generalize its value. I thought of it as education by numbers. The Internet had hardly begun, and computers in the early 1980s had to be programmed. Typewriters still ruled, paper galleys were mailed to authors and resent to publishers, and around 1978 new graduate students in education were advised to delay any qualitative and ethnographic work until after tenure. It was indeed a hostile, defended, and bossy education. It was a time when gay and lesbian teachers were fired from schools and where, in U.S. universities, faculty were asked to take patriotic loyalty oaths. But it was also a time of AIDS, social and governmental disavowal, and the beginnings of Queer activism, and ACT-UP in the street, in academic journals, films, and novels. Eve Kosofsky Sedgwick's (2011a) "Thinking Through Queer Theory" reflected on her academic beginnings as a new English Professor at Hamilton College, a small liberal arts college in New York State. Sedgwick was first hired with a short-term contract, and this, she argued, brought her intellectual freedom. Here is what it felt like to Eve:

> In the period around 1980 in the United States, feminist theory was at a particularly exciting, almost reckless, juncture. After a certain amount of additive scholarship in various disciplines, in which the writings or other achievements of a few women were simply added to the existing male canons, this was a time, instead, of very basic feminist challenges to the conceptual roots of the disciplines themselves. It was at this time that the claims of gender-free objectivity in the sciences, of phallic privilege in psychology, of the exclusive importance of statesman and warriors in history, of purely stylistic value judgments in literature were all subject to feminist attack at a radical level. A few big concepts, such as patriarchy, seemed to offer a lot of new critical leverage across disciplinary boundaries. (Sedgwick, 2011a, p. 192)

Later, Sedgwick (2011b) stated that learning and pedagogy felt like theory when she advised, "Take advantage of an understanding of theories as theory" (p. 160). This principle is one of contingency, plurality, and error, another definition of what theory, as well as learning, is like.

Lather began university teaching in those days. I came a few years later. In the early to mid-1980s, I was a graduate student in the theory/method wars in education. By the mid-1980s, these wars had to do with the status of identities in research, the methodologies praised and demonized, the conflicts of gender wars, racism, and inequality in representations of educational research, and with our choices of subjects and theoretical frames. Still, one could be involved in epistemological revolutions and in theoretical analysis of education by way of cultural studies, feminism, African American studies, Ethnic Studies, Marxism and structuralism, poststructuralism, and from the late 1980s on, new developments drew from psychoanalysis, queer theory, decolonization, and deconstruction. Such were the environmental influences and where margins became the frame.

Lather's many research interventions occur within this cacophony of history. Studies in education could then ask: What makes education intelligible? Why consider research as embodied? What happens to research when new vocabularies enter its fray? And what kind of science for what kind of policy for what kind of politics, and for what kind of life? (Lather, 2007; 2009). In Lather's work, research is representation's forensic and its praxis.

The quest for praxis began with Lather's claim in her 1986 *Harvard Educational Review* article, titled, "Research as Praxis." This was a paper that not only proved to become an extraordinary discourse effect, but it was also the only paper in the *Review* that quoted the lesbian songwriter, Chris Williams, quite a surprise to say nothing of opening research with the margins of erotic life. The novelty was that quoting would be akin to free association, that you could bring coded life into your discussions and fray the lines between high and low research cultures and play between the major and minor chords of education. The novelty was that "Research as Praxis" made us happy, for it posited the work of research as an open field of theoretical world-making, affected by that world, and affected by discourse.

I can say that around 1986 the character of educational research went through a significant change, even an epistemological break with the intelligibility of measurement. Lather's paper "Research as Praxis" was published at the beginning of the research wars in the field of education. It was a battle between quantitative and qualitative research and a breaking point in the hegemony of education's ties to measurement, intelligence testing, and justification of its own practices. It would take about 40 years to see qualitative work as normal and now, its methods, too, suffer from what we now can say is the crisis of representation, founded in the AIDS pandemic, feminism, homosexualities, Black liberation movements, demands for human rights, and First Nation reconciliation movements, to name some of the protests for difference and psychosocial transformations that have affected the way we do research now. Yes, something happened to paradigms. Research becomes both terminable and interminable.

Those educated in the late seventies and early eighties learned of 'Paradigm Wars' and the problems of discourse in the education of the human professions. These contentions of paradigm can now be considered as opening gambit for the education of the scientist, an important claim of John Forrester's (2017) study, *Thinking in Cases*. Forrester's concern was to treat research as a method of the close reading of transference, and so research became a means for encountering the fissures of knowledge behind the scenes. When reading any case study, Forrester advises readers to ask themselves questions such as what the researcher is responding to, what research invests in, and how the shape of its interventions admits the limits of knowledge. The issue was how we then read research: is our focus on diagnostics, experience, identificatory attachments, confirmation, or research as symptom? And, from whatever approach, would readers then be able to consider the ways they now read?

Lather and I have been friends for over 39 years. We have worked together on so many panels and sat through so many presentations at the American Educational Research Association, the Association for Educational Studies, the Philadelphia Ethnography Forum, and the Bergamo Conferences. We have published in the same journals and have book chapters in the same books. And we have struggled to have our say, even when what is said is not immediately understood. We have fought the wars in vocabulary and questioned the measures of legibility. We have asked, what is the use of theory? And, in our respective ways, we have enjoyed extracting experience from the anchors of compliance. We have each educated generations of doctoral students and saw them into their worlds. We remain good friends with warm attachments that should and do happen in research and in life. And over these many years, in listening to her many keynotes and reading her work, there are always surprises in citations, in ideas, in vocabulary, and in theories. And always, there is a care for thinking at the limit with what I have mentioned earlier as negative capabilities, or the toleration of frustration of experience without having to reach for quick solutions or without repressing the constitutive uncertainties of life's adventures and its underbelly of meanings.

And yet, even with my backward glance into time no longer, it must be admitted that qualitative research, even if one wishes to do this, is not easy to learn. Engagement within the qualities and negations of existential life is not simply writing down what others have said, finding the proper means to code, and then presenting the 'real' story. It is not a corrective but rather, qualitative research is a symptom of life in education. After all, in doing research one is already in life and cannot momentarily bracket out the larger world in which one lives. The surprise is that research is a relationship to both the self who searches and the one who tells the story. Data, then, has already been through the sieve of multiple structures of experience as well as carrying the aftereffects of institutional life and the fate of listening, speaking, reading, and writing. There is something utterly personal in finding one's way through the words and scenes of others. Almost unmentionable is what the interviewer learns about the self. What occurs is not quite portraiture or autobiography. And only later can researchers grapple with their preconceptions to learn of unconfirming theory. So, the amassing of details is other than the style of engagement. In getting to know, one may have to loosen anticipatory ties to representation and wrest oneself away from the nice story and the ideality of politics. One may have to admit that experience cannot be seen, that it can just as easily be obscured in the anxieties of appearance. With language, one may have to play in a field of confusion, indirection, mistaken views, and uncertainty. Language will not hold still, meaning escapes notice. Nor will the demands for representation be the end of the work.

Coda

Around 1998, Alice Pitt and I developed a qualitative research program around the question of what makes knowledge difficult in teaching and learning. Looking back, we were telling a story of impossible research (Pitt & Britzman, 2003). Our approach was psychoanalytic, and we wished to listen to data with a 'third ear,' meaning we tried to focus on the aporetic, with notice for fantasies that support knowledge claims of experience, attending to what was not being said and with metaphors indicating the hurdles of or defenses against narrative. We were interested in the gaps and breakdowns of memory. The issue was how to study resistance to learning as an aspect of learning. And, because anyone who studies education was once a child in school, we were interested in where childhood theories of learning showed in contemporary observations on what learning should and should not be. Our problem was first how to solicit and study aporetic narratives of learning, a rather ironic quest as the imaginary of learning is representation, one of the fundamental pillars, so to say, of how to account for education.

We called on Patti Lather to help our doctoral students learn the work of in-depth interviewing across the disciplines with teachers, professors, and graduate and undergraduate students, and during what was known as the crisis of representation in education. Alice Pitt and I created a phenomenological interview protocol, a sort of thematic perception experiment that invited participants to explore their times of learning when meaning breaks down, when one feels education as impingement, when one senses isolation or feelings of revenge, and also, when there are attempts at repair (Pitt & Britzman, 2003; Britzman & Pitt, 2004). We wanted to study love and hate in learning and how research expresses what education feels like. So, we asked what makes knowledge difficult in teaching and learning. And we wanted to study the texts of the interviews by way of the participants' metaphors, analogies, defenses, and wishes.

For Lather's workshop, the graduate students who would go on to do some of our interviews were introduced to the protocol, interviewed one another, and then returned to the group to discuss their experiences. Lather led the discussion. Just as with many new experiences with qualitative research, our graduate students were enamoured with gathering and retelling their data. They desired to adequately represent their stories without having to interpret their quest for significance or their anxieties in getting interviewing right. They may have thought that the stories would convey the stability of experience and may have worried they would somehow misrepresent their participants, or perhaps ruin the clarity of storytime. For some, they may have been frightened by what their participant described as the 'trauma of education' and felt if only more details could be invited, bad feelings would disappear. While none of the students had a background in qualitative research in education they were, of course, affected by a life in education. And yet, Pitt and I were surprised by how easily these students repeated the assumptions of instituted life and normative qualitative work. They were drowning in a sea of details in an effort at protecting a cohesive story of experience. They were not yet doing what Forrester (2017) advised, that is, to imagine that thinking in cases is like climbing inside someone's head. Looking back at this workshop so many years ago, I have to wonder if my surprise is a defense against research. My partial retelling involves my implication: I too was an adolescent researcher, thinking more about the conclusions and what could be used before I even knew what the research was about (Britzman, 2003). Learning comes late.

At the time of the workshop, Lather listened to the students as they reported back and finally said, "We don't care about that!" By which she meant that the students were stuck in their stories. Instead of playing with ideas, they kept asking for more and more details. They had difficulty discerning the fantasies of learning that attempted to hold experience together, and indeed these details defended against a learning story, or a story of having to learn, before they could understand. We were asking students to do something difficult for us all: to study their desires for narrative as clouding the problems of learning that does involve unexpected and unresolvable experience. We were interested in what happens to the researcher who overidentifies with the story, who becomes enmeshed in a rescue fantasy, or who is afraid to consider research as interference and as transference.

We were beginning to learn firsthand that our interest emerged from the difficulties of representing learning against the romance and ideality of representation. We were learning from qualitative life without foundations. Here, Lather would note the problems of "getting lost." Ours would be a losing of certainty by accepting a fundamental indeterminacy in practice and theory with breakdowns of meaning—our own and those of the students. And this shared emotional situation that could not be known in advance brought us to the paradoxical situation that learning was unrepresentable but nonetheless still existed as a search. We were learning there is no such thing as data when it comes to grasping the atmosphere of learning. Learning is not data. What there is involves an educational apparatus, communities of agreement and disagreement, revolt and compliance, and a history of biographical and social conflicts to repeat and unconsciously transfer onto new situations. Here, we can see that foundations easily become our quicksand. But so, too, can our stories of our stories. Qualitative research without expectations may only occur once researchers meet their foil or the question of belief (Britzman, 2003). Tolerating the frustrations of experience, the researcher's negative capabilities, are also a needed quality of research.

Research should leave us with better questions. What then can science without foundations mean for the present generation of researchers compelled by the problematics of representation, identity, decolonization, difference, and the binary politics of education, and so with debates over the ethics of presence and absence? Can research become a third space, or again, as Sedgwick noted, concern for theory as theory? What resources and attitudes might be created that would allow for interest in the deeper paradoxes of empowerment sown when the obstacles to meaning become embroiled in or even collapsed with demands for social change? What then becomes of the identities of researchers working the ruins of experience, as Lather has presented? And, what if these fragments are still alive, affecting what can be thought of as history's return?

It seems to me that one of the missing pieces in our discussions of research, there all along, concerns the ways we come to be affected by our areas of concern, the ways the world and the vulnerabilities of knowledge come to matter to thinking over transitory experience. Lather's work has opened such dilemmas. I now think a science without foundations is comparable to an education without foundations. They are both situations of need, vulnerability, conflict, and desire, but only if each can permit their difficulties and dreams of knowledge to affect their procedures. And such may occur to us only if science and education care for a fundamental indeterminacy that affects our unconscious communication with one another and plays through our transferences to knowledge and perception. A science without foundations and a learning without foundations remain beholden to what is utterly human, and this includes the pleasures of analogy, the capacity to tell time, the desire for friendships, the toleration of frustration, and the care for life and death.

References

Benjamin, W. (1999). *The arcades project.* Harvard University Press.

Bion, W. (1994). *Learning from experience.* Jason Aronson.

Britzman, D. P. (2003). *Practice makes practice: A critical study of learning to teach* (Revised ed.). State University of New York Press.

Britzman, D. P. (2009). *The very thought of education: Psychoanalysis and the impossible professions.* State University of New York.

Britzman, D. P. [Pedagogy and Psychosocial Transformation]. (2018, April 19). Patti Lather at York University [Video]. YouTube. https://youtu.be/crkqnsOuLww?si=6x5vKcEx Bzv6_tfg

Britzman, D. P. (2024). *When history returns: Psychoanalytic quests for humane learning.* State University of New York Press.

Britzman, D. P., & Pitt, A. J. (2004). Pedagogy and clinical knowledge: Psychoanalytic observations on losing and refinding significance. *JAC: A Quarterly Journal for the Interdisciplinary Study of Rhetoric, Literacy, Culture, and Politics,* 24(2), 353–374.

Certeau, M. de. (1988). *The writing of history.* Columbia University Press.

Certeau, M. de. (1993). *Heterologies: Discourse on the other* (B. Massumi, Trans.). University of Minnesota.

Forrester, J. (2017). *Thinking in cases.* Polity.

Freud, S. (1939). Moses and monotheism: Three essays (1939 [1934–1938]). In A. Freud, A. Strachey, & A. Tyson (Eds.), *Standard Edition* (Vol. 23) (J. Strachey, Trans.) (pp. 3–140). Hogarth Press.

Kuhn, T. S. (1970). *The structure of scientific revolutions* (2nd ed.). University of Chicago Press.

Lather, P. (1986). Research as praxis. *Harvard Educational Review, 56*(3), 257–278.

Lather, P. (1991). *Getting smart: Feminist research and pedagogy within the postmodern.* Routledge.

Lather, P. (1999). Drawing the line at angles: Working the ruins of feminist ethnography. In E. St. Pierre & W. Pillow (Eds.), *Working the Ruins: Feminist Poststructural Theory and Methods in Education* (pp. 284–311). Routledge.

Lather, P. (2007). *Getting lost: Feminist efforts toward a doubled science.* State University of New York Press.

Lather, P. (2009). *Engaging science policy: From the side of messy.* Peter Lang Press.

Lather, P. (2010). Troubling clarity: The politics of accessible language. *Harvard Educational Review, 66*(3), 525–546.

Lather, P., & Smithies, C. (1997). *Troubling the angles: Women living with HIV/AIDS.* Avalon Press.

Pitt, A. J., & Britzman, D. P. (2003). Speculations on qualities of difficult knowledge in teaching and learning: An experiment in psychoanalytic research. *International Journal of Qualitative Studies in Education, 16*(6), 1–22.

Reed, G. S., Levine, H. B., & Scarfone, D. (2018). Introduction: from a universe of presences to a universe of absences. In H. Levine, G. Reed, & D. Scarfone (Eds.), *Unrepresented States and the Construction of Meaning: Clinical and Theoretical Contributions* (pp. 3–17). Routledge.

Rose, G. (1996). *Mourning becomes the law: Philosophy and representation.* Cambridge University Press.

Sedgwick, E. K. (2011a). Thinking through queer theory. In J. Goldberg (Ed.), *The Weather in Proust* (pp. 190–203). Duke University Press.

Sedgwick, E. K. (2011b). Affect theory and theory of the mind. In J. Goldberg (Ed.), *The Weather in Proust* (pp. 144–163). Duke University Press.

Stengers, I. (2018). *Another science is possible: A Manifesto for slow science.* Polity Press.

CHAPTER TWELVE

Bringing Down the Menses: My Abortion Story

PATTI LATHER

July 7, 2022[1] "... something more like deploying her own experience as an engine for thinking that spins out into the world and backwards and forwards in time."

Christian Lorentzen (2015, from review of *The Argonauts*)

IF DWIGHT D. EISENHOWER had not died on March 28, 1969, I would have gotten married and borne a child that year when I was 21.

Eisenhower's death meant that the Denver city offices were closed and the hastily planned marriage could not happen. Hasty, perhaps, but I had brought what I thought was to be my wedding dress and even a headpiece. I could tell you every detail of that dress that I had made back in South Dakota with Easter as a cover.

I come from a background of fierce Catholicism and a time when unwed mothers were so looked down upon there was a sort of greyish film over them and their names and families. I surely did not understand this as a child, but I still remember in my bones such occasions in the small South Dakota towns of the 1950s.

Part of the shame regarded sex, of course, which I had religiously held off on until I didn't at 20, mad for him.

So instead of getting married, we went to the house of his friends who were pregnant with a third, or was it fourth (?), child and played the Ouija board to see if our children had souls. Hers did, mine didn't, it was determined by all but zombie-me. And she had a doctor who would set up an abortion in Juárez.

Abortion—I had never heard the word. Nor birth control except for what he thought he knew.

And so we drove off to El Paso for the Mexican abortion, illegal of course. And met the contacts at a designated corner in Juárez, got in a car, were blindfolded, and driven to the "clinic."

Which was a house in a nondescript neighborhood. I remember chairs in a waiting room and being ushered into a sort of medical room where there were, as I remember, hundreds of people. I was laid on a sort of medical bed and a very real gas mask came toward me. And no one spoke English. And I thought "here I go, maybe to die but at least no baby."

And I woke up on another bed in another room. And he was there in his own zombie space, he who had paid the $400, thank you very much. And we were driven back to the border.

And we had a sort of loving evening where he was most solicitous and we went to a strip club, my first, and he bought me a very large orange flower that I kept through various stages of decrepitude until I didn't.

And I was surprised I didn't hurt at all.

And we returned to Denver, a long drive, where he went into an uncommunicative funk with his own black film around him.

Which remained and grew blacker and so I flew back to South Dakota early and crying and I remember the plane was delayed. And in the long wait a young cowboy very kindly befriended me and I can't remember if I told him the truth or not.

I returned to college life in South Dakota. Some of the zombie haze started to lift until a terrible discharge began to ooze from me. The student health center had the good sense to do a pregnancy test after I came clean with them.

I was hospitalized in the infectious disease ward where everyone had to wear a hazmat sort of suit until the pregnancy test came back positive and they knew what they were dealing with.

I expelled a tiny red jello fetus in the night, on the toilet, glad for the emergency button right there.

Following a D&C procedure in a clean, well-lit room where there were not a hundred people, I rested. I don't remember communicating with medical staff other than telling them to not notify my family. I do remember three girlfriends coming to visit, shocked at least as much by my not being a virgin (!) as the abortion/miscarriage. Having had an irritant implanted in Mexico that took three-ish weeks to do its work, I was released back into my life.

I told myself I would quit smoking in honor of that baby, a promise I did not keep.

My relationship with the father of the fetus did not survive.

Freed from Catholicism, I became religious about birth control. I began my move into feminism. I marched in the Doo Dah parade each 4th of July as a Concerned Lady Against Women (CLAW) with a "Protect the Unconceived" sign. I donated to NARAL but never served as a clinic protector although I raised my fist at every "Unwanted Pregnancy Crisis Center" I drove by.

I never said a word to my mother.

In 2013, as women were just starting to "come out" with their abortion stories, I came out in a clause, in a sentence of an intellectual autobiography that I read aloud to a small academic group: "blindfolded, desperate, life shattering," to quote myself, as my heart raced.

And now with the Supreme Court going back to the 18th century to misread history as instigated by the forced birth crusaders, I am moved to expand upon that earlier clause.

And my Mom is dead, so here—

Note

1. Editors' Note: On June 24, 2022, in *Dobbs v. Jackson Women's Health Organization*, the Supreme Court struck down fifty years of precedent protecting abortion rights. This devastating ruling ignores medical science, dismisses bodily autonomy, and forces countless Americans to seek dangerous alternatives—just as Dr. Lather did over fifty years ago. Her powerful testimony reminds us what is at stake when we deny access to safe, legal abortion care. We publish her story as both historical document and urgent warning.

CHAPTER THIRTEEN

Response to Beyond Measure: Studying the Educational Logic of Patti Lather's *Getting Lost*

PATTI LATHER AND TYSON LEWIS

A Response to a Review: Patti Lather

TYSON LEWIS (2016) WROTE an incisive critique of *Getting Lost*, the kind of review one can only dream of that helps one see both what was accomplished and where one ran into limits. While it is, unfortunately, not included given permission costs, I include my response nonetheless. The editors invited Tyson to respond to my response, and it is included below.

Arguing persuasively for "study" versus "learning," Tyson probes the educational logic of *Getting Lost* as "a most peculiar book." It is, he argues, peculiar in being a kind of "inoperative" text, "a learning that un-learns itself in its learning." In other words, he sees what I saw: a book about a book, research about research, complicated by it all being about one's own highly invested research. Down, down the rabbit hole he goes with me, seeing, feeling, *visiblinzing* my experience of it all. In the ruins/runes of a project where "philosophical troubling" was on both our minds, he leads me to a much clearer sense of what I attempted, accomplished, and ultimately undercut, or, in his words, *hesitated* to fully embrace. "The unmeasurable potentiality" of the book is undercut by my own reinsertion of calculability via its "toward" move, as noted in the title, its reinsertion into a progressive narrative, instead of the "precious and precarious" potentials involved in the very getting lost I am endorsing.

Oh yes, Tyson. I see it when I read you. But I cannot help myself. I am no "Bartleby the Scrivener," able and willing to forego the drive toward (there's that word) socially useful and productive research. My "I prefer not to" would be in terms of the "interminable activity" I would have to embrace. I see that this is, indeed, "sacrificing potentiality in the name of actualizing." I feel the "suspension" I get so close to but then cannot fully endorse. The book, Tyson argues, has more going on in terms of what it is teaching than the author realized.

This is what criticism is supposed to do: help us all—readers, authors, everyone—see deeper into a text's unconscious, "the real gift the book has to offer." What *Getting Lost* performs, its pedagogy, uses Derrida's ghosts and Benjamin's angels in ways that unleash way more than an author can understand, let alone control/calculate. Energies and paralyses push into one another, closures are prolonged, (de)creations abound; all toward getting lost in the inoperatives and suspensions sustained by proliferations. Hey! These are the words for what I did know inchoately in the time of writing, "instantiating the potential of research to be *and* not to be or to do *and* not to do at the same time."

But then I falter at the "toward" of the title, failing to understand the very movement of Benjamin's Angel of History (2003): moving as a capacity rather than an actuality; moving in potential; "a frozen grace despite the winds of change." Here I miss the opportunity Benjamin offered, and Buddhism too, what "the architecture of angels" offered: an ethic of potentiality let loose from the dialectic. Too quickly foreclosing on the very "educational unique-ness" of *Getting Lost* (2012), I offer a sort of "postmodern improvement project," smuggling the calculable back in, rescuing too quickly, falling back into learning and out of the studying where the very potentiality of resisting all calculation falters. And I get found, and a familiar narrative structure, purposes, methods, and validity testing all get re-inscribed. And not in the "otherwise" way to which the text got so close, although the text does exceed my intentions as its rhythms instantiate a "subaltern educational logic" for which I did not know I yearned. So . . . thanks for the best review ever, Tyson.

A Response to a Response to a Review: Tyson Lewis

As I read it, *Getting Lost: Feminist Efforts Toward a Double(d) Science* (2012), never—despite its title—provides an orientation toward progressive development so much as a (dis)orientation around the very question of what it means to study one's own research. And through this gesture of study, Patti opens up a space and time to dwell with research and discover new uses for old words that might, in the end, be unrecognizable in terms of initial orientations toward a specific intervention or goal. The precarious position of a studier of one's research is uncomfortable and even stupefying. This is a difficult state of being to describe, let alone expose to the world. More often than not studying is concealed or erased through the process of writing and publishing. It is a kind of embarrassment that reveals the researcher to be a non-sovereign subject, caught up in a process that exceeds them, lost in interminable rhythms of thought that resist any (prescribed) end. Yet Patti does not flinch and instead commits to the page her many recursive movements around questions, themes, concepts, and political urgencies. This is not an infinite deconstruction of meaning or deferral of a plan of action. For me, *Getting Lost* is a making present of the act of studying and the potentiality which studying can find in the ruins. This potentiality means that the text can always be otherwise than what it is and that the text is not a necessary fact so much as a contingent threshold for becoming. Thus, Patti's text reminds us that what we write and give to the world is full of potentialities, even if we are too wedded to our own "towards" to recognize them. And while some might critique the book for losing sight of its "towards," I fully embrace such weakness as an honest portrait of studying as a unique form of educational life beyond learning. This is a fragile gift that Patti has given us, one that does not contain a lesson so much as an opportunity to continue to wrestle with the gestures of the studier. My essay was (and is) an attempt to take up this opportunity and celebrate the inoperative and weak features of her work that others might easily dismiss. Thanks, Patti, for inviting us to join you in studying. And in this sense, we don't have to be isolated Bartlebys or lone angels anymore. . . .

References

Benjamin, W. (2003). On the concept of history. In H. Eiland & M.W. Jennings (Ed.), *Selected Writings* (pp. 389–401). Harvard University Press.

Lather, P. (2012). *Getting lost: Feminist efforts toward a double (d) science.* State University of New York Press.

Lewis, T. (2016). Beyond measure: Studying the educational logic of Patti Lather's *Getting Lost. Qualitative Inquiry,* 1–9.

CHAPTER FOURTEEN

Concluding Remarks

PATTI LATHER

IT IS BOTH THRILLING and humbling to read these contributions to this book. In 2017, I published my own selection of my work and much enjoyed writing the "forewords" that were a kind of looking back on how each essay came to be, with sections on validity, feminist research and pedagogy, and the various posties (Lather, 2017). But this is a very different experience of intersecting with how others see and use my work over their own quite varied enterprises.

My goal from the beginning, as Egon Guba's student at Indiana University in the early 1980s, was to **re-inscribe** the terms that legitimized qualitative research as scientific as well as to provide roadmaps for counter-practices of the social sciences. Such practices were in keeping with commitments to research as praxis, research that helps to bring into being the world in which we want to live. This has resulted in such key terms in my work as "voluptuous validity" and "the validity of angels" and, really, the concept of "research as praxis" itself with which my career got its start. For example, Peter McLaren once told me that he had put the entire article on overhead and taught it line by line to his students.

This was back in the day before Peter and I fell out over the bro-ish dimensions of critical pedagogy and the fear and loathing of the posties on the part of many of the Marxist boys, as we feminists called the critical pedagogy guys.

But perhaps that is as good a place as any to turn from my work to, as Bette Midler says, "enough about me, what do you think about me?"

Gabe and Rob's introduction: Let me begin with a thanks to Gabe and Rob whose careers I have followed over the years, Rob, ever since one of the first AAACS pre-AERA conferences, in New Orleans as I remember, and Gabe, since Rob began bringing him to Bergamo where they eventually ran the conference for a few years. It is a generational thing spanning Madeleine Grumet, Bill Pinar, Janet Miller, and myself over many AERAs and even more Bergamos and much good whiskey and even better conversations.

Their introduction to the book as a "labor of love" tracks their combined engagement with my work over its many years and what they term its "continual movement" as it puts theory to work in the context of struggles for social justice. I particularly appreciate Gabe's course organized around my work as it allowed both Janet Miller and myself to gather at my home around the Zoom and engage with Gabe's curious and on-point students. Their varied ways of using my work show up on this panel with Elissa's paper on jiu-jitsu, a direction I never would have anticipated!

Janet Miller: Janet's chapter foregrounds what she calls "shimmers of a thinking differently" across our mutual exchange of ideas over 40-some years and counting. Janet's chapter is also a primer on the history of Bergamo *JCT* conferences, the reconceptualist movement, and what she terms "curriculum feminists." Across psychoanalytic, phenomenological, and critical theory perspectives, these scholars, Janet and myself included, studied the representation of women in education history, gendered meanings with such concepts as "the feminization of teaching," and the pervasive impacts of patriarchy including what I called in an early paper "the jockocracy" of educational administration. I especially appreciate Janet's autobiographical focus on the "unhinging" that my work created in her work. Channeling Judith Butler, as we all did then, Janet gives evidence in the very way she writes the chapter to a kind of disequilibrium that did justice to this field of education. Refusing to tell the "straight ahead" story, she complicates both the teller and the tale as she highlights and probes my emerging body of work including a re-telling of the naked methodology encounter from her own situated perspective. All in all, what Janet offers is a kind of long-term engagement with my work across varied contexts and a friendship that abides. Her presence in Columbus is a comfort in my old age and for this I am beyond thanks!

Chris Smithies is my strongest experience of collaborative research, so she knows stuff. Her chapter well captures both the grace and the struggle of that many-years project on women, AIDS, and angels; the kind of project that changes a researcher's life. Chris brought me to the women in their already extant support groups and I brought her to qualitative research. She held my feet to the ethical fire, and I made her dance with angels and theory as we both benefitted from the "naked methodology" that emerged. Chris saved the book from me in many ways, especially her insistences on the women's narratives that kept the theory angels in check as we struggled toward a "K-Mart book" that was deconstructive to the core. And feminist too, including the ways of our lives over the years. I am so thankful she got over her writer's block, as this book would have been quite incomplete without her chapter. We were writing history although we did not know this at the time. But we did know wisdom and grace were gifted to us and, we hoped, made their way into the pages of a book that has traveled far and wide as both model and testament.

Susan Adams' paper traces a crash course in my research as praxis article where she both resisted and got lost in its implications for her work as an ESL teacher and teacher educator as well as an emergent researcher at the front end of a dissertation. Taking "an unexpected detour into philosophy" at a rather late stage in her doctoral work, she became angry, lost, and exhilarated as she recognized herself in that early article of mine, knowing this meant a much deeper dive than she had anticipated into all sorts of things. Reading (and) reading (and) reading, as Bettie St. Pierre urges, stalking me at conferences and on the Internet, she moved through the dissertation with a "dark turn" toward the end as she grappled with what it all meant in the context of "the failures of representation" and the inevitabilities of betrayal in telling other people's stories. This brought up my own dark grapplings with the implications of Derrida's thesis of "necessary complicity" in my journey of "knowing both too much and too little" about what Susan calls "the transactional nature of the academic game." She came out of it with not only a Ph.D. but a feet-on-the-ground empathy for herself and all of us as we struggle to do work that can make a difference, and I ended her paper with a tear in my eye as she sort of exploded into my life as I had in hers.

Lisa Mazzei is one of those students who shows up in your classes from somewhere else and then proceeds to do the kind of work that blows your socks off. With a background in workforce development and instructional technology before it met any sort of cultural studies, somehow she worked and worked and published in excellent journals. She also set herself up for an informal post-doc with John Caputo at Syracuse where she immersed herself in some of the best of deconstruction. And then Lisa went off to Manchester Metropolitan University with Maggie and Harry and Deleuze Camp, more than once as I remember. And then Oregon, where Jerry Rosiek finally got her to come work with him where she has produced not only field-defining work but excellent teaching and mentoring.

All of this is to say that the chapter she contributes is testimony to herself as much as me, although I am thrilled to hear about the weight of me in her. Lisa (and Alecia) have taken the concept of thinking with philosophical concepts in the context of empirical work to wonderfully pedagogical heights with their book(s) on thinking with theory. Lisa was witness to my early efforts to bring "a poststructural reckoning" to many areas and she was in on the Foucault course and the immense luxury of the Derrida course, where we did, indeed, spend a semester reading the 100 pages of Spivak's introduction to *Of Grammatology*: two co-teachers and five students, a dream class for us all that got deconstruction in our bones. I love the Top Ten List and could come back at her with the big lesson she taught me: never underestimate a student on fire no matter how seemingly quiet the fire.

Harry Torrance sees and appreciates my "policy turn" more than most, given his own years of work to move educational policy analysis in fruitful, or in his words, "less dumb," directions. Sharing a background in program evaluation (which paved the way for the incursions of qualitative research into the field in ways not often acknowledged), Harry provided quiet guidance as I ventured into the policy arena. This is especially the case as I began to fuzz the qualitative/quantitative boundaries, areas Harry had troubled much longer than I myself had. And his U.K. perspective was always a necessary corrective to my narrow U.S.-focus as we joined in resisting positivist resurgence and governmental incursion. Sharing many stages across time and conferences, Harry's endorsement of my democratic ambitions for policy analysis has kept my sense of intellectual project both grounded in necessary constraints and exactly on task: a never-completed praxis of enacting an inclusive scientificity. More iterative and dynamic, certainly messier, such policy and practice is never settled but always in process and relational in its time and place. And good whiskey never hurts, although the cigars are all his.

Reading **Sam Rocha** made me laugh. He has pictured me as a teacher like no one else: busy, loud, stern, direct, there. I am so glad the story of the necessity of Thomas B. Kuhn is included and the "places where you can/cannot say fuck"—great stories. And I had never put my worries about whether Sam got the quality education he deserved into British vs. USA models, so that was interesting, although I would argue UBC is much more along USA lines than U.K. And I am pleased to be admitted into at least the fringes of the heights of the philosophy of education club and maybe even the humanities club, especially given my social science hegemonies. This chapter reads like an insider's exposé of teaching in the kindest sense. I see the bones of some of my ways of being in the role and recognize myself indeed.

Elizabeth de Freitas: Liz's focus on my late-blooming interest in the qual/quant relationship brings the new materialist turn and my refusal of a qual/quant binary into consideration. Given her background in digital media, computational culture, and philosophy of mathematics, she takes my work to a higher level. And, always, she provides me with my next reading list so that I can keep getting smarter about what the hay she is talking about, which might as well be French! Rethinking the quantitative alongside the qualitative becomes much more philosophically interesting once I begin to get Liz's concepts under my belt. Entanglements run amok, to the benefit of both qual and quant. Her articulation of my emerging focus on "the incalculable" is but a prime example of how her engagement with my work deepens my own work, and I always feel smarter after engaging with hers.

Maggie MacLure: Receiving the great compliment of being read so very closely by Maggie, I come to see my own work in almost magical terms as she writes that I am both "seismographer" and "sorcerer" of developing (post)qualitative research methodology. And then, through a gestalt of erudition and poetic thinking/writing, she traces the arc of my work and its ins and outs of theories across time and influences. Zeroing in on my critiques of heroic imaginaries and my hauntings by the incalculable, Maggie helps me see what I have done in terms of both skating a bit too close to the perils of privilege and my various disabusements. She nails my use of a doubled science, my efforts toward self-deconstructing, and my attraction to the more affirmative not-knowing of Barad and "the queer logics of quantum mechanics," after the necessary mourning time with Benjamin and Derrida. There is a shift in the chapter from "Lather" to "we" as Maggie articulates "a new architecture for qualitative inquiry," probes "what inhuman relationality" might be, and delineates the cost of the "colonial orthodoxies" still at work in our work. Quoting my response to what new sensibility might be brewing for research, she cautions against "extractive and superficial" uses and abuses of efforts toward inclusion of Indigenous work and claims of "bad girl" trouble. Ontological trouble indeed. "Divinatory," I can only hope.

Elissa Bryant's chapter on jiu-jitsu is perhaps the most unexpected use of my work in the book. She puts into play many of my key concepts—impossibility, aporia, thinking the limit, demastering, effacement, incommensurability, and getting lost, to name a few—in order to explore her white settler identity in the context of anti-racist work. Enacting a narrative of a methodology via an embodied practice, she invents a "lost practice of somatic inquiry" to navigate such fraught territory. Using many of the textual practices of *Troubling the Angels*, Bryant uses Indigenous temporal heterogeneity to unsettle linearity and urges us toward a de-colonial whiteness that is both impossible and necessary. This helped me in my own wrestling with such issues where I have explored Afro-pessimism and the work of Fred Moten toward a sense of the limits of reflexivity and even getting lost in de-centering my own whiteness (Lather, 2023). Coining, I believe, the term "Latherian," Elissa also taught me a lot about jiu-jitsu and provided me with a bibliography for learning more, and for this as well as her creative extension of my work into unexpected realms, I thank her.

Sarah Sterner: In her dissertation, Sarah coins the "Latherian Theorizing" concept to which I have some resistance, much preferring a more networked, rhizomatic, relational, or entangled account. Nonetheless, Sarah puts it all to work in the context of a study of "reading whitely" in order to find a methodological and writerly home in the academy. Through a sort of hacking move, Sarah puts me in conversation with a phenomenology I have followed Foucault in leaving. This, however, does appear to be a deconstructive sort of phenomenology where subjects are reflexive, narratives are troubled, and multi-layered texts solve perhaps too many problems. While Sarah surely gets the "fleeting, shifting, whispiness" of what we study and embraces getting lost, I would encourage her to think of "situated methodology" as a possibility where "thinking with" anything or anyone is but a direction, and neither arrival nor transfer.

Deborah Britzman's penetrating chapter tells a story of a long-time academic friendship with benefits of spilling into the rest of our lives. Across both too many or maybe not enough AERA conferences, we shared many a stage and witnessed one another grow into our professornesses. We shared Marxism at the front and surely feminism and then, in my case, a psychoanalysis I could bear to learn from, in Lisa Weems' felicitous words, as Deborah opened that field up for education. And she nails it that our work was situated in the science wars of our times, specifically in our field of education with its measurement manias and hegemonies in which we were mostly more than marginal. But we survived and even thrived as the times met us and we found not only one another but an audience for work that shared much while differing in productive ways. I am more than glad to have a reader who appreciates my gerunds, my citational practices, and my fields of theory including Benjamin and queer theory, both of whom were sharpened and deepened for me via Deborah. As did the psychoanalysis always at work in her and, in a way I could bear, myself. Maybe "ruining Marxism with deconstruction" is not such a bad legacy!

References

Lather, Patti. (2017). *(Post)Critical methodologies: The science possible after the critiques: The selected works of Patti Lather.* Routledge.

Lather, Patti. (2023). Culturally responsive post-qualitative research. In P. Pasque & E. Alexander (Eds.), *Advancing culturally responsive research and researchers: Qualitative, quantitative and mixed methods* (pp. 30–47). Routledge.

ABOUT THE AUTHORS

SUSAN R. ADAMS is professor of education and faculty director of Diversity, Equity and Inclusion and professor in the College of Education, Butler University. A former secondary ESL teacher and instructional coach, Susan's research interests include race, critical pedagogies, and transformational adult learning. Her publications are included in *Theory into Practice, Critical Literacy, English Journal, Writing and Pedagogy, The Brock Education Journal, SAGE Sociology of Education,* and *The New Educator.* She is co-author of the 2016 book, *Race and Pedagogy: Creating Collaborative Spaces for Teacher Transformations,* with Jamie Buffington-Adams and co-editor of the 2024 publication, *Exploring Meaningful and Sustainable Intentional Learning Communities for P–20 Educators,* with Angela Breidenstein.

DEBORAH P. BRITZMAN is distinguished research professor emeritus at York University, Toronto and a working psychoanalyst. Her recent book with SUNY Press is: *When History Returns: Psychoanalytic Quests for Humane Learning* (2024).

ELISSA BRYANT (she/her) earned her Ph.D. in curriculum studies with additional certifications in both Women and Gender Studies (WGST) and Comparative Race and Ethnic Studies (CRES) at Texas Christian University in 2023, and is currently an independent researcher and director of the program evaluation and qualitative research company, EdAffect LLC. Her work centers emancipatory (post)qualitative methodologies, critical theories, and collectively conscious action through radical Love and trans-religious Queered spiritualities toward inclusive and hopeful futurities. Prior to her academic career, Elissa taught in Title 1 (low-income) Texas public elementary schools for seven years, where she witnessed the present crisis in education first-hand, and after working towards her school administrator certification in Texas while having two young children of her own in public schools, she remains committed to finding innovative and cooperative ways to bridge the gap(s) between her academic and community-oriented research enactments.

ELIZABETH DE FREITAS is a writer and professor at Adelphi University. She works across disciplines, developing creative and critical research methodologies for the social sciences, including mapping and other spatial methodologies. Two of her current projects are focused on the affective atmospheres in school buildings. With expertise in the history and philosophy of mathematics, her research explores the power of speculative thought in STEAM imaginaries, and the role of algorithmic thinking in control societies. Her work has been funded by the Canada Council for the Arts, the Toronto Arts Council, the Social Sciences and Humanities Research Council of Canada, the U.S. National Science Foundation, the U.K. Economic and Social Research Council, and the Spencer Foundation.

GABRIEL HUDDLESTON is an associate professor and department chair of Counseling, Societal Change, and Inquiry in the College of Education at Texas Christian University (TCU). He is also the director of the Center for Public Education and Community Engagement, one of three research centers and institutes housed in the College of Education. Additionally, he is affiliated faculty with both the Women and Gender Studies (WGST) and Comparative Race and Ethnic Studies (CRES) departments. In 2018, Gabe collaborated with other TCU CRES scholars to design a K–12 social studies curriculum overlay focusing on Latinx cultures and histories. He teaches classes in curriculum studies, qualitative inquiry, teacher education, and a Deconstructing Disney class for the John V. Roach Honors College. His work in curriculum studies utilizes a cultural studies theoretical framework within qualitative research to examine the intersections between schools and society, with a particular focus on the relationship between neoliberal education reform and teachers. His research interests also include popular culture, spatial theory, new materialism, and postcolonial studies. Gabriel has published in several journals, including *Taboo: The Journal of Culture and Education, The Journal of Curriculum and Pedagogy, The Review of Education, Pedagogy, and Cultural Studies, Critical Literacy: Theories and Practices, International Review of Qualitative Research*, and *The Currere Exchange Journal*. He has also contributed to several book chapters, including "Welcome to Zombie City: A Full-Service Community School and

School Choice" in *Deterritorializing/reterritorializing: Critical Geographies of Educational Reform*, and "The Zombie in the Room: Using Popular Culture as an Apparatus" in *Pedagogical Matters: New Materialisms and Curriculum Studies*. Additionally, he has co-authored several entries in the *Oxford Research Encyclopedia of Education* regarding curriculum theory/studies. Gabe has actively participated in the American Education Research Association (AERA) annual conference from 2012 to 2023. In 2020, he received the Critical Issues in Curriculum Studies and Cultural Studies SIG Early Career Scholars Award and was inducted into the Professors of Curriculum. His current projects involve various community-based research studies with partners such as Dallas Truth, Racial Healing, and Transformation, and All-Pro Dads, as well as internal evaluation research studies for the Honors College, the TCU/FWISD Counseling Clinic, and the Koehler Center for Instruction, Innovation, and Engagement. He is a member of two research teams: one focusing on a National Science Foundation (NSF) funded study on how universities can better support women faculty in the STEM fields, with a particular emphasis on intersectional identities, and the second analyzing data from a statewide survey of Texas Latino Male K–12 teachers, believed to be the largest of its kind, along with conducting focus groups with some of the survey respondents. From 2013 to 2018, he served as the managing editor of the *Journal of Curriculum Theorizing (JCT)*, during which time he also acted as the program chair and co-organizer for *JCT*'s annual conference, The Bergamo Conference on Curriculum Theory and Classroom Practice. Gabriel has also held positions such as the program chair for the Critical Issues in Curriculum Studies and Cultural Studies SIG from 2015 to 2018, and the section program co-chair of Section 1 of Division B from 2017 to 2019 (AERA). He served as the chair of the Critical Issues in Curriculum Studies and Cultural Studies SIG from 2020 to 2022.

ROBERT HELFENBEIN is professor of curriculum studies in the Tift College of Education and has published numerous pieces about contemporary education theory in journals such as *Curriculum Inquiry, The Journal of Curriculum Theorizing, The Review of Education, Pedagogy & Cultural Studies, Educational Studies, The Urban Review*, and co-edited the books *Unsettling Beliefs: Teaching Theory to Teachers* (2008), *Ethics and International Curriculum Work: The Challenges of Culture and Context* (2012), *Deterritorializing/Reterritorializing: Critical Geographies of Education Re-*

form (2017) and the single-author text *Critical Geographies of Education: Space, Place, & Curriculum Theory* (Routledge, 2021). From 2013 to 2019 he served as editor of the *Journal of Curriculum Theorizing* and organizer of the annual Bergamo Conference on Curriculum Theory and Classroom Practice in Dayton, Ohio. His current research interests include curriculum theorizing in urban contexts, cultural studies of education, postfoundational research, and the impact of globalization on the lived experience of schools.

PATTI LATHER is professor emerita in the School of Educational Studies at the Ohio State University where she taught qualitative research, feminist methodology, and gender and education since 1988. She is the author of five books, *Getting Smart: Feminist Research and Pedagogy With/in the Postmodern* (1991, Critics Choice Award), *Troubling the Angels: Women Living with HIV/AIDS*, co-authored with Chris Smithies (1998, CHOICE Outstanding Academic Title), *Getting Lost: Feminist Efforts Toward a Double(d) Science* (2008, Critics Choice Award), and *Engaging (Social) Science: Policy from the Side of the Messy* (2011, Critics Choice Award), and *(Post)Critical Methodologies: The Science Possible After the Critiques: The Selected Writings of Patti Lather* (2017). She was the recipient of a 1989 Fulbright to New Zealand. She is a 2009 inductee of the AERA Fellows and a 2010 recipient of the AERA Division B Lifetime Achievement Award.

TYSON E. LEWIS is a professor of art education in the College of Visual Arts and Design at the University of North Texas. He has published on a wide variety of topics including philosophy of education, arts-based research, aesthetics, critical theory, critical phenomenology, posthumanism, and philosophy for children. He is author of many books, most recently *Walter Benjamin's Antifascist Education* (SUNY Press, 2020) and with Peter Hyland, *Studious Drift: Movements and Protocols for a Postdigital Education* (University of Minnesota Press, 2022). For an introduction to his body of work, see the collection of his previously unpublished public lectures titled *Educational Potentialities: Collected Talks on Revolutionary Education, Aesthetics, and Organization* (Iskra Books, 2023).

MAGGIE MACLURE is professor emerita in the faculty of Health and Education, Manchester Metropolitan University, U.K., and a former member of the Education and Social Research Institute (ESRI), where she led the Theory and Methodology Research Group. Her interests include theory and methodology in qualitative inquiry, and early childhood research. She is founder-director of the international Summer Institute in Qualitative Research.

LISA A. MAZZEI is alumni faculty professor of education at the University of Oregon, United States, where she is also affiliated faculty in the Department of Philosophy. She is interested in philosophical inquiry that opens thought to the not yet. Recent books include *Thinking with Theory in Qualitative Research*, 2nd edition, co-authored with Alecia Jackson (2023) and *Postfoundational Approaches to Qualitative Inquiry*, co-edited with Alecia Jackson (2024).

JANET L. MILLER, professor emerita, Teachers College, Columbia University. Founding managing editor of *JCT: Journal of Curriculum Theorizing* and director/co-director of its Bergamo Annual Conferences (1978–1998). In 2010, Professor Miller was elected an American Educational Research Association (AERA) "Fellow." She also was awarded AERA's Division B-Curriculum Studies' Lifetime Achievement Award (2008) as well as The Curriculum & Pedagogy Project's "Lifetime Impact Award" (2022). Janet was elected AERA vice president for Division B (1997–1999); secretary of Division B (1990–1992); and president of the American Association for the Advancement of Curriculum Studies (2001–2007). Single-authored books: *Sounds of Silence Breaking: Women, Autobiography, Curriculum* (2005); *Creating Spaces and Finding Voices: Teachers Collaborating for Empowerment* (1990). Her co-edited book, with William Ayers: *A Light in Dark Times: Maxine Greene and the Unfinished Conversation* (1998). Forthcoming books (Routledge): *Maxine Greene and Education* as well as *Curriculum Studies: Communities without Consensus*.

KATE O'BRIEN is a post-doctoral researcher at the University of Georgia (USA) and honorary research associate at the University of Manchester (U.K.). Trained as an artist, educator, and minor mathematician, her work explores creative, collaborative, and contextually responsive mathematical practices. https://orcid.org/0000-0003-2830-7656

SAMUEL D. ROCHA is associate professor in the Department of Educational Studies at the University of British Columbia. His most recent books are *The Syllabus as Curriculum: A Reconceptualist Approach* (Routledge, 2020) and *Philosophical Research in Education: An Introduction to a Phenomenological Approach to the Philosophical Study of Education* (Brill, 2023).

NATHALIE SINCLAIR is distinguished university professor at Simon Fraser University, which is on unceded Coast Salish Territories (Lhu̱kw'lhu̱kw'áyten). Her most recently funded research project is The Colonial Legacy of European Mathematics in the Americas (with Elizabeth de Freitas). She is co-editor of the forthcoming book *Speculative Pedagogies for a Pluriverse Education amidst Extinction Challenges* (with Petra Mikulan). Her research in mathematics education involves both the design and study of new tools (her gestural software for mathematics learning, TouchCounts and TouchTimes, with Nicholas Jackiw) is used around the world, (with over 700,000 downloads) as well as the philosophical and historical study of the aesthetics of mathematical practice.

CHRIS SMITHIES has been a clinical psychologist in private practice in Columbus, Ohio for over 30 years. A feminist by age four, she has committed her professional life to serving the developmental, psychological, and educational needs of marginalized and diverse people. She completed a psychology internship at the University of Florida and worked at the University of Cincinnati as a staff psychologist at The Center for Eating Disorders. In the late 1980s, when HIV/AIDS was spreading among women, Dr. Smithies started Womancare, one of the first support groups for women. She extended her involvement in the HIV/AIDS communities in Cincinnati and Columbus, providing counseling, weekend retreats, education, and leadership. This work became the trajectory for meeting Dr. Patti Lather, co-researching and publishing *Troubling the Angels*, and becoming lifelong friends.

SARA K. STERNER is an associate professor at California State Polytechnic University, Humboldt (formerly Humboldt State University) in the School of Education. She serves as the Liberal Studies Elementary Education Program leader, working with undergraduate preservice educators and credential candidates. Additionally, she works closely with first year education students in a place-based learning community, Educators for Social Justice. Sara serves as the chair of the Integrated Curriculum Committee at Cal Poly Humboldt and is a member of the Children's Literature Assembly (NCTE) board. Sara earned her Ph.D. in curriculum and instruction: literacy education from the University of Minnesota in 2019. She is a teacher educator and qualitative researcher using post-intentional phenomenology, arts-based research, and narrative inquiry practices. Her research interests include preservice teacher development, the promotion of inclusive children's and adolescent literature, and disrupting white supremacy in education through anti-bias pedagogies and white teacher identity studies. Sara's scholarship stems from her experience as an elementary educator, passion for literacy education, and commitment to creating equity in education.

HARRY TORRANCE is professor emeritus and formerly director of the Education and Social Research Institute (ESRI), Manchester Metropolitan University, U.K. His research interests include: the inter-relation of assessment, teaching, and learning; testing and educational standards; the role of assessment in educational reform and policy development; qualitative research methodology; and the relationship between research and policy, research governance, and research management. He has undertaken many research projects investigating these topics funded by a wide range of sponsors. He is editor of the four-volume *Routledge Major Themes in Education* collection *Educational Assessment and Evaluation*, the four-volume *Sage Handbook of Qualitative Research Methods in Education*, a former editor of the *British Educational Research Journal*, and a fellow of the U.K. Academy of Social Sciences. He was a member of the 2021 U.K. Research Excellence Framework (REF) Education panel.

INDEX